# Railway Towns

# Railway Towns

## An Overview of Towns That Developed Through Railways

### David Brandon

First published in Great Britain in 2024 by
Pen and Sword Transport
An imprint of
Pen & Sword Books Ltd.
Yorkshire - Philadelphia

Copyright © David Brandon, 2024

ISBN 9781399051071

The right of David Brandon to be identified as author of this work has been asserted by him in accordance with the Copyright, Designs and Patents Act 1988.

A CIP catalogue record for this book is available from the British Library.

All rights reserved. No part of this book may be reproduced or transmitted in any form or by any means, electronic or mechanical including photocopying, recording or by any information storage and retrieval system, without permission from the Publisher in writing.

Typeset in INDIA by IMPEC eSolutions
Printed and bound in the UK on paper from a sustainable source by
CPI Group (UK) Ltd., Croydon, CR0 4YY.

Pen & Sword Books Ltd. incorporates the imprints of Pen & Sword Books: After the Battle, Archaeology, Atlas, Aviation, Battleground, Discovery, Family History, History, Maritime, Military, Naval, Politics, Railways, Select, Transport, True Crime, Fiction, Frontline Books, Leo Cooper, Praetorian Press, Seaforth Publishing, Wharncliffe, After the Battle and White Owl.

For a complete list of Pen & Sword titles please contact

PEN & SWORD BOOKS LIMITED
47 Church Street, Barnsley, South Yorkshire, S70 2AS, England
E-mail: enquiries@pen-and-sword.co.uk
Website: www.pen-and-sword.co.uk

or

PEN AND SWORD BOOKS
1950 Lawrence Rd, Havertown, PA 19083, USA
E-mail: Uspen-and-sword@casematepublishers.com
Website: www.penandswordbooks.com

# Contents

| | | |
|---|---|---|
| *Introduction* | | 7 |
| **Chapter One** | The Historical Context | 23 |
| **Chapter Two** | Some Railway Towns of New Creation | 33 |
| **Chapter Three** | Some Smaller Railway Settlements of New Creation | 53 |
| **Chapter Four** | Towns Predating the Railways | 71 |
| **Chapter Five** | Cathedral Cities and Railway Towns | 99 |
| **Chapter Six** | Railway Industrial Districts in Provincial Cities | 108 |
| **Chapter Seven** | London's Residential Railway Suburbs | 116 |
| **Chapter Eight** | London's Railway Districts | 131 |
| **Chapter Nine** | Major Industrial Towns | 140 |
| **Chapter Ten** | Railways and Suburbs in Provincial Cities | 151 |
| **Chapter Eleven** | Railways and Seaports | 164 |
| **Chapter Twelve** | Inland Watering Places | 179 |
| **Chapter Thirteen** | Some Major Seaside Resorts | 190 |
| **Chapter Fourteen** | Some Smaller Seaside Resorts | 213 |
| **Chapter Fifteen** | Railways and Smaller Towns | 229 |
| **Chapter Sixteen** | Navvy Settlements | 248 |
| *Select Bibliography* | | 251 |
| *Index* | | 253 |

# Introduction

An acute observer of changing Britain wrote in 1850:

> Railways have set all the towns of Britain a-dancing. Reading is coming up to London, Basingstoke is going down to Gosport or Southampton, Dumfries to Liverpool and Glasgow; while at Crewe and other points, I see new ganglions of human population establishing themselves ... Reading, Basingstoke, and the rest, the unfortunate towns, subscribed money to get railways; and it proves to be for cutting their own throats. Their business has gone elsewhither ... They are set a-dancing, confusedly waltzing, in a state of progressive dissolution, towards the four winds; and know not where the end of the death-dance will be for them...

The observer was Thomas Carlyle and for him the railways epitomised so much that he passionately loathed; the evils of unfettered capitalism, the worship of mammon and the dependence upon the cash nexus. Was he right in identifying what he clearly saw as the baleful effect of the railways on Britain's towns?

Carlyle was not alone in deprecating the advance of Britain's railways. Earlier, *John Bull*, first published in 1820 and at that time a Sunday weekly magazine of robustly traditional views, laid in to the railways:

> Does anybody mean to say that decent people, passengers who would use their own carriages ... would consent to be hurried along upon a railroad ... or is it to be imagined that women ... would endure the fatigue and misery and danger ... of being

dragged through the air at the rate of 20mph, all their lives being at the mercy of a tin pipe, or a copper boiler, or the accidental dropping of a pebble on the line of way? ... Railroads will do incalculable mischief. If they succeed they will give an unnatural impetus to society, destroy all the relations which exist between man and man, overthrow all mercantile regulations, overturn the metropolitan markets, drain the provinces of all their resources, and create, at the peril of life, all sorts of confusion and distress.

One part of the complex activity known as history consists of asking questions. This is easy. Answering them with a sufficiency of solid supporting evidence is frequently difficult. In the current work we will ask what is meant by the phrase 'railway town'. We probe into odd corners of the socio-economic impact of railways, of urban geography, and topography, for example, as we attempt to reach, if not exactitude, at least some element of a greater understanding of the concept. To do this, we will consider a wide variety of places in mainland Britain where the railways had both a presence and influence.

The concept of a 'railway town' is not a simple one. Simmons (1986) argues that on occasions it is possible to say without doubt that the railway caused urban growth, as when it established locomotive or carriage works of its own, importing employees for the purpose thereby creating a new community, a 'railway town'. He states that, in his opinion, there are not many places that can with certainty be described as 'railway towns', partly because of the difficulty of establishing a definitive answer to how far the railways contributed to the growth and changing nature of any specific place. Clearly a complex and unique mix of economic, social, geographical and other factors contributes to the growth of any urban community.

Perhaps a start could be made with places like Swindon or Crewe. Swindon was an old and small country town. It stood on an eminence overlooking an area of flattish land on which the Great Western Railway (GWR) chose to build what became an enormous industrial complex.

This required a large workforce and the GWR built housing and the amenities of a not inconsiderable town in order to attract, accommodate and retain the workers and their families who mostly migrated from elsewhere. Crewe, prior to the coming of the railway, consisted of little more than a smattering of farms and hamlets. It became a major railway junction and had large engineering workshops. It became a key hub of the mighty London & North Western Railway (L&NWR) and, as with the GWR at Swindon, the L&NWR had to build the infrastructure of a town to supply many of the needs of what became a very large workforce, again moving there from elsewhere.

Swindon and Crewe satisfy any proposed criteria for defining the term 'railway town'. A small number of other places, on what could be described as 'green field sites', might qualify similarly. Wolverton, Horwich and Shildon come to mind. All the five places mentioned grew enough to be regarded as towns, if not large ones. At all of them there had been limited human habitation before the railway came. The railway was the major employer, its physical presence was immediately obvious as was its influence on the social and cultural life of the town. There were other smaller settlements, not usually described as towns, which met the same criteria. Melton Constable, Woodford Halse and Hellifield spring to mind. Perhaps they could be described as 'railway villages'. That might take us into the murky waters of attempting to define what distinguishes a town from a village.

Did a place qualify as a railway town simply because it was the meeting point of several lines, had a large passenger station, extensive sidings, goods depots and other infrastructure, and provided much employment locally? By such a yardstick, Preston, for example, would certainly be a railway town. So would its near neighbour Wigan. This had three significant passenger stations in the town centre, three engine sheds, extensive marshalling yards and a web of interlinked lines of quite amazing complexity. The railway would have employed much local labour. Preston and Wigan have rarely, if ever, been described as railway towns. Ely, never a large town, was the meeting place of lines converging from six directions. It even had an avoiding line! There was considerable passenger interchange business there but little in the way of sorting and shunting activity. It would never have been a major local employer. Railway hub it might have been. Railway town it was not.

Another category of railway-associated towns includes Peterborough, York and Carlisle. These were all ancient ecclesiastical centres which had developed before the railways into places of importance even though small by today's standards. All were cathedral cities and market towns, all stood on rivers which were navigable, and all were the focus of many roads. York had great importance as an administrative and judicial centre as well as hosting lively activities for Yorkshire's social elite. It began to develop something of an industrial character in the nineteenth century as well as becoming a major railway junction with engineering workshops, engine sheds and extensive shunting and marshalling yards. Carlisle's strategic position had provided it with a troubled history. It became a major railway hub served by no fewer than seven important pre-grouping railway companies. The railway had a huge presence in the city with each of the companies tending jealously to have their own locomotive facilities and goods depots. Other industries developed in the city, but the railways remained major local employers. Neither York nor Carlisle have generally been considered as railway towns, but Peterborough has frequently been put in that category. This was a small cathedral city and market centre on which seven lines eventually converged. It had two stations, several engine sheds and numerous shunting yards. The Great Northern Railway (GNR) occupied vast siding space where the sorting of coal trains from Yorkshire and the East Midlands took place before their contents were despatched largely to supply London's huge demand for fuel from both domestic and industrial consumers.

What for convenience will be called 'railway clusters' need to be considered. These were districts, usually on the fringe of large cities, where railway activity in the broadest sense set an indelible stamp on their appearance and character. This may just have been a spaghetti of through lines with associated junctions and sidings dense enough to preclude much else in the way of land use in the area involved. Something similar and more modern can be seen today at some motorway and trunk road intersections where there are often tracts of underused or virtually unusable land. Examples of such clusters were in south-east London around New Cross and Bricklayers Arms and around Selhurst and Norwood Junction where there was a complicated web of lines and junctions formerly belonging to the London, Brighton and South Coast Railway (LB&SCR). Glasgow had a similar district around Shields Road to the south-west of the city and Birmingham likewise with the Saltley and Bromford Bridge area.

Another kind of urban area greatly influenced by the presence of railways was what could be described as an 'industrial suburb'. These adjuncts to cities had a complex network of lines, engine sheds and railway engineering works requiring large workforces tending to be housed nearby. In such areas much or most employment would have been related to the railways. Sometimes the tradition they developed encouraged other engineering and heavy industries to locate close by. Examples of such industrial suburbs were the Gorton and Openshaw district of Manchester and the Springburn area of Glasgow. Battersea in south-west London had railway-related engineering works, large engine sheds and a convoluted network of railway lines.

Railways contributed to the growth of suburbs close to many cities and large towns. It may be convenient to call these 'railway suburbs'. Some served by railways grew into substantial towns even with populations over 100,000. Ealing could be taken as an example, developing many of the services and amenities expected of large established towns. Before the railway era, Ealing had numerous large country houses enjoying the attraction of rural seclusion as well as proximity to London. In the nineteenth century, Ealing became a favoured residential outlier of London. Acton, close by, had ancient origins and drew wealthy residents for the same reasons as Ealing. It grew very rapidly in the nineteenth century from a population of 3,000 in 1861 to 38,000 in 1891 by which time it had excellent canal, road and railway links to central London. Unlike Ealing, however, it became highly industrialised location with a large working-class population. Although both Ealing and Acton came to be well served by railways it would be simplistic to ascribe their rapid growth in the nineteenth century simply to railway development. Historical causation is a complicated process.

There are, however, residential suburbs that almost certainly do owe their growth primarily to the intervention of railways in the historical process. Perhaps the place most often mentioned in this connection is Surbiton which was once known tentatively and fortunately not for long as 'Kingston-on-Railway'.

Some larger provincial cities have suburbs where undoubtedly railways contributed substantially to their growth. To the south of Manchester, Alderley Edge, Wilmslow, Sale, Altrincham and Bowdon experienced significant growth as fashionable outer suburbs in the nineteenth century. Similarly, just north of Manchester the growth of Heaton Park, Prestwich and Whitefield was greatly encouraged and aided by the Lancashire and Yorkshire (L&Y) line to and from Manchester Victoria. North of Glasgow, Bearsden and Milngavie owe much to the North British Railway (NBR) into Glasgow, passenger services commencing in August 1863. South of Birmingham the GWR built stations along its lines to Stratford-upon-Avon and Leamington Spa which encouraged the spread of desirable speculative residential development in more countryfied areas than were to be found north and east of the city. Care needs to be taken when considering what contribution, if any, railways made to the development of Edinburgh's suburbs. In the second half of the nineteenth century there was intense largely high-quality residential development south of the city centre in such districts as Merchiston, Morningside and Grange. The former was catered for by the Caledonian Railway's (CR) line to Edinburgh to Edinburgh Princes Street Station while the latter districts were served by the South Suburban Line of the NBR to and from Waverley but much more directly and quickly to Edinburgh's city centre by what became a formidable network of tram services. The presence of a railway intended to provide passenger facilities for suburbs was no guarantee that the citizenry would not prefer alternative forms of transport. These suburbs in south Edinburgh cannot be described as railway suburbs.

Britain was the nineteenth-century export and trading nation par excellence and the period 1830 to 1914 saw the expansion of many earlier ports and the development of some entirely new ones. Railway companies had a major physical presence in, and contributed significantly to, the economic development of many of these. At the risk of over-simplification, some ports can be described as handling imports and exports and a few, such as Barry, concerned almost entirely with exports, in this case, of coal. Some ports were engaged mainly in servicing ferries to and from the Continent and Harwich, Dover and Newhaven fall into such a category. Others such as Southampton and Liverpool were involved in servicing long-haul voyages and handled both passengers and cargo. Hull, Fleetwood, Grimsby and Lowestoft may be thought of as archetypical fishing ports but the first two also acted as ferry ports. Immingham was a major exporter of coal but also served European ferries. Weymouth acted as a ferry port and doubled as a seaside watering place as did Folkestone. Railways served all these places and unquestionably contributed to their growth and yet it is by no means easy to decide which, if any, could usefully be described as railway towns.

Mention of seaside watering places leads on naturally to a consideration of the relationship between railways and coastal resorts. Given the vagaries of the British climate, the classic British seaside resort could be seen as an unlikely development, but those climatic vagaries favoured Britain's transformation into a pioneering industrial society and eventually generated a demand by working people for an escape from their everyday drudgery. People living near the sea were used to dipping in the briny, often naked, but the idea of the health-giving effects of bathing in and drinking seawater only caught on, at first among the well-to-do, in the later part of the eighteenth century. Places like Brighton and Scarborough attracted a well-heeled clientele before the age of the railway. It was only from around the middle of the nineteenth century that towns came into existence largely to cater for what we would now call the leisure market and began to attract a more demotic type of visitor and in larger numbers. Some of these towns grew with extraordinary rapidity to provide an escape for the better-off workers from the grim mining and industrial settlements inland. Blackpool and Southport were early northern examples. Southend-on-Sea and Margate catered for 'escapees' from the metropolis. The seaside resorts that grew into large towns in the nineteenth century, often from almost virgin sites, were served by railways which provided the efficient means for transporting the masses who wanted sea, sand and, where possible, a bit of sin, at first just on day trips. It is always risky trying to quantify the exact impact of the railways on such towns given the frequent paucity of concrete evidence. It would be possible to argue that Blackpool was a railway town, every bit as much an industrial town in its own way as one manufacturing textiles or metal goods. Its prime purpose was to provide services, on an industrial scale, for working people and their families. Blackpool depended on the railways for bringing these leisure consumers in their tens of thousands and would not have developed in the way it did without the railways. It could be argued Skegness and Cleethorpes, for example, can be regarded as railway towns because their function as resorts was for decades dependent on railways bringing them the visitors, and railway companies had invested large amounts of money in making them what they became.

The habit of 'taking the waters' in locations where there were mineral springs with supposedly therapeutic properties, is ancient. The springs at Bath, for example, have certainly been used for bathing since at least Roman times. Bath's popularity as what we would now call a spa, dates from the eighteenth century when the rich and powerful, often synonymous with the lazy, over-indulgent and hypochondriacal, converged in large numbers on the town for the 'season'. At the end of the nineteenth century, the Duke of Devonshire developed Buxton as a northern rival to Bath. Britain's spas were losing their fashionable character by the time railways were spreading across the country and some found a new function as sedate, select inland resorts and residential towns for gentlefolk of comfortable but not unlimited resources. Many of them also became the locations of prestigious schools and later played hosts to events such as conferences. The railways played a role in facilitating this modified function by providing easy access.

Towns such as Swindon and Crewe which were virtually created by the railways and dominated by their need for engineering and support services, have already been mentioned. Railways played a major role in assisting the growth of many other towns with heavy industries. They often brought in the raw materials and fuel required by the local industries and carried away what was produced. Sometimes the transportation of the raw materials by rail may have been over long distances as, for example, coal and coke from the Durham mining districts to ironworks in Cumberland and around Barrow-in-Furness. Another example was iron ore imported through Tyne Dock to supply ironmaking at Consett. Unquestionably, such towns would have developed differently had railways not played a crucial role in assisting their industrial development. Do such places merit being described as railway towns? Burton-on-Trent is another highly specialised industrial town which benefitted greatly by the railways bringing in its raw materials and fuel and taking away its beery products often to distant markets, especially that of London. It brewed beer long before the railways arrived but was at the forefront of the move to concentrate the brewing industry in the hands of ever fewer highly capitalised, high-output industries marketing their products not just locally but across the country, particularly through the possession of large numbers of tied houses. It was impossible to be in the centre of Burton-on-Trent and not beware of the dominating presence of the brewing and ancillary industries. Is there a case, then, for regarding Burton-on-Trent as a railway town?

Something should be said about the navvy settlements erected as temporary headquarters and accommodation during the construction of Britain's railways. Where construction work was likely to be prolonged, as, for example, at Woodhead where the barrier of the Pennines had to be penetrated by a long tunnel, these settlements could be large and, although frequently highly squalid, also sophisticated given their essentially temporary nature. They were created by the requirements of railway building. Is there a case for saying that they were a particularly specialised type of railway settlement?

It would be easy to fall for an assertion that railways caused economic growth and that places that had railways grew faster than those that did not. The railways were both products of economic growth and generators of that growth, but their influence was uneven. We could state that the population of place X grew by 25 per cent in the twenty years after the railway arrived, implying that this growth was the result of the coming of the railway and its beneficial effect on wealth generation in the town. Certainly, the transport facilities afforded by the railway were likely to attract new business and a booming town encouraged inward migration because of the jobs that were created. However, this apparent 'win-win' situation was not inevitable. Some individual case studies would support the assertion and others call it into question.

The first national census of the British population took place in 1801 since when the normal pattern has been for them to be carried out every ten years. Those held from 1841 to 1921 are available for public scrutiny. There are some concerns about the accuracy of the early returns but with that reservation they provide useful evidence for historians, not least because the growth of any specific place can easily be traced over the years. The censuses also provide information about the occupations of those who are enumerated although not, unfortunately, details of their employers. Therefore, descriptions like 'labourer' are not necessarily very helpful in determining whether the person was employed on the railway. The railways of the nineteenth century were extremely labour-intensive. Where the population of a town grew very fast between, say, 1850 and 1914, and we know from other information that the railway had a significant presence, it may be reasonable to assume that a substantial proportion of the increased population consisted of railway employees and their families. We do know of course even without reference to census returns that in some places which were built on green field sites, the railways created communities from scratch in which, at least initially, virtually the whole of the local economy and society was orientated around railways.

Some deeply researched monographs on specific localities can provide detailed information about the impact of the railway in terms, for example, of its social, economic, cultural, political and environmental impact. Within the confines of this book, probing the question of what we understand by the term 'railway towns', we are restricted largely to more general observations and conclusions albeit sometimes with more specific detail where it is available.

Only individual studies can help to determine whether this or that place was decisively shaped as a result of railways. Examples can be given of places well-served by railways which grew and prospered after the railways arrived. This does not necessarily mean that they qualify as railway towns. Conversely, there are places which expanded rapidly in the nineteenth century but only became rail-connected at a later stage. An infinite number of factors influence urban development of which railways may be only one. In a few places, Swindon and Crewe for example, what happened to them in the nineteenth century was clearly dependent on them becoming centres of railway activity. They are correctly recognised as railway towns and the prosperity they experienced in the nineteenth century was greatly expedited by the railways. While being served by a railway could bring added prosperity and growth to a place, it did not necessarily bring either. It might even have a damaging effect. The ancient town of Horncastle, for example, was harmed by the opening of railway connections to Lincoln in 1855. Local shopkeepers and the market quickly noticed trade falling as townspeople took themselves off to sample the greater retail choices offered in the county town.

Some established towns found their populations falling after they gained a place on main line railways. Examples are Cambridge and Bath. Clearly this fall was not due the coming of the railway but to factors peculiar to each of these towns. The population of Britain's towns in the pre-railway age sometimes fluctuated considerably over time for reasons unique to the specific location or, of course, sometimes caused by such factors as visitations of epidemic disease. When the railways began to spread across the country, we can safely say that most towns wanted to be connected, many believing that an age of far greater prosperity would follow. Not to have a railway was thought to be the path to stagnation or decline. Prosperity did not necessarily follow. Faringdon in Berkshire desperately wanted to be placed on a railway but was loftily avoided when the GWR was building its line from London to Swindon, Bath and Bristol. It became the terminus of a short branch from that line in 1864 by which time the town's population was in decline. It continued this pattern until the end of the century. It seems that the railway's presence failed to provide a hoped-for boost. Westerham in Kent was another small town which fruitlessly agitated for years to be put on the railway map. It eventually succeeded in 1881 but the town experienced no significant growth before the First World War.

The cases of Kendal and Frome are interesting. These towns were deemed important enough to gain their own representation in Parliament under the 1832 Reform Act. When the Lancaster & Carlisle Railway opened throughout in 1846, Kendal, to its great chagrin, found itself on the end of a 2-mile-long branch line from Oxenholme rather than on what became the West Coast Main Line. It therefore had to bear the consequences of being a railway backwater even after the line from Oxenholme was extended to Windermere. Frome was on the line from Bath to Weymouth which came under the thrall of the GWR and gained its station in 1850. This was a classic rambling secondary line. What Frome wanted was quick access to London and it finally gained this in 1906 when the GWR opened its line from Taunton via Westbury to Reading and Paddington. Now firmly on a main line, Frome found itself relegated once more to secondary status when the GWR built a short avoiding line to the south of the town in 1921. Even if both these towns did not stagnate, they remained small and their relatively lowly position on the railway system was probably at least partly responsible.

Tewkesbury was another old country town prospering from its role as a market centre with some rural industry and being a coaching centre of importance. When the Birmingham & Gloucester Railway received parliamentary authority in 1836, there were two towns situated close to each other which would have expected to be directly served by this line. These were Tewkesbury and Cheltenham. The latter was growing very rapidly and already boasted a population four times that of Tewkesbury. The burghers of both towns lobbied hard for the company's favours. It was Cheltenham that won, albeit with a rather awkwardly placed station, and the town's fortunes continued to blossom. Tewkesbury, to its intense disappointment, found itself on the end of a short branch from the Birmingham & Gloucester at Ashchurch. Later it was placed on a branch line of the Midland Railway (MR) to Great Malvern via Upton-on-Severn. This was very much a backwater. Tewkesbury went into relative stagnation, and it was little compensation that the Birmingham & Gloucester likewise chose to route its main line to avoid the considerably larger city of Worcester.

We can safely say that railways were usually built to serve places that the promoters thought would generate useful business although in some cases they were disabused because some lines never became viable. Sometimes railways were built for territorial reasons in the hope of keeping other companies out. Such lines might prove to be hopelessly uneconomic ventures. Some railways were built to snatch a share of business being done by a company or companies that had got there earlier. This explains at least some of the over-provision of lines that made railways vulnerable when serious alternative means of transport became available in the twentieth century. We can safely say that railways contributed to urban growth in Britain in the nineteenth century. We need to exercise care, however, when we consider the contribution of railways to the growth of any individual community in the absence of indisputable quantitative evidence.

Census returns gave the birthplace of the inhabitants, and it is evident that many places served by railways required labour and drew extensively on migration from surrounding rural districts. Peterborough, for example, which needed a particularly large railway workforce, drew widely on Lincolnshire and the Fens where modernised agricultural practices were achieving greater productivity and output but doing so at the expense of manpower. This short-distance migration is entirely understandable, but the census returns also show individuals or families who have come from as far away as Ireland and the Scottish Highlands in search of work. The expanding railway network helped to facilitate this process.

Railways could assist existing industries to expand or encourage new industries to be established. They played a vital role in bringing in fuel and raw materials and carrying manufactured products away. In turn, railways were themselves great consumers of the products of other industries. This was backward linkage which might stimulate towns to specialise in supplying the needs of the growing railway system. Middlesbrough and Stockton-on-Tees, for example, gained a name for producing the iron chairs used for anchoring rails on their supporting sleepers. Workington had iron and, later, steelworks engaged in the mass-production of rails. Ferrous items for rolling stock and other uses were manufactured in South Wales, South Yorkshire, the Black Country and elsewhere.

We have briefly mentioned some of the ways in which railways brought change to human settlements, but it is difficult to quantify exactly the extent of that change except perhaps in a few places such as Crewe or Swindon, these probably being the most widely recognised examples of railway towns. It is even more difficult to assess exactly the part played by the railways in the qualitative changes created by the twin processes of industrialisation and urbanisation. There is even opaqueness when considering the exact extent of the employment provided by the railway in any specific location. A host of occupations is enumerated in census returns which could, but do not necessarily, involve employment on the railway but may well have. 'Carter' would be an example.

There was a possible precedent for the railway towns in the earlier transport hubs which were those places whose prosperity came to depend heavily on the coaching industry, and others, on the canals. The network of Royal Mail and long-distance stagecoach services had become extraordinarily complex and widespread by the 1830s after which it went into rapid decline with the spread of the railways. The industry depended on the use of vast numbers of horses. These were changed frequently en route before they became winded. The changeover usually took place at a wayside inn and could be completed remarkably quickly with the coach and its new horses on the way again within minutes. Periodically on a long journey a stop would be made not only to change the horses but for refreshment purposes. Some inns provided overnight accommodation. There were places along the major roads where there were several inns, the hospitality usually being graded according to what the customer was prepared to pay. Among these were Hounslow, Stony Stratford, Stamford and Doncaster. The provision of hospitality and the servicing of the horses and coaches were both labour intensive and they created large numbers of jobs. The local economy could become dangerously dependent on the coaching trade and many coaching towns went into the doldrums as long-distance coaching declined.

Britain's canals were built primarily to move heavy, bulky, low-value items such as coal and other minerals which they were capable of doing with great efficiency. At some places, often junctions with navigable rivers or other canals, settlements could develop where goods were loaded and unloaded, sometimes transhipped, and where warehouses for storage were built. Workshops, boatyards and waterside inns could contribute to a complex of canal-related buildings which could provide useful local employment. Examples were Shardlow, Stourport-on-Severn, Gloucester, Ellesmere Port and Brentford. Some of these places attracted further industrial premises because of the cheap transport offered by the navigable waterway or canal.

Settlements along the major roads, navigable inland waterways and canals, therefore, provided a precedent for the places later loosely described as railway towns. The coaching towns and the hubs of inland water transport activity may have excited awe in their heyday, but their impact was necessarily far less than that created by the railways at places that became important railway junctions and the site of engineering works like Crewe, Derby, Swindon or early major termini like Euston or what became Curzon Street Station in Birmingham.

The railways were great employers of labour, much of their operations being immensely labour-intensive although this was, admittedly, at a time when semi-skilled and unskilled labour was cheap. To attract labour, the railways frequently had to offer housing. Some of this was provided by the private sector but many of the pre-grouping companies built their own housing. This could be anything from a couple of cottages to a terrace, several streets or even whole districts. This housing was often superior to that provided by other contemporary industrial employers or by private speculative builders. The overall scale of the housing operations of the railway companies is often not appreciated. Before the grouping just after the First World War, collectively they were the largest housing landlords in Britain, owning about 27,000 dwellings occupied and rented by their employees and families.

In the current work, the period being considered is that from 1830 to 1914. By the latter year the railways of Britain had reached their peak.

*Chapter One*

# The Historical Context

A historian's perception of the past is necessarily very different from that of the people who lived through and experienced the events being considered. Using hindsight, we can see that the century leading up to the 1830s when railway development began in earnest was one of far-reaching change in which many of the preconditions were created for Britain's remarkable transformation into a predominantly urban industrialised society by the middle of the nineteenth century.

The Liverpool & Manchester Railway (L&MR), which opened in 1830, showed the world the potential of the steam-hauled railway but it did so in a period of great political volatility. 1815 marked the end of over twenty-five years of more-or-less continuous war with France and her satellites and was followed by sharp political tensions when huge numbers of men from the army and navy were abruptly released into the labour market precisely at a time when the country was hit by a sharp economic recession as industry lost the boost so often provided by wartime requirements for arms and munitions. Wages fell and unemployment grew. Widespread anger was reflected in the spread of radical demands for political reform; ordinary people being virtually powerless at the time. The response of the governments of the 1820s was to increase their means of repression. Crime was almost out of control and the official response was to implement a penal code of barbaric savagery. The middle classes wanted political rights commensurate with their increasing importance in the economy and headed up a movement with much working-class support for a widening of the franchise. The political tensions were evident at the opening of the L&MR when it was decided that the first train from Liverpool should stop short of Manchester because the Duke of Wellington was on board. The authorities could not guarantee his safety given the angry crowds who were waiting at the Manchester end. The Duke, far from being revered as a great military leader, was seen as a reactionary opponent of political reform. Such was the level of political and social disaffection around this time that many of Britain's ruling elite thought that the country was on the brink of revolution.

A new historical era necessarily contains within it many elements inherited from the previous period. It was not until around the middle of the nineteenth century that the earlier almost total domination of political power by the landowning elite was threatened. It was now challenged by 'new wealth', that of the rising industrial and commercial bourgeoisie. The more progressive elements among the landed interest had played a major part in transforming agriculture into an efficient, modern high-productivity, high-output industry through processes such as enclosure, the ending of peasant farming, the investment in and application of scientific and technological methods and the creation of a wage-earning workforce – an agricultural proletariat. These processes had a major impact on country-dwellers, large numbers of whom had had little option but to migrate to areas where extractive and manufacturing industries were increasingly drawing on the use of steam power and requiring large supplies of labour. The agricultural improvements helped to feed this increasingly urban population.

Numbers of landowners handsomely enriched themselves through encouraging agricultural innovation or by exploiting minerals on their lands. To further increase their incomes, they and many early industrialists invested in improvements to rivers to make them into navigable waterways. They also invested in the building of canals which enabled the easier and more efficient transportation of raw materials and fuel and the despatch of the products of the factories, mines and quarries to the consumers. The cost of coal and of necessities such as iron ore, clay, bricks and fertilisers could be substantially reduced.

The canal system, though far from perfect, gave both agriculture and industry access to a far wider national market and, in conjunction with rivers and ports, even to an international market. Improved internal waterways, by facilitating communication between producers and consumers, encouraged industries to develop where conditions were most favourable. This in turn acted as an incentive for progressive entrepreneurs to employ ever more sophisticated machinery to increase the efficiency and productivity of their workforces.

As industrialisation expanded, an improved transport infrastructure of canals and navigable waterways and, to a considerably lesser extent, of roads, proved inadequate for the seemingly unquenchable demand of industry for improved internal communications. Something better than canals was needed; something that was faster, more efficient and more flexible.

This something was to be found in the railway. Plateways, tramways and primitive railways had appeared as early as the seventeenth century, but the quantum leap occurred when steam engine technology was adapted to create locomotives which could not only move themselves but haul a payload. The pioneering days in the early nineteenth century were fraught with trial and error as ingenious men, usually colliery engineers with little formal education, strove to improve the sometimes strange contraptions they built. They were assisted by advances in ironmaking which enabled rails to be manufactured which were strong enough to bear the considerable weight of locomotives. Their efforts may be said to have culminated on 15 September 1830 with the official opening of the Liverpool & Manchester Railway. This can be described as the first modern railway. It possessed a double track of iron rails designed to support regular services for passengers and freight hauled by steam locomotives between two major provincial cities.

Railways proved to be very efficient movers of heavy, bulky loads such coal, iron ore and limestone. They also tapped successfully into an almost totally unexpected market of people travelling for leisure and pleasure. It had correctly been thought in relation to the Liverpool &

Manchester Railway, for example, that people engaged in industry and commerce might use railways in following up business possibilities. Few people in the early days of railways had considered that people living in, say, Manchester, and having the money to do so, might enjoy travelling by train to find out more about that mysterious seaport about 30 miles away called Liverpool. Before the railways came, travelling across country was far slower and, in the case of roads at least, expensive and often hazardous. The idea of travelling to Liverpool and back to Manchester in a day would previously have seemed little more than a fantasy for most people.

The railways, by providing a far more efficient transport infrastructure, facilitated the further exploitation of Britain's enormous coal resources and of previously untapped iron ore deposits such as those in Cleveland and parts of Lincolnshire and the East Midlands. Steel is an essential material for modern industrial economies and its production on a large scale became possible after the Bessemer process was introduced in 1856. Indeed, the mighty L&NWR was among the first users, if not the pioneer, of utilising this process which it did in its steelworks at Crewe. Steelmaking became a major industry, and the railways played a crucial role in bringing the necessary raw materials to the manufacturing plants and moving the finished steel to where it was needed. The railways were also major consumers of the output of the steel industry. This was a prime example of 'forward linkage'. The railways expedited demand and assisted the integration of markets by providing an effective transport infrastructure. The railways were also responsible for 'backward linkage' in creating demand from producers for materials and artefacts that were needed for their construction, operation and maintenance. Felicitously, they also provided the means of transport necessary for these operations. The railways became major employers – not only of the huge numbers who worked directly for the railway companies but also by creating a demand for coal, iron and steel, and rolling stock and for the specialised products provided by the mechanical and constructional engineering industries, for example.

Railways carried the iron and, later, the steel that was needed in the construction of steamships. Britain gained an early lead in developing them and their inherent advantages over sailing vessels for many purposes allowed Britain to assume the position of world leader in shipping as well as shipbuilding, thereby further enriching herself. The railways contributed to this process by transporting the materials from which the ships were built and handling the movement of many of the goods that were imported and exported. They also carried the coal that fuelled the steamships. The railways became major players in the movement of coal and by 1867 were moving more coal to the almost insatiable market presented by London than was moved by water and sea.

Care must be taken, however, not to over-emphasise the contribution made by the railways to Britain's economic growth in the nineteenth century. Although it would be difficult to quantify, much of this growth would have happened even if the railways had not been built. Historians attempt to record, analyse, explain and evaluate actualities. Concretely, it cannot be denied that railways took their place as the dominant form of inland transport in the period under review and unquestionably made a significant contribution to the expansion of the economy and, concomitantly, to the process of urbanisation and the generalised rise in living standards.

It is significant that the L&MR opened during a period of political turmoil which was to see the passing of the Reform Act of 1832. This extended the franchise to include the middle class of the growing industrial towns such as Manchester and Birmingham. Most men and all women, of course, remained excluded from the vote. However, the 1832 Act should be judged not on its incompleteness but by its marking a crucial demarcating point between a society in which wealthy, often aristocratic, landowners dominated society and a different sort of society in which the industrial and commercial capitalists came to gain a major position in economic and political decision-making. This was a profound transformation and one which was essential for Britain if it was to undergo its Industrial Revolution and proceed, for a period of decades, to become the leading economic and political power in the world.

The Industrial Revolution is an imprecise, possibly inadequate, term for a process of change of immense complexity. It involved a great increase in human control over nature, an extraordinary growth in the productivity of human labour and in the intricacy of social organisation and interaction. It has been called an industrial revolution, but it was much more than that. It was also a social revolution because it effected a profound transformation in the lives of untold numbers of people. During the period 1750 to 1850 which is most often quoted as the heroic period of industrialisation, the population of Britain increased exponentially. Overall, standards of living rose. Many existing towns and cities expanded rapidly, and many smaller towns and villages followed suit. New industrially based settlements appeared on what were previously green field sites.

In these emerging urban settlements, social conditions were vastly different from those in pre-industrial communities. Long-standing semi-paternal social relations between squires and tenants, farmers and labourers, and masters and servants were replaced by markedly more impersonal relationships between employers and employees, producers and consumers, haves and have nots. The common people had to adjust uncomfortably to the harsh new reality of life in overcrowded urban settlements involving new and uncongenial forms of social control. Governments had to implement many radically new public policies in order to deal with the myriad problems thrown up by the processes of industrialisation and urbanisation. Railways were an integral part of this process and a cause and effect of it. The railway provided the efficient form of transport essential for a modern industrial, commercial and urban society.

It is convenient, although not necessarily accurate, for historians to give a snappy name to a period they are studying. This can provide a simple pointer to the underpinning feature they wish to emphasise of the period under consideration. Thus, Eric Hobsbawm in his masterly and well-received trilogy gave us *The Age of Revolution* dealing with 1780 to 1848; *The Age of Capital* relating to 1848 to 1875 and *The Age of Empire* for 1875 to 1914. Harold Perkin gave us *The Age of the Railway* and Michael Robbins almost followed suit with *The Railway Age*. I would not pretend to the eminence of these authors but suggest that as far as the nineteenth century in Britain is concerned, a case could be made for calling it 'The Age of Urbanisation'.

Urban societies can be characterised as those where most of the population is a town-dwelling one not depending directly for its living on agricultural and other rural occupations. Such a society requires a decreasing proportion of the population to feed an increasing proportion which is engaged in manufacturing, mining and quarrying and commerce, trade and other services. To undergo the allied processes of industrialisation and urbanisation it is necessary that there is a substantial transfer of population from dependency on rural-based activities to various kinds of industry, commercial and other business activities of a predominantly urban character in communities which are themselves recognisably urban.

Industrial activity was, of course, not unknown in Britain before the eighteenth and nineteenth centuries. Rural settlements in various parts of the country were engaged in small-scale industrial activity frequently on a domestic outwork basis and in mining and quarrying, for example. The commercial aspect of such activities, however, was frequently town-based which increased the importance of towns in the national economy. Britain at the beginning of the nineteenth century with around 25 per cent already had proportionately more town dwellers than countries on the European continent. This figure was to increase to 50 per cent in the middle of the century. By 1900, Britain was a predominantly urban society.

Among the factors contributing to this remarkable change was the widespread application of steam power to factory production, mining and to transport. Harnessing the power of steam enabled much industrial activity to be freed from dependence on waterpower and encouraged the concentration of productive industry at places where coal or other favourable factors were present. Industrial production on a factory scale needed a large supply of labour and the operatives usually had little option but to live within walking distance of their workplace, often in newly built settlements, many of which developed into towns.

Textiles and various metal-based industries were among those employing steam power efficiently in large mills and factories by the first quarter of the nineteenth century. At the same time gifted mechanical engineers had advanced considerably down the demanding path of designing and building effective steam-powered railway locomotives. The potential of such machines was clearly demonstrated at the Rainhill Trials on the L&MR in 1829. This was the first modern railway in the sense that it was a long-distance line connecting two major cities, owning its own track and running its own trains. It was designed for the use of steam motive power except for on a short steep incline at the Liverpool end which was initially cable operated. The immediate success of the Liverpool & Manchester initiated a heroic era of railway promotion and building. The increased extraction and use of coal as a fuel, the application of steam power for factory production and in mining and for railway haulage and the development of an urban society were interlinked and interacting processes that transformed Britain. They formed the basis by mid-century of what Britain could justifiably boast about being – 'The Workshop of the World'.

In 1801, London, with a population of 865,000 was the only British town with over 100,000 inhabitants. Just fifteen other towns had 20,000 or more population. By 1851, sixty-three towns had populations over 20,000 and eight of these had 100,000 or more residents. The process of urban concentration had, however, started earlier. Some places which went on to become great industrial and/or commercial centres had grown considerably before railways started making their impact. Between 1821 and 1831, Sheffield had grown by 41 per cent, Birmingham 42 per cent, Liverpool 46 per cent, Leeds 47 per cent and Bradford a prodigious 66 per cent. In 1891, town-dwellers constituted 72 per cent of Britain's population. Towns with more than 100,000 citizens rose from eight to twenty-four over the same period. Ancient towns such as Exeter and Norwich, whose populations had been fairly static, began to grow significantly. Many long-established small country towns which attracted little industry grew only marginally if at all, particularly if they did not manage to secure a place on the railway system. The percentage of the population that could be described as 'rural' fell in real terms. Several settlements that can be regarded as virtually new appeared in the eighteenth and nineteenth centuries. These tended to be associated with steam-powered factories. They included Cromford and New Lanark, but they did not necessarily grow into towns of significant size. Many of the fastest growing towns proved to be those in which railways gained a major presence. London, many rapidly developing ports, iron manufacturing settlements in Wales, the West Midlands, Central Scotland and the North East, textile manufacturing centres especially in the West Riding of Yorkshire and in Lancashire and a few seaside resorts expanded, sometimes with feverish speed. What they had in common was the railway. It brought in fuel, raw materials, food and other necessities. It carried away the towns' manufactured goods. It was also a huge consumer of the iron and, later, the steel which some of these towns manufactured. If the town was a resort, its visitors came and went by train. The ports flourished as British built and owned ships carried the country's industrial goods to every corner of the globe.

The process of urbanisation was very evident in Scotland. There, towns with populations of over 20,000 grew from five in 1801 to nine in 1851 and seventeen in 1891. By 1891, two-thirds of Scotland's population was urban. Glasgow was on the crest of a wave. It managed to be both a port and a manufacturing centre particularly for textiles, ships and machinery. By 1891 it housed 19.4 per cent of Scotland's population. Even London only had 14.5 per cent of England's population.

In general terms, railways tended to stimulate the growth of those settlements that were already advantaged in terms of location or other factors and to do so faster than other places that were smaller and less advantaged at that time. If we use this hypothesis in relation to seaside resorts, we can see that it was true about large seaside resorts like Brighton, Blackpool, Bournemouth, Scarborough and Southend, all of which grew more rapidly than smaller places such as Newquay, Hornsea, Aberystwyth or Hunstanton.

Railways were a major player in the in the revolutionary changes that occurred in British life in the nineteenth century. Millions of people travelled who had never travelled before. Even those who did not travel by train used them indirectly. Railways provided the means for the mass distribution of newspapers, periodicals and cheap literature. They had a significant impact on the diet of the people, especially in the towns and cities, as the railways provided a cheap means of bringing meat, fresh vegetables and fish to the urban consumer. They provided huge numbers of jobs. They reduced transport costs not only for fuel and raw materials but for finished goods, vast quantities of which were exported. They brought in the building materials used in the construction of new communities. We could continue but having indicated aspects of the context in which urbanisation became such a major societal factor, it is time to examine a variety of places, large and small, in our attempt to establish some understanding of what the phrase 'railway town' means.

*Chapter Two*

# Some Railway Towns of New Creation

P rofessor Jack Simmons (1986) argued that the term 'railway town' should be restricted to just that small number of places which were developed by the railways either on greenfield sites or as adjuncts to existing settlements and where the presence of the railway became an absolutely dominating one economically and socially. Those on greenfield sites might be termed 'towns of new creation'. He proposed just six towns for such a description. They are Swindon, Crewe, Shildon, Horwich, Wolverton and Eastleigh. Let us consider each of these in turn.

## Swindon

The origin of what became the mighty Great Western Railway lay in the building of a main line from the prominent provincial city and seaport of Bristol to London. About halfway between these two, a subsidiary line was planned which would strike off in a north-westerly direction towards Gloucester. A junction and station were therefore envisaged, located just to the north of an existing small hilltop market town called Swindon. The line connecting London and Bristol was superbly engineered, with only gentle gradients from London to Swindon after which much steeper gradients could not be avoided as the line descended towards Bath on its route to Bristol. It was decided, given the state of development of steam locomotives at the time, that Swindon should be the changing point for the locomotives best suited to work the two very differently graded sections of the line. It was a natural outcome to consider locating locomotive servicing and maintenance facilities at Swindon. A logical further step was the decision that Swindon, where plenty of cheap suitable land was available, should be the location for the company's main engineering works and support facilities. A bonus was that a nearby canal, the Wilts & Berks, provided the means to bring in coal and coke cheaply and easily through its connections with other canals.

The GWR opened in 1840. The nucleus of a new town was about to be created. The company had no option but to attract labour from outside the district and it therefore had to provide accommodation for workers and their families. An estate of 300 cottages was constructed close to the station. These were substantial stone-built dwellings of distinctive appearance, and they provided what, for the time, was high quality working-class housing. John Betjeman in a burst of enthusiasm once described it as 'one of the first garden cities in the world'. The contractor involved also erected the initial buildings of the engineering works, the station and what became its somewhat notorious refreshment rooms. The GWR then found itself engaged in social engineering. It was not enough to attract a labour force; it had to retain it. The company built a school and gave moral support for a church, completed in 1845. Both were shrewd investments. The company needed literate and numerate employees. The church helped to create some social cement and to inculcate the deferential attitudes demanded of company servants. Despite these early efforts at social control, 'New' Swindon gained a reputation for being a somewhat rough district.

The community around the works and station grew quite rapidly and the railway village and other local accommodation tended to become overcrowded and somewhat negated the GWR's attempt to attract and keep staff by offering them good quality accommodation and a range of social facilities. It took some time for the works to develop production and although 2,000 jobs were planned, as late as 1851 there were only 600 available and the requirement for labour had fluctuated through the difficult financial years of the 1840s. As the GWR's system grew, so the workload and the workforce at Swindon Works increased and downturns in the economy could create considerable local hardship in a town so dependent on the fortunes of one major company.

Before Swindon Works opened, the GWR had tended to buy much of its rolling stock and other equipment from outside contractors. As the company expanded, the engineering facilities of companies it had absorbed became available. Some of these works built rolling stock. Wolverhampton, for example, manufactured locomotives until 1908 and carriages and wagons were constructed at Worcester and at Saltney, near Chester, until 1874. Repairs also took place at these and a small number of other locations, so Swindon never had a monopoly of such work. Limited numbers of locomotives, rolling stock and other equipment continued to be brought from outside suppliers.

The GWR, like many railway companies, especially the larger ones, aimed for, but never quite achieved, self-sufficiency but the growth of the company saw an increase in the functions performed at Swindon. Evidence of the desire to do things 'in-house' saw the opening of a rolling mill for rails in 1861. This required some specialist workers and saw men experienced in the production of iron and steel moving to Swindon from South Wales. Inhabitants with Welsh origins and Welsh habits and culture were long a feature of Swindon society. By 1905 the GWR employed just over 14,000 workers at Swindon out of a population of about 45,000.

Relations between the pre-industrial world represented by Old Swindon, a small, sleepy market town serving a deeply rural area, and the ultra-modern New Swindon with its noise, bustle and sense of restless modernity, were not particularly cordial. The GWR seemed content to let the new town get on with what it was built for. It was a company town totally devoted to serving the needs of a dynamic, ambitious modern capitalist company. For at least ten years after Swindon Station opened, the residents of the Old Town repeatedly tried to persuade the GWR to construct a new road to give them access to the station. They got a frosty reception. Inevitably, however, Swindon's two distinct neighbourhoods eventually merged. New Swindon, growing remorselessly through most of the second half of the nineteenth century, was a functional, planned industrial community.

Old Swindon, with a thrusting, growing population on its doorstep, could not help being deeply influenced by what was going on down the hill. The GWR was anxious not to waste any of the land it had purchased by using it for purposes it regarded as superfluous. Old Swindon found itself being transformed and modernised whether it liked it or not to become the place where Swindon's new population did their shopping. The collective spending power of the GWR's employees demanded an expansion of Old Swindon's retail services. This, in turn, boosted its existing function as a regional market centre. It had been somewhat overshadowed by Marlborough in that respect but by the 1870s had usurped that town as the focal point of north Wiltshire, and not just for retailing. The Old Town was transformed functionally and physically to serve the needs of the new one. The community around the station and the works bore the indelible stamp of the GWR having been developed over a matter of decades. The Old Town looked more diverse, elements of the past mixing, not necessarily harmoniously, with planless modernity.

Public health policy was recognised as an urgent necessity by the early years of the nineteenth century. However, this was the age of laisser-faire and it proved difficult in the face of entrenched opposition to implement effective measures to improve sanitation and housing conditions and to combat the epidemic diseases which spread so rapidly, especially in overcrowded conditions. Old Swindon, despite so much of it being newly built, suffered from outbreaks of smallpox, scarlet fever and typhoid. Its water supply was notable for its poor quality. In the New Town things were somewhat better, the GWR being prepared to take some responsibility for public health issues. Premises were found for a surgery in 1847 when a Medical Fund was also established. In 1849, the GWR began to operate excursions for employees and families during the annual holiday week. This provision, which became known as 'The Trip', went from strength to strength and in 1914 no fewer than 25,616 employees, families and friends made use of free trips on special trains or with excursion tickets. These trips earned dividends in terms of employer loyalty.

Planting a new town on a greenfield site with a largely imported workforce inevitably meant that the GWR at Swindon and the L&NWR at Crewe had to take on responsibility for directing the moral, educational, medical and social welfare of those they employed. Hence the provision at Swindon of housing, the building of a church, a hospital, of swimming and Turkish baths, of a school twenty-five years before it became a legal requirement, a recreational park and a Mechanics' Institute. The latter opened a public library well before local authorities took on that responsibility.

In 1868, the Swindon Permanent Building and Benefit Society was established. Its primary intention was to contribute to the provision of housing of a good standard for employees of the GWR and their families. Not only was much working-class housing in Swindon of poor quality but it was also in short supply. Daniel Gooch, a dominant figure in the GWR, was instrumental in obtaining funding for the Society and persuading the GWR to sell land to the Society for better quality residential development than private speculative builders were likely to erect.

The Old and the New Swindon merged physically about 1890 and Swindon metamorphosed into a municipal borough in 1900. It speaks volumes for the influence of the GWR that the borough's first mayor was George Jackson Churchward who, at the time, was the works manager.

Many railway companies supported the idea of self-improvement among their workers and, as at Swindon, established Mechanics' Institutes. One was established very shortly after the works opened but its functions were greatly enhanced when it moved to much larger premises indirectly sponsored by the GWR and on land owned by the company. It had a well-stocked library and a range of recreational facilities of the sort then considered as being of a 'wholesome' character. From the point of view of the company, this was enlightened paternalism. The sceptic might say that it was all about controlling the workforce. Even among the railway companies of Victorian and Edwardian times, the GWR was noted for its rigid disciplinary code and hostility to trade union organisations among its workforce. Those employees who were happy to keep their heads down and mouths shut and to be viewed by management as steady and conscientious, knew that they had good prospects of a job for life. Undoubtedly, the GWR and many other companies generated what seems today like extraordinary loyalty among their workers. It was not a good idea for a footplate worker to let it be known that he considered the conditions on the footplate almost intolerable. GWR locomotives were known for their awkwardly arranged cab fittings and minimal shelter from the elements for the footplate crew. The work of shunters and track workers was inherently dangerous, and many suffered injuries and death. Even so, railway employment was sought after.

Swindon never developed into a major railway junction to match somewhere like Crewe. It became the point at which the secondary GWR main line to Gloucester and Cheltenham left the London to Bristol and South Wales route and there was a short branch in a north-easterly direction to Highworth. There was also the rather low-key presence of what became the Midland & South Western Junction Railway with its town station opened in 1881. There was physical connection between it and the GWR. Despite its potential value as a connection from the West Midlands towards Southampton and other places on the south coast, the 'Tiddley Dyke' as it was sometimes called, never grew up.

The works boasted a stentorian hooter which announced the beginning and end of shifts and could be heard several miles away. The locals cursed it but got used to it. Not so the 5th Viscount Bolingbroke whose estate at Lydiard Park was over 3 miles from the works. He also cursed it because it allegedly disturbed his pheasants when they were sitting on their eggs.

## Crewe

The Grand Junction Railway (GJR) was authorised in 1833 to build a line from Curzon Street in Birmingham through Wolverhampton, Stafford and Warrington to join the L&MR via the Warrington & Newton Railway which it was to absorb in 1834. The line was opened in 1837. An intermediate station was opened close to the small settlements Monks Coppenhall and Church Coppenhall. This station took the name 'Crewe' after a nearby country house, 'Crewe Hall'. In 1837, the Chester & Crewe and the Manchester & Birmingham Railway were authorised. They would also serve Crewe which was then on its way to becoming a major railway junction.

There has always been a question about why the GJR chose to serve Crewe and make a railway town of it when logic might have assumed that Nantwich, an old-established market town 4 miles south-west of Crewe, might have offered prospects of greater originating traffic. Nantwich was already served by inland waterways and a network of roads. However, there was considerable opposition from local landowners. Additionally, it seems that large quantities of relatively cheap land were available in the Coppenhall area.

Crewe was building locomotives by 1843 and soon capacity in the works was at a premium so the wagon making facility was run down and eventually transferred to a new works built on a virgin site at Earlestown, north of Warrington. This in turn became a railway town albeit on a much smaller scale than Crewe. The L&NWR, successor to the GJR, decided to concentrate all work on carriages at Wolverton.

From the start, aspects of town planning had to be applied by the GJR from 1840 when construction of its new engineering facilities at Crewe began. There was little suitable labour available locally so, in 1843, the GJR took the sensible but expensive decision to transfer a sizeable number of its experienced employees and their families from Edge Hill at Liverpool. They needed housing and the provision of the infrastructure for a cohesive community. Streets of terraced houses were built to what was a high standard for the time and the nucleus of a town had been created by 1848 when wider economic problems caused a slowdown in business activity throughout much of Britain.

The first 32 cottages were occupied by the end of 1842; in 1848 there were 520 and well over 700 in 1858. *Chambers' Edinburgh Journal* in 1846 wrote of the housing at Crewe:

> The dwelling houses arrange themselves in four classes: first, the villa-style lodges of the superior officers; next a kind of ornamental Gothic constitutes the houses of the next in authority; the engineers domiciled in detached mansions, which accommodate four families, with gardens and separate entrances; and last the labourer delights in neat cottages of four apartments.

The last railway-built housing was erected about 1859 and after that new working-class housing was provided by private speculative builders and generally of a poorer standard.

In 1850, *Chambers' Edinburgh Journal* wrote:

> The general appearance of Crewe is very pleasing. The streets are wide and well-paved; the houses are neat and commodious, usually of two stories, built of bricks, but the brick concealed by rough-cast plaster, with porches, lattice windows, and a little bit of garden ground before the door ... The accommodation is good and it would be difficult to find such houses at such low rent even in the suburbs of a large town.

The indefatigable traveller by train, Sidney Smith, writing in the middle of the century, said:

> Crewe is a wonderful place; sixteen years ago, the quietist of country villages, now intersected in every direction with iron roads pointing from it to almost every point of the compass

... The railway village of Crewe is on the same plan as that of Wolverton, but situated in much prettier scenery; and includes a church, infant, boys' and girls' schools, a Library and Literary Institution.

The GJR, and its successor the L&NWR, also built gas works, public baths, provided a water supply, dealt with sewage and refuse disposal, let out land for allotments, established a surgery complete with a doctor, a superbly equipped Mechanics' Institute, opened a savings bank and set up its own fire brigade. It was happy to provide funding for the establishment of Church of England places of worship because it was felt that these would assist in inculcating the 'correct' values in the workforce. They were less enthusiastic about assisting nonconformist groups and Roman Catholics to set up their own bases. The first Anglican church was Christ Church, paid for by the GJR and opened in 1843. The *Railway Gazette* in 1845 enthused over this building saying that endowing churches 'is one among many signs ... which seem to foretell that great, noble and national works, incidental only to railways, will come out of railways; such works as may chance to compete with our ancient cathedrals'.

The GJR merged with three other companies to create the L&NWR. Each of the giant L&NWR's component companies had its own engineering works and the decision was taken to concentrate locomotive construction and overhaul at Crewe. Typical of the large railway companies at this time, the L&NWR aimed to achieve a high level of self-sufficiency. As far as possible it eschewed buying from outside contractors. It developed facilities for making its own rails. Crewe was a very early location for a plant using the Bessemer steel-making process. The Crewe installation was unusual in having a facility for making bricks on a mass scale. The construction of railways required vast quantities of bricks.

Not everything was done by the L&NWR in-house. It built a factory for a firm specialising in the manufacture of uniforms for railway staff.

This gained a monopoly of L&NWR business and supplied many other companies. Everyday railway operation consumes huge quantities of paperwork, and it made good sense, if not doing the printing themselves, at least to have a very close relationship with a reliable printing company. This was McCorquodale of Liverpool. This concern built a works in Crewe and another at Wolverton and supplied all the L&NWR's printing needs.

Although these activities provided some diversity in employment, Crewe was very much a one-industry town and vulnerable to fluctuations of the economy. There were at least two occasions in the second half of the nineteenth century when Crewe was in the doldrums and LNWR employees had to be laid off. The population increased from 19,000 in 1871 to 45,000 in 1911, admittedly after an extension of its boundaries to embrace nearby Nantwich, an ancient town of a totally different character. Employment at the works went from 4,000 in 1870 to approaching 8,000 at the turn of the century.

Despite homes being built by the GJR for many of the workers needed in the early days of the town, its successor, the L&NWR, soon ran out of enthusiasm for this activity and Crewe's housing needs were then largely provided by private builders. This may seem odd given that the L&NWR was determined to put an indelible stamp on the town, to give it an identity as a company town. It also gave Crewe the very fine Queen's Park in 1888, a Jubilee tribute to Queen Victoria and celebration of fifty years since the opening of the GJR. Railway companies were not philanthropic organisations but some of them, the L&NWR included, reckoned that involvement in this kind of provision paid dividends in terms of employee loyalty and industrial relations.

This enlightened practice contrasted with its everyday disciplinary activities which tended towards the draconian. Senior management figures, most notably Francis William Webb, were martinets who demanded absolute obedience from the workforce. For many years they pursued a political line strongly supportive of the Conservatives and they were prepared to dismiss company employees who were known to be pro-Liberal. In the 1880s, as trade unions attempted to gain a foothold in the workforce, activists were peremptorily sacked. The newspapers and other material available in the Mechanics' Institute was carefully vetted. On the other hand, the Mechanics' Institute provided technical, cultural, educational and recreational facilities for several generations of the company's employees.

Crewe was an outstanding example of a town utterly dominated by the presence of railways. Some of the L&NWR's early activities in urban planning were undoubtedly progressive but over time its ubiquitous presence became a heavy hand, even a stultifying one. The makings of a model industrial town in the 1840s evolved over time into a rather mundane and even backward place. Despite a population of about 45,000 people just before the First World War, the town had not even introduced electric trams, a mode of urban public transport in widespread urban use elsewhere.

A comparison may be appropriate, if only because both places are so often cited as archetypes of railway towns. In both Swindon and Crewe, the dominating GWR and L&NWR both believed unequivocally in the right of management to have the monopoly of controlling every aspect of the business. This extended to playing a major role in the lives of their workforces and their families. Such managers were naturally authoritarian and exceptionally loyal to their companies but high office in these companies did not necessarily equip them for treating their employees with respect and humanity. A great mechanical engineer, for example, may not have been the person to bring out the best in those he employed. Here we would have to say that Daniel Gooch seemed to be able to combine virtuosity in progressing from an engineer to the heights of General Manager of the GWR while retaining a reputation for humanity. He had no match among the senior management of the L&NWR. Francis Webb was an autocrat. As Locomotive Superintendent he dominated life in Crewe on behalf of the company and himself, being mayor, a magistrate and alderman, he was a staunch opponent of trade unionism on the railways. Autocrat he may have been, but he left money in his will to establish the Webb Orphanage for the children of L&NWR employees.

The name of the main early trade union for railway workers encapsulates the nature of the relationship between management and labour. This was, of course, the Amalgamated Society of Railway Servants. Servants were expected to do as they were told. If they did not like the terms and conditions of their employment, they were free to leave. Except that it was not usually as easy as that.

Crewe became the hub of the L&NWR's extensive empire as it came to be the focus of its lines from Holyhead and Chester, Scotland, Carlisle, Preston and Liverpool, Manchester, London, Rugby and Birmingham, Northwich, and Shrewsbury and the West Country. Despite the L&NWR's domination of operations at Crewe, there were three interlopers. The first was the enterprising North Staffordshire Railway working in from Kidsgrove and Stoke-on-Trent and opening in 1848. Despite some early disagreements, the relations with the North Staffordshire Railway were generally amicable, perhaps because that company had no great territorial ambitions and was largely content with its own compact system. The L&NWR was extremely ambitious and made several takeover bids for the North Staffordshire Railway. Relations settled down and each company enjoyed running powers over parts of the other's system. Viewed very differently was the GWR which gained access to Crewe in 1863 by virtue of running powers over the L&NWR's Shrewsbury to Crewe line from Nantwich. A considerable amount of long-distance freight traffic especially from the West Midlands, ran over the GWR's line from Wellington to Nantwich via Market Drayton. Trains of the Cambrian Railways from the Oswestry direction also made their way to Crewe after joining the line from Shrewsbury at Whitchurch. The GWR's foray into Crewe was viewed with great distaste at the centre of the L&NWR's operations. Adding insult to injury was the opening of a pub at Crewe called *The Brunel Arms*.

An enormous quantity of traffic was handled at Crewe – passenger, mails and freight – but Crewe never had a station of architectural distinction like Carlisle or York, for example. It was extended time and time again but without evidence of any grand vision. Essentially, its main function was as a station where people changed trains and a large percentage of the passengers it handled never entered or left the premises. Very close to the station was the *Crewe Arms Hotel* which was bought by the L&NWR in 1877 and this was a prestigious establishment from which uniformed flunkeys would emerge to meet the principal trains and assist those passengers who were staying at the hotel.

By the late 1890s the L&NWR employed 10,000 people in Crewe which was about a third of the population. Crewe was a true railway town.

## Shildon

This town in County Durham possessed what can be described as the grandaddy of railway company workshops at which locomotives were manufactured. The primitive workshops here opened in 1826 for the Stockton & Darlington Railway (S&DR) and were the first in the world on a railway serving the public. The first locomotive completed at Shildon was *Royal George*, designed by Timothy Hackworth. This may never have shared the celebrity of *Rocket*, for example, but deserves recognition as the pioneering locomotive to be built by a railway company in its own workshops. By 1832, seven more locomotives had been completed at Shildon. A tradition of engineering skill and expertise built up there, building locomotives not just for the S&DR but, through the firm of Hackworth at the Soho Works, locomotives for other customers.

In the 1820s, Shildon was little more than a scattered village, having a population of around 900. New Shildon was close by, and this is where the S&DR made a considerable investment and showed its confidence in the future by creating the infrastructure of a town. This involved a gas works, clean water supplies, a school and a Railway Institute having an educational and social function. What developed was very much a company town in which the directors owned most of the land and decided what was to be done with it. Strangely, as the place developed, it seemed to lack any sense of actual planning or of a corporate hand being involved. There was a sizeable engine shed and what became a large marshalling yard. There were coal mines and other industrial works and all in all, they made Shildon an unpleasant place, environmentally blighted even by the standards of the time. Among the adjectives used by contemporaries to describe its appearance were 'ugly' and 'hideous'.

In 1863, the S&DR became an important component of the North Eastern Railway (NER) and in the 1870s the works ceased to build locomotives. The NER preferred to concentrate its locomotive work at Darlington. Shildon thrived, however, as the main wagon-building and repair facility of the NER which was a notably progressive company enjoying a near-monopoly of the eastern side of England from the Humber to the border with Scotland. In 1902 it employed 1,000 workers at Shildon and the town had grown to have a population just short of 2,500. Shildon remained largely dependent on the railway for employment, but it never grew into a town of any great size. Indeed, for all the validity of it being described as a railway town, it remained comparatively little-known. It was never located on any major passenger-carrying route and the lines that served it and its vicinity were largely given over the lucrative but unglamorous function of moving coal and other minerals.

## Wolverton

Most early railway companies bought their locomotives from private manufacturing contractors. The London & Birmingham Railway (L&B) was among those that moved to bring such work in-house. It chose a location in open countryside at Wolverton in Buckinghamshire which was about halfway between the two cities. The L&B had the same problem as other companies establishing themselves on virgin sites, that of providing accommodation for an inward-moving workforce. The old market town of Stony Stratford, about 2 miles away, might supply some workers but the L&B decided to build a town of its own to house what was likely to become a sizeable workforce. The result was that by 1844 this previously bucolic spot had become a small, planned town containing seven residential streets, a church, schools and a market hall serving an initial population of about 1,000.

The works at Wolverton built and repaired locomotives for the L&B and then the L&NWR into which it was absorbed. About 180 locomotives were erected at Wolverton between 1845 and 1863 when the L&NWR decided to rearrange its locomotive and rolling stock construction and repair facilities. Crewe became the major centre of locomotive work and Wolverton gained a virtual monopoly of the L&NWR's carriage building and repair work. It soon became the largest railway carriage works in Britain.

Samuel Sidney in *Rides on Railways* (1851) was a shrewd and observant if somewhat quirky early enthusiast for railways who travelled extensively visiting many places served by the L&NWR. His comments on Wolverton provide a particularly instructive description of an early railway town. He starts by describing Wolverton as 'the first specimen of a railway town built on a plan to order'. He continued:

> The population entirely consists of men employed in the Company's service, as mechanics, guards, enginemen, stokers, porters, labourers, their wives and children, their superintendents, a clergyman, their wives and children, schoolmasters and schoolmistresses, the ladies engaged on the refreshment establishment, and the tradesmen attracted to Wolverton by the demand of the population ... This railway colony is well worth the attention of those who devote themselves to an investigation of the social condition of the labouring classes.

> We have here a body of mechanics of intelligence above average, regularly employed for ten and a half hours during five days, and for eight hours during the sixth day of the week, well paid, well housed, with schools for their children, a reading-room

and mechanics' institution at their disposal, gardens for their leisure hours, and a church with clergyman exclusively devoted to them. When work is ended, Wolverton is a pure republic – equality reigns. There are no rich men or men of station: all are gentlemen.

... At Wolverton may be seen collected together in companies, each under command of its captain or foremen, in separate workshops, some hundreds of the best handicraftsmen that Europe can produce, all steadily at work, not without noise, yet without confusion. ... Among all it would be difficult to find a bad-shaped head, or a stupid face – as for a drunkard, not one. ... Although locomotives are built at Wolverton, only a small proportion of the engines used on the line are built by the company, and the chief importance of the factory at Wolverton is as a repairing shop, and school for engine-drivers.

The men employed at Wolverton station in March 1851, numbered 775, of whom four were overlookers, nine were foremen, four draughtsmen, fifteen clerks, thirty-two engine-drivers, twenty-one firemen and 119 labourers; the rest were mechanics and apprentices. ... Of course, these men have, for the most part, wives and families, and so with shopkeepers, raise the population of Wolverton to about 2,000, inhabiting a series of uniform brick houses, in rectangular streets, about a mile distant from the ancient parish church of Wolverton, and the half-dozen houses constituting the original parish.

As the works grew, it expanded its workforce, many of whom lived in Stony Stratford and walked to and from Wolverton. Early in the 1880s it was decided to build a light railway connecting the station and the works with Stony Stratford. Not only would this make life easier for those employed at the works who lived in Stony Stratford but give the latter town a much-needed economic boost. The result was the opening in 1887 of a street tramway using odd-looking steam locomotives which at one time hauled impressive tramcars with seating for up to 100 passengers.

## Horwich

The towns mentioned above were first generation railway towns. Horwich and Eastleigh belong to a later generation of railway towns.

The L&Y was the result of the merging of several small northern railway companies in 1847. The consolidated company initially concentrated its engineering facilities at Miles Platting, close to Manchester, but soon found that the location of the site virtually precluded expansion. This problem was exacerbated by a serious fire and the decision was then made to remove the carriage and wagon operation to nearby Newton Heath. Locomotive work remained at Miles Platting, but the site was constricted and so 350 acres of land were bought at Horwich, north of Bolton, in 1884. Some of this land was surplus to requirements and was quickly disposed of but a brand new, high-tech factory was built primarily to handle the L&Y's locomotive building and repair work. This work came on stream in late 1886.

Although the land on which the works was built was a greenfield site, Horwich was already in existence as a small town involved in bleaching and cotton-spinning. These activities were in the doldrums when the L&Y decided to relocate to Horwich and the company was able to take advantage of a large number of unlet dwellings. These were occupied by workers' families, many of them transferred from Miles Platting. As well as the company-built housing, speculative builders targeted the town, keen to put up homes for the sizeable numbers of other incomers who would need to be accommodated. Several streets were built close to the works which were also adjacent to the trunk road from Bolton to Preston and these new streets were named after prominent engineers, most, but not all of whom, had made their name from work associated with railways. Horwich's housing was well regarded at the time. The 'new' town was some distance from the pre-railway nucleus and remained distinct from it. Various amenities were built close to the works, including a hospital, a hotel, a bowling green and what became an extremely impressive Mechanics' Institute. This was open to all local people but was mostly used by L&Y employees and their families. Although the emphasis was on technical education, classes in the arts and social sciences were available. Instruction in practical skills like cooking and dressmaking were also provided but, in keeping with the mores of the time, these were aimed at a female audience.

The railway proved to be just the fillip Horwich needed. Its population grew rapidly, and some other industries started up in the town, particularly employing female labour. It never became a large place, but it was dominated by the presence of the giant works of the L&Y. It was a hard, northern town standing in the lee of Winter Hill and Rivington Pike. These are outriders of the Pennines. With the prevailing winds from the west, the town got more than its fair share of rain. It was no beauty spot, but it had a community spirit encouraged by the L&Y which subsidised recreations for its employees and their families such as football, cricket, angling, horticulture, musical and dramatic arts, brass bands and orchestras.

## Eastleigh

The L&Y was not the only railway company to encounter problems when outgrowing the space available for their engineering activities especially where these were in districts becoming increasingly built up. Little land might be available for expansion or spare land could be excessively expensive and so it made sense to transfer operations to sites which avoided such difficulties.

The London & South Western Railway (L&SWR) had a works at Nine Elms, Battersea, established in 1839 on a constricted site and the impossibility of expansion saw the carriage and wagon work transferred to a new facility at Eastleigh in Hampshire, not far from Southampton. This had already become something of a nodal point because it was the place where the L&SWR's main line from London to Southampton made a junction in 1840 with secondary but important lines to Portsmouth and Salisbury. Growth had been slow, but some cottages housed railway employees before the new works began to be built. We have seen how some companies engaged in social engineering in the planned urban developments for which they were responsible, but Eastleigh soon drew opprobrium for the poor quality and unplanned nature of the housing that was built to accommodate the incoming workforce. The L&SWR transferred locomotive stabling and maintenance operations from its depot at Southampton and many of its workers and their families moved to Eastleigh where they obviously required housing.

Changes in local government regulations around the end of the nineteenth century helped environmental conditions in Eastleigh to improve by the time the L&SWR took the plunge and transferred its heavy locomotive work from Nine Elms to Eastleigh in 1910. There were 1,500 staff involved in this move and housing had to be built for them. Eastleigh was now a fully-fledged railway town dominated by the presence of extensive railway engineering works and a large locomotive shed but it remained a formless place lacking the sense of semi-paternalistic pride and identity that was evident in Swindon and Crewe, for example.

## Tuxford

Tuxford was a little-known large village in Nottinghamshire before the Lancashire, Derbyshire and East Coast Railway (LD&ECR), a hopelessly optimistic company which never managed to reach either Lancashire or the East Coast, decided in 1896 to establish its workshops there. A passenger station was opened by the LD&ECR served by trains mostly running to and from Chesterfield and Lincoln. The GNR had already opened a wayside station in 1852 on its 'Towns Route' between London King's Cross, Peterborough and Doncaster. This was also called Tuxford and was inconveniently sited for its namesake. In 1897, the LD&ECR and the GNR opened a two-level exchange station where the former company's line crossed the GNR. This was called Dukeries Junction and high hopes were entertained at least by the LD&ECR that healthy tourist traffic would develop to the Dukeries close by. It did not. The GNR seemed much less interested particularly because its own Tuxford Station was only about three-quarters of a mile away. Only a handful of trains called on either line and, Dukeries Junction can be regarded as something of a white elephant. A curve north of Dukeries linked the LD&ECR and the GNR and there were some exchange sidings alongside the GNR.

The engineering works was small as befitted the company that owned it but at its peak it employed 130 men. With some irony it was known locally as 'The Plant' given that the similarly nicknamed Doncaster Works of the GNR was not too distant. There was also a small engine shed and some housing for railway workers. The LD&ECR was absorbed by the Great Central Railway (GCR) in 1907 and it is not surprising that Tuxford Works soon began to be run down. It finally closed in 1927.

*Chapter Three*

# Some Smaller Railway Settlements of New Creation

## Woodford Halse

Woodford & Hinton was the name originally given to the station, opened on the GCR London Extension in 1899, from where, soon after, a branch line diverged in a south-westerly direction to Banbury and a connection was made with the Stratford-upon-Avon & Midland Junction Railway's rambling cross-country line from Ravenstone Wood Junction to Stratford and Broome Junction. Woodford Halse was almost 70 miles from London and 34 miles south of Leicester.

The GCR specialised in acting as a conduit for an intensive service of freight and mineral trains largely from the north-east and the East Midlands which made their way onto the GWR's system at Banbury with onward connections to South Wales and the West Country. At Woodford, a sizeable marshalling yard was constructed for the sorting of this traffic and a substantial engine shed was built to service the locomotives involved. A passenger station was opened but freight traffic absolutely dominated operations.

The railway obtained a large amount of cheap land for its business at Woodford, and this involved the creation, on a greenfield site, not exactly of a railway town, more a village. Before the railway came, the locality consisted of two hamlets, Hinton and the rather larger Woodford Halse. Work was mostly in agriculture but also with female employment in lacemaking as a cottage industry. The GCR proceeded to build a settlement containing housing and some social facilities and having much of the appearance of a scaled-down industrial settlement.

The local building material was a brownish ironstone of which most of the pre-railway vernacular cottages and other structures were composed. Woodford became a rather strange hotch-potch of the old stone buildings juxtaposed to the harsh red brick of the railway housing and other new buildings that followed the coming of the railway. The streets of railway housing may have been plain and utilitarian, but they were well-built, having piped water and gas which made them better places in which to live than the picturesque but crumbling cottages that had survived from the days of yore.

As elsewhere in railway settlements, the housing was designed on strictly hierarchical lines allotted according to the status of the occupant's employment. Of the artisan grades, engine drivers were always seen as the elite, and they were provided with markedly more spacious houses boasting bay windows. The road on which they were located was known as 'Piano Row' because the bays of several of them displayed a piano, very much a status symbol of 'respectability' at the time. Lodging accommodation was available in four of the 136 dwellings built for railway employees who moved to the area or traincrew whose rosters required them to sleep between their outward and return duties.

Woodford never grew to be much more than a village. It had a population of just 1,220 in 1901. Although it is beyond our time frame, the station was renamed 'Woodford Halse' in 1950. The population reached around 3,500 in the early 1960s of whom between 500 and 600 worked on the railway. It was therefore a severe blow when the GCR closed in September 1966 but the place, although much changed, has survived. Woodford had been a perfect example of a settlement completely owing its existence to the railways.

## Riccarton Junction

Even smaller than Woodford Halse, there really was nowhere else quite like Riccarton Junction. This remote spot in the old Scottish county of Roxburghshire was the junction of what became the NBR's Carlisle to Edinburgh main line commonly known as the 'Waverley Route' and the same company's Border Counties branch line to Hexham via Reedsmouth. The station opened as 'Riccarton' in 1862, the suffix 'Junction' being added in 1905. As well as the sparse Border Counties line passenger trains, some stopping trains on the Waverley Route called.

The station was in the most desolate and remote of fell country, far from the nearest road. Riccarton stood over 850 feet above sea level and was 65 miles from Edinburgh and 32 miles from Carlisle. A small engine shed was built for banking freight trains on the climb towards Whitrope and Hawick. A workforce had to be assembled to service the locomotives and maintain the permanent way and other railway installations in this bleak spot. There was no alternative to the building of a largely self-contained company settlement. A railway village was created. All the residents were dependent on the railway for their livelihood. No other employment was available.

The theoretical boss of the small community that was created was the station master. As well as the duties attached to that position, he ran a sub-post office located in the booking office. Takings in the booking office must have been frugal. Railway staff and their families would have been able to buy privilege tickets, but members of the general public would have been few and far between. Any intending passengers would have had to clamber over rocks and wade through gorse and other unforgiving flora to reach the station which, incidentally, housed the local branch of the Hawick Co-operative Society, the only retail outlet.

A schoolroom was built by the NBR and rumour has it that the spiritual needs of the residents were met in the engine shed which was a few hundred yards from the station. There was no doctor in such a small community and in the event of any resident needing urgent medical attention, they would be conveyed on the footplate of any handy locomotive to receive attention at Newcastleton or Hawick. It did not do to fall ill at Riccarton! Its inhabitants even missed out when they died. There was no place of interment at Riccarton so they were forced to make their last journey by train. The NBR graciously transported the cadaver for free while the mourners, if they were railway employees, could take advantage of privilege tickets.

Few railway employees wanted to live at Riccarton Junction and it is said that in NBR days the place was used as a 'sin bin' to which errant workers were sent as a punishment.

## Hellifield

In 1800, Hellifield was a small, rather obscure village with some employment in agriculture and in cotton weaving. It stood on a turnpike from Keighley to Kendal and teams of horses were changed at the *Black Horse Inn* which was the focal point of the village.

Hellifield's first railway was the 'Little' North Western Railway. This small but ambitious company wanted to connect the West Riding of Yorkshire via Skipton and Hellifield with the main line of the L&NWR to Carlisle and Scotland, at Low Gill. From Clapham it built a line as far as Ingleton which was intended to be the first stage of the line to Low Gill. This opened in July 1849. The problem was that the company was in a dire financial state and could not afford to build beyond Ingleton. Worse, it could not even afford to run the short section from Clapham and it closed for eleven years. In 1861 the L&NWR opened the line from Ingleton to Low Gill. A few weeks later, the MR which had taken over the lease of the 'Little' North Western, reopened the Clapham to Ingleton section. From Clapham what was originally intended to be a branch proceeded westwards to Lancaster and Morecambe and this had opened throughout in June 1850 and was proving to be a more viable venture. A small and rather insignificant station for the North Western was built outside the village, opening in 1849. This had little impact on the village except for providing some railway jobs and helping to compensate for the loss of employment in cotton weaving and farming, both of which were in the doldrums. The population fell slightly for a few years.

In 1880, the L&Y completed its line from Blackburn. This immediately changed the status of Hellifield as it now became a junction. A new and better-appointed joint station came into use on 1 June 1880. The L&Y

built exchange sidings and a small engine shed. The MR also had a shed. Railway activity at Hellifield now required an increasing workforce. Both companies needed to recruit and had little option but to provide housing for a substantial number of incomers. This housing, in common with much of that provided elsewhere by other railway companies, was of superior quality by general working-class standards. In 1881 the population was about 250 but rose to 670 in 1895 of which 60 per cent were employed on the railways that now dominated the modestly growing community. In 1875-76 the MR had opened the monumental Settle and Carlisle line and Hellifield's status was enhanced as it now found itself on an Anglo-Scottish main line. The level of railway activity at Hellifield grew rapidly as the Settle & Carlisle was a major freight artery and heavy traffic used the line. Much of this additional traffic had come along the L&Y metals from Manchester and industrial south Lancashire. The amount of sorting and shunting activity increased as did the workforce the two companies required.

Certainly not a town, Hellifield became a railway village, its economy depending almost entirely on the railway. Between them, the two companies provided much of the infrastructure of a small railway settlement such as housing, running water, gas supplies, places of worship and allotments. Railway-built housing and other social facilities symbolised the power of railway companies and the breadth and diversity of the activities in which they became involved. It could be useful public relations, seeming to be philanthropic. However, railways were hard-nosed businesses, and they undertook these activities strictly for financial and not for social reasons. Ironically, in the case of Hellifield, the station refreshment room became something of an informal village community centre.

By 1914, Hellifield was served by ninety passenger trains a day, the railway absolutely dominated the economic and social life of the place and a constant sight was that of railway workers walking the streets to and from their shifts at all times of the day and night. If not a town, Hellifield was certainly a railway village.

## Rowsley

In 1849 the small settlement of Rowsley in Derbyshire, embracing less than 500 inhabitants, found itself the temporary northern terminus of the ponderously named Manchester, Buxton, Matlock & Midland Junction Railway from Derby and Ambergate. In 1860, construction began of the line to Bakewell and Buxton. At that time the original station went over to goods use and a new passenger station was built. Eventually the line was opened throughout and became busy with freight and mineral traffic. Rowsley gained an engine shed for locomotives whose job it was to bank northbound trains climbing to Peak Forest. It also gained sidings which expanded into a larger marshalling yard where much shunting and sorting activity took place. This required more locomotives and the shed was enlarged, eventually being designed to accommodate sixty locomotives.

This embryonic railway was situated in a beautiful but isolated and very rural dale containing the River Derwent. It became necessary for housing to be built and the MR, successor to the Manchester & Buxton, constructed several blocks of modest but well-built cottages which greatly increased the housing stock of what remained a small community.

Passenger traffic was a subsidiary activity to freight and minerals at Rowsley and consisted of a basic service of stopping trains but Rowsley was located in what might be described as a smaller version of the Dukeries in Nottinghamshire. Within reach were the residences of the Dukes of Devonshire and Rutland, and the Marquis of Granby. Such grandees used trains for longer distance journeys and often requested that express trains be stopped at Rowsley for their convenience. Intimation of this was, for the MR, not so much a request as a demand, although one that would not have been entertained regarding ordinary passengers of lower social standing. The Royal Family sometimes visited Chatsworth House, the residence of the Duke of Devonshire, and then the bunting flew on Rowsley Station.

Despite being a nodal point for freight traffic and providing much local employment, Rowsley never grew into a large settlement but can fairly be described as a railway village.

## Didcot

Didcot was a small, quiet village until the GWR arrived in June 1840. It was located on the London to Bristol main line where a branch line was built northwards for about 10 miles to Oxford. When this line opened in 1844, Didcot became an important interchange station. It gained another line in 1882 with the opening as far as Newbury of the Didcot, Newbury & Southampton Railway. It is easy to feel that the potential of this line was never really fulfilled; that it could have been a major traffic artery instead of spending much of its life as a lightly used cross-country branch line.

In 1856, an eastern curve allowed trains to and from the Oxford direction to bypass the station and in 1886 a west curve performed a similar function for trains to and from the Swindon direction. Sorting sidings opened and an engine shed and various other items of railway infrastructure including a vast provender store providing sustenance for the GWR's 3,000 horses, so railway employment became a vital part of the local economy. In the period up to 1914, the town expanded but not to the extent of being much more than an overgrown village. Although the GWR provided jobs, it was less forthcoming with housing for its employees, building just thirty-two in 1903. In 1914, Didcot became a place of strategic importance when a vast army ordnance depot was opened which eventually had no less than thirty-two miles of track.

It was almost by accident that the railway came to Didcot at all. The original plan was for the line from London to Bristol to pass through the market towns of Wallingford and Wantage as it made its way west from Reading. Brunel, as engineer of the line insisted, however, on a cheaper and more easily graded route which happened to pass through Didcot. Didcot was a railway town in the period being examined.

## Westbury

This Wiltshire town developed in much the same way as Didcot, also courtesy of the GWR. It had been a thriving market town but had declined to being little more than a village. The Wiltshire, Somerset & Weymouth Railway, later a constituent of the GWR, arrived in 1848. This was a small section of a much grander scheme and ran from Thingley Junction, near Chippenham on the main line from London to Bristol. An initial outcome of the opening of the railway was some depopulation as the railway widened the opportunity for people to migrate in search of work in more prosperous districts. Westbury became a junction when a line was opened to Frome in 1850 and another to Warminster in 1851. Not long after, Westbury found itself on more important lines via Frome to Yeovil and Weymouth, through Warminster to Salisbury and via Bradford-on-Avon and Bath to Bristol. This made Westbury into something of a nodal point and with sidings for the exchange of goods traffic, an engine shed was built.

Westbury's importance as a railway centre was greatly enhanced in 1906 when the GWR opened its direct main line from Reading to Taunton thereby making access to the West Country considerably easier. The siding provision grew as did the allocation of the engine shed and interchange became a larger function of the station. Westbury expanded, enhanced by the opening of an ironworks, but it did not grow into a large town. However, employment on the railway was a major contributor to the town's economy.

## Normanton

Normanton, a few miles east of Wakefield, was a mere scattering of dwellings with a population of less than 300 before the railway came in 1840. The population was 12,300 in 1899. The railway was a major factor contributing to this growth.

Normanton was often referred to as 'the Crewe of the Coalfields'. It became the focal point for traffic from London, Lancashire and the

Midlands making its way to Hull, Leeds, York and the North East. Normanton was initially located on George Hudson's North Midland Railway which made an end-on connection with his York & North Midland Railway (Y&NMR) at Altofts Junction about a mile north-east of Normanton. This meant that express trains on Hudson's circuitous route from York to London Euston called at a temporary station at Normanton right from the start of operations on 1 July 1840. Shortly afterwards the Y&NMR opened a short spur from Methley Junction on the North Midland to Whitwood Junction which enabled access from Normanton to Leeds. In October 1840, the Manchester & Leeds completed its line from Wakefield and points west that joined the North Midland at Goose Hill Junction just south-west of Normanton. This link gained in importance in 1841 when through Manchester to Leeds trains started. These had running powers over the North Midland metals to Leeds. The North Midland became part of the MR's empire; the Manchester & Leeds became a component of the L&Y, and the Y&NMR was absorbed into the NER.

Normanton was becoming an increasingly busy railway centre and the three companies involved in operations there agreed to share the cost of a new, more capacious station which would, however, be managed only by the North Midland. This station became well-known for its Normanton Hotel and Refreshment Rooms which opened in 1842 with the hotel having the luxury of being joined to the station by a covered footbridge. Normanton was chosen as a place where long-distance passenger trains stopped and passengers could obtain a meal – usually half an hour was allowed. Normanton also became a nodal point for the interchange of mails and frenzied activity frequently took place during the hours of darkness.

Extensive sorting sidings were used mainly for sorting coal wagons belonging to the many collieries in the district. An engine shed was built close to the station and at one stage had an allocation of over 100 locomotives. All this meant that employment in the mining and railway industries dominated in Normanton and close to the station there was much housing occupied mainly by the families of railway employees. Before the First World War, the railways provided an estimated 1,000 jobs. Normanton grew in this period but did not become a major town. However, such was the influence locally of the railways, Normanton warrants being described as a railway town.

## Langwith Junction

Langwith Junction was the point at which the route of the Lancashire, Derbyshire & East Coast Railway (LD&ECR) from Chesterfield to Pyewipe Junction near Lincoln was joined by a line of the same company from Beighton, just south of Sheffield. Operations at Langwith Junction commenced in 1896/97. The place was on the north-western edge of the highly productive Nottinghamshire coalfield and was a critical location for the LD&ECR the main purpose of which was taking away the 'black gold' mined in the district. When it opened, Langwith Junction was somewhat isolated and a rather inconvenient station for Shirebrook. Its name was changed to Shirebrook North by the LNER in 1924. The company built an engine shed and some streets of houses for the employees they needed to bring into this somewhat unglamorous district. A railway village was therefore created. It lacked much in the way of superstructure, but it did have 'The Mission' which doubled as a place of worship and a centre for social activities. The shed, which, as it grew over the years, became increasingly difficult to operate without remodelling, always had as its main function the conveyance of coal from the various pits in the area and the returning of the empties.

The contribution of railways to Langwith's economy was enhanced by the presence of the wagon works of W.H. Davis & Sons on a site close to the engine shed.

## Tebay

This place was entirely the creation of the railways – a small and isolated settlement in the fells of what was then Westmoreland. It was located on the Lancaster & Carlisle Railway (later the L&NWR), the opening of which in 1846 saw a start in creating a railway-based community. This was because a locomotive depot was needed for providing rear-end assistance for trains heading northwards up the notorious climb to Shap. A passenger station was opened in 1852. Tebay became a junction with the South Durham & Lancashire Union Railway's line across the Pennines to Barnard Castle and West Auckland. This later came into the ownership first of the S&DR and then of the NER. Although a limited number of passenger trains used this line over Stainmore Summit, its primary purpose was to carry coke from the Durham mining districts to be used with the rich haematite ores available in the Furness area. Mineral traffic started in July 1861 and passenger services in August. The station in due course became jointly owned by the L&NWR and the NER.

Tebay had several terraces of houses for the L&NWR's local employees and families. About eighty in number, they were built of red brick, alien to their surroundings but stock materials for the L&NWR. The NER houses were made of a rather more sympathetic local stone. Tebay had a large and dominant pub called *The Junction Hotel*. A market hall, an institute, assembly rooms, a brass band and basic facilities for worship also provided services for the community. By 1900, Tebay had a population of about seven hundred. It was the perfect example of a railway village.

Tebay originally possessed two engine sheds. That of the L&NWR was the main establishment but the NER also had a small depot which closed as early as 1902 after which any NER locomotives were serviced at the L&NWR shed.

## Some other small railway communities

There are a number of other places which were 'made' by the railways but which never grew into substantial towns or ever became anything much more than small villages. Craven Arms in Shropshire was a significant junction where the L&NWR's long and rural line towards

Swansea left the joint route of the GWR and the L&NWR from Shrewsbury to Hereford. Just north was Stretford Bridge Junction where one of Britain's most penurious and eccentric backwater branch lines headed off to Bishop's Castle. Beyond was Marsh Farm Junction, where a branch line of the GWR struck out in a north-easterly direction towards Buildwas and Wellington.

Craven Arms took its name from a well-known nearby coaching inn. A large, rather industrialised village developed, the railway links contributing to the success of a busy cattle market and attracting a little industrial development. A small motive power depot opened and this, with a busy goods depot, ensured that employment on the railway was a major factor in the life of the local economy.

Llandudno Junction opened in 1858 at the point where a short branch to Llandudno left the Chester to Holyhead main line. In 1879 it became a junction for the exquisitely scenic branch line southwards to Blaenau Ffestiniog. A motive power depot was built and provision made for accommodating and servicing carriages, there being limited space for such activity at Llandudno itself. The station became a busy interchange point and a large village developed much of which consisted of privately built housing for railway workers.

Builth Road was the point at which the L&NWR's Central Wales line from Shrewsbury and Craven Arms to Swansea crossed the long and deeply rural line of the Cambrian Railways from Moat Lane Junction to Three Cocks Junction and Brecon. The L&NWR station opened in 1866 and that of the Cambrian in 1889. A short spur was put in connecting the two lines. The L&NWR built three terraces for the workers it needed at this rural spot.

The station called Pontypool Road was over 1½ miles from the town of Pontypool to the west. This location opened in 1854 and then named 'Newport Road', was on the Hereford to Newport main line and came to have an extremely busy passenger station at which virtually all the long-distance expresses stopped, sorting yards that were active around the clock and an engine shed with an allocation of around ninety locomotives. Pontypool Road became the focus of a network offering two routes to Newport, a line westward to Crumlin and Aberdare, the main line to Abergavenny and the north-west and a branch eastward to Monmouth. All this would have required a sizeable input of labour but as far as is known, no housing or other social facilities were built in the immediate vicinity. So, at Pontypool Road, we have intense railway activity but not even an associated settlement worthy of being called a railway village.

Carstairs in Lanarkshire was an example of a railway complex some distance from the village whose name it borrowed. It became an important junction on the CR's system where its main line from Carlisle divided, with one route heading for Glasgow and the other for Edinburgh. Services started in 1848. Its importance as a railway centre increased as connections were laid in for Lanark and the mineral-rich area around it and a short branch was built to Dolphinton in 1867. Extensive sidings were installed and a medium-sized engine shed constructed. To meet the requirement for a labour force, the CR created a basic settlement which remained separate from the older village of Carstairs itself. It always seemed a cheerless place.

Inverurie was a small and ancient Scottish Burgh which might have slumbered on in relative obscurity for all time had it not been chosen by the Great North of Scotland Railway for the location of its main engineering workshops, the company having run out of space at the previous site at Kittybrewster, just north of Aberdeen city centre. Construction of the works at Inverurie started in 1897. The company not only built the workshops but was faced with the same problem that other companies had in similar places, that of recruiting a suitable workforce. There was no option but to build housing since workers with the right skills would have to be tempted to move from elsewhere. A small town was created, the housing accommodation having traces of the Scottish baronial style. It was well built and appointed by the standards of workers' homes of the times and was known locally as 'The Colony'. A park, a playing field, social, recreational and educational facilities were added and the scheme was completed in 1905. The company built a small power station and even its housing accommodation had electric lighting, very progressive for the time. The coming of the works caused an increase of about 1,200 in the local population and would have done much to change the character and culture of the town. Inverurie, however, did not grow very large. The Great North of Scotland was, after all, quite a small railway company and was financially challenged. It deserves great credit for not only creating a model community at Inverurie but also an exemplary railway engineering works using the most modern technology to expedite its business.

## What sort of towns were these?

We have mentioned several places where railway companies created new communities virtually from scratch. In each of these new settlements, the railway had a dominating physical presence with considerable space being given over to workshops and ancillary engineering buildings, sidings and housing provided for railway employees. Of the three, Swindon, Crewe and Eastleigh also had large engine sheds.

It will be argued in Chapter Five that a good case can be made for Peterborough being regarded as a railway town. In the nineteenth century, it was the butt of acerbic comments from several visitors. William Morris, who visited in 1887, was not favourably impressed:

> You travel by railway, get to your dull hotel by night ... You go out into the street and wander up it: all about the station, and stretching away to the left, is a wilderness of small, dull houses built of a sickly-coloured yellow brick pretending to look like stone ... and roofed with thin, cold, purple-coloured slates ... a kind of sick feeling of hopeless disgust comes over you...

Earlier, Sidney Smith had been, if anything, even more jaundiced in his judgement:

A city without population, without manufactures, without trade, without a good inn or even a copy of *The Times* except at the railway station ... and which, by the accident of situation, has had railway greatness thrust upon it in a most extraordinary manner ... There is, therefore, the best of consolation on being landed in this dull, inhospitable city, that it is the easiest possible thing to leave it.

Clearly there was some planning associated with the early towns, but it is evident even with the given examples that the enthusiasm for companies being involved in creating model communities diminished somewhat over time. Such activities cost money and the directors were ultimately responsible to their shareholders. Many railway companies were only able to pay them frugal dividends for much of the period up to 1914. It was therefore understandable, although not very philanthropic, that shareholders were not enthusiastic about companies engaging in ventures the cost of which might erode already marginal profits. The railway companies implemented very strict control over their employees when they were at work, safety being such a major issue in the industry. They took a far more liberal attitude towards their activities outside work. As we have seen, they were sometimes prepared for the company to spend money on educational and some recreational activities, but the idea of creating a model environment for their workforce such as that at Saltaire near Bradford was a step too far. Companies in many other industries could find themselves competing for labour, so making some social provision might help in recruiting and retaining workers.

Where companies did create some social infrastructure, it was usually for reasons that were not altogether altruistic. Well-equipped mechanics' institutes and libraries, and perhaps other recreational activities such as sport, brass bands and allotments might be encouraged with some financial support. These all fitted into the category known as 'rational recreation'. They could encourage identification with the employer and with fellow employees. Companies might pay for churches, most obviously Anglican, and chapels where they would expect the virtues of sobriety, diligence, obedience and respectability to be taught. This could make such expenditure a canny investment by helping to create a compliant workforce. The provision of social facilities such as housing gave the companies a strong hold over their workforces and, of course, their families, because serious misdemeanours could mean dismissal and eviction.

Large numbers of employees brought together working and often living close to hundreds or even thousands of others might develop an awareness that they shared common interests. Such interests could conflict with those of company officialdom. A particular source of grievances lay around safety. Injuries and deaths were all too common among railway workers and the companies went to great lengths to blame carelessness on the employees' part rather than accept that they had any share in the blame. Some railway workers were auto-didacts of great intellect, signalmen often being regarded as sages by other railway workers. Engine drivers saw themselves as men at the top of their profession and were respected as such. Some became involved in local government politics as councillors after most working men had gained the vote in the 1880s. At that time, they often supported the Liberal Party as having some sympathy with the cause of working people. The same men might become local trade union activists although in this role they were likely to encounter unremitting hostility from their employees and might put their employment in jeopardy. Despite weighty opposition from most railway companies, trade unions gradually became established on the railways although it took longer for most companies to recognise them for collective bargaining purposes.

Railway workers were found among those unions that helped to create the nucleus of the Labour Party at the beginning of the twentieth century. They intended it to be a party speaking in Parliament for the interests of working people. In towns where the railway had a major presence, railway workers were often on the local council in large numbers, usually but not always, under the flag of Labour from that time. Some railwaymen of a particularly ambitious bent climbed the greasy pole from local trade union activist to full-time union official and then to the lofty heights of Parliament. Perhaps the best known of these was J.H. Thomas, who had worked on the footplate in South Wales and eventually became a cabinet minister. His ambitions and career path did not bring him undiluted admiration from others in the trade union and labour movement.

In the towns we have talked about, besides the obvious presence of the railway in terms of passenger stations, sometimes large and busy, and other items of infrastructure such as goods depots and warehouses, engine sheds and engineering facilities, there would usually be many streets of humble housing often placed close to the railway activity. There might be some uniformity in the early housing where it was provided by a railway company, but later housing was likely to be speculative and not to bear the stamp of any specific railway. Sometimes, such as at Crewe and Swindon the homes of senior staff might be in a more select area a little further from the noise and pollution created by the railway. Not so far, however, that they lost the sense of keeping an eye on whatever was happening.

Railway employment was not particularly well-paid, but it was steady and a job for life was usually to be expected for a worker who kept a clean disciplinary record. There were clear pathways to promotion for those with ambition and there was status attached to railway employment. Although railways using steam locomotives were innately dirty and much operating activity was noisy, the railway locations mentioned were certainly no worse and possibly environmentally preferable to many other industrialised places.

Inverurie, Melton Constable and Highbridge are examples of small towns in deeply rural areas in which railway workshops happened to be located. As places of employment, they would have stood out because some at least of the workforce would have been skilled men earning high wages in a district where low-paid work on the land predominated. Men who moved from agricultural work to railway employment were upwardly mobile in terms of wages and often of social status. Railway employment was hardly a bed of roses, many operating staff, for example working antisocial hours and often in potentially dangerous conditions. However, working for the railway in one of these places was probably preferable to the trauma of migrating to the developing industrial districts with their pollution and manifold social problems. In many villages and small towns, a railway worker was a countryman first and an industrial worker last.

*Chapter Four*

# Towns Predating the Railways

In this chapter we will consider a few places that were towns of some substance before the coming of the railways. They became major centres of railway activity occupying large amounts of land, providing much employment and having a major local presence. However, although the railways played a significant role in their development in the nineteenth century, they maintained an economic diversity and other functions which meant that they were never totally dominated by their railways. They were, however, usually thought of as railway towns.

## Derby

Derby was an ancient place where the Romans once had a presence and was already a large town by the standards of the time, with a population of 25,000 in 1831. It was a county town with the administrative, legal and social functions of such towns. It had ironworks and textile factories. It was a progressive, bustling sort of a place.

Derby initially found itself the focus of attention from three railway companies. These were the Midland Counties Railway with lines to Nottingham and Rugby; the Birmingham & Derby Junction Railway, to and from Burton-on-Trent and Birmingham, and the North Midland Railway to Leeds. These lines had opened by 1840. The town council was eager to get on the railway map but unhappy with the prospect that three railway companies might operate three separate stations. The companies took some persuading but eventually agreed to locate a joint station on land that the council was prepared to sell cheaply. This was on a site liable to flooding and inconveniently located nearly a mile east of the town centre.

The Birmingham & Derby Junction Railway ran from Derby to Hampton-in-Arden where it had a junction with the L&B thereby providing access to London. When this line opened, one traveller, apparently aware of the historic nature of the occasion, bought the very first ticket and commented that the facility to travel to London opened 'a mine of wealth'.

Although the triumvirate of companies somewhat reluctantly agreed on a joint station, they displayed sturdy individualism by insisting that they each had their own engineering workshops. That of the North Midland was a sizeable establishment; the others were small. When the amalgamation of the three companies took place in 1844 and the MR was created, the other two small works were merged with the former North Midland's site.

A large railway enclave was therefore established to the east of the town. This district contributed to the economic and social life of the town but was separate from it and formed a physical barrier beyond which lay an area of wasteland. Topographically, something similar happened at Cambridge where the station was likewise distant from the centre and on the east side of the town and at Exeter where the railway installations around St David's Station formed the edge of the city but were on its western side.

The passenger station at Derby became large and very busy and sported a magnificent façade, a statement that Derby was the headquarters of what became the MR's formidable empire. The MR was the third largest of Britain's railway companies after the GWR and the L&NWR. The locomotive and the carriage and wagon workshops eventually developed on different sites but were very extensive, as expected of such a gigantic railway company and they employed thousands of workers, becoming far and away the largest employer in Derby. A smallish 'village' of well-built houses for North Midland Railway employees was created near the station. This was one of the earliest railway villages to be built and one of the most exemplary. Ninety-two dwellings were erected including four shops and a pub.

Over the years, other railway workers and their families came to occupy massed streets of terraced housing on the eastern and southern side of the town. Most of this housing was of a poorer quality. A later development which involved the demolition of some of the MR cottages was the Midland Institute opened in the early 1890s. Paid for by the MR, it was an imposing building with a lecture and concert hall which could seat 500, three classrooms, a library containing 14,000 volumes and reading games and coffee rooms. The MR, like many other railway companies, was keen to encourage 'rational recreation' among its employees who could enjoy the facilities for a small subscription.

A feature of the imposing station at Derby was the opening in 1841 of the equally splendid *Midland Hotel*. An elegant building adjacent to the station. It was designed by Francis Thompson, the architect of the station itself and, over the years, of many other fine structures built for railway purposes. The hotel was a private speculative venture and had proved very successful by the time it was acquired by the MR in 1862. This was possibly only the second purpose-built railway hotel in Britain. Hotels were something of a new concept in the world of hospitality. Stagecoach travellers had used inns but establishments calling themselves hotels in Britain were largely restricted to places taking in well-off visitors in spa towns such as Bath or Buxton. The hotel's facilities were high class and were clearly aimed at least partly at long-distance travellers who wanted to stay overnight when they made a break in their journeys. A precedent was established whereby major provincial stations that were some distance from the towns they served would often have a grand hotel close to the station. As at Derby, there might also be several other hotels and pubs in the vicinity catering for those using or working at the station. Some might be of a 'respectable' nature, but it was not uncommon for the neighbourhood of big stations to assume something of a seedy nature over time.

The settlement of housing for railway employees close to the station at Derby was the work of the North Midland Railway and was initially composed of North Street, Midland Terrace and Railway Terrace, thereby spelling out the initials of the railway company. Two small adjuncts were named Leeds Place and Sheffield Place. Such housing provision made good sense for the companies that engaged in it by creating the nucleus of a workforce close to where it was needed and generating a useful small but steady rental income. It also gave the railway company some control over its workers who, as tenants, might think twice before engaging in actions that might get them dismissed and risk losing their homes. The village contained ninety-two houses. The 1851 Census indicated that the houses were occupied by 586 people. The houses were of a high standard by contemporary standards and the settlement even included a pub, the *Brunswick Inn*, built in a uniform style. Fifteen of the original houses were demolished in 1892 by the MR to build the Institute mentioned above.

It was almost as if two communities existed in Derby. That containing the railway in the east; and the rest of what was admittedly an expanding town carrying on much as it had been doing before the railway arrived. Admittedly some railwaymen were elected as councillors, but it was 1914 before one became the mayor. As the MR became such a large player in Derby's economy, concern grew that the town was dangerously dependent on the company for jobs and general economic well-being. The council deliberately sought to diversify the town's economic base and was very pleased when Rolls-Royce decided to build a factory in the 1900s.

The men who were really powerful figures in the MR tended not to live in the town or to become much involved in local affairs. In terms of the land the railway occupied, the employment it provided in the town and the importance of Derby as a railway hub, we can say that Derby was indeed a railway town but just as there was often tension between 'town and gown' in Oxford and Cambridge, so the railway and the rest of Derby were not relaxed bedfellows during this period. The MR was a mighty commercial concern. Derby was its administrative centre, but the company extended its activities on its own, with partners or running powers to places as far afield as York, Carlisle, Edinburgh, Glasgow,

Liverpool, Manchester, Brecon, Swansea, Bristol, Bournemouth, London, Great Yarmouth and a host of places in between. It is difficult not to sense that the company's directors tended not to look inward to Derby but outward to defend and develop such a massive railway empire.

This apparent schism between the men of the railway and the men of the town does not detract from the very significant contribution that the railway played to the development of Derby in the nineteenth century. From a population of nearly 33,000 in 1841, Derby expanded to a figure of 100,000 sixty years later although admittedly some of this growth can be attributed to the extension of its boundaries. The population of the Litchurch district, close to the railway, increased from 855 in 1841 to 6,560 in 1861. Much of this growth consisted of housing for railway workers and their families. During this same period, Derby increased and diversified its industrial base and it is likely that this area also contained the homes of workers in other industries. Even without quantifiable evidence, it is likely that its effective railway links were at least one factor encouraging industrial development and therefore the creation of jobs in the town. The local firm that later became the well-known Handysides Foundry, is just one example of a company that expanded on the back of contracts won for the MR and other railway companies for all manner of iron castings. The firm of Bemrose was set up before the railways came to Derby but obtained contracts to do printing work for the North Midland Railway in 1840 and grew as it won major contracts with the MR from 1844. One local man in the tailoring business, James Smith, in 1844 won a contract to supply uniforms for MR personnel. This coup launched him onto more success producing uniforms for many police forces and the military. In 1907, Rolls-Royce opened a plant in Derby attracted particularly by the town's tradition of engineering.

In 1900, the railway was by far the largest employer in Derby. About 20,000 workers were employed by the MR at that time. We can hypothesise that Derby would have grown in the nineteenth century without the presence of the railway but that the economy and general character of the town would have been considerably different. It should be mentioned that the GNR also had a foothold in Derby on lines from Nottingham giving access westwards to Burton-on-Trent and Stafford. Its station at Friargate was very convenient for the town centre but it was a backwater compared to the MR's establishment. Derby can be regarded as a railway town.

## Darlington

The prosperity of Darlington in medieval times is evident in its fine parish church and it thrived as a market centre for a prosperous agricultural area. Its fame, however, lies in its pioneering role in the development of early railways built as more than just a short feeder line from a mine or a quarry to the nearest navigable water. The S&DR was an altogether larger affair, initially built to convey coal from pits in south-west Durham via Darlington to the River Tees in Stockton. Its early traffic was hauled by horses. It was on this line that Timothy Hackworth worked with the S&DR's first resident engineer, George Stephenson, groping by trial and error towards the building of steam locomotives that were powerful, reliable and efficient enough to supplant horse traction. The S&DR and Darlington therefore play a key role in the history of the development of railway steam traction. The S&DR was to widen its operations considerably and to become a very profitable business by 1863 when it was taken over on amicable terms by the NER.

Basic railway repair and maintenance facilities were established at Darlington in 1844 but the S&DR transferred much of its locomotive work from Shildon in 1863 to a new site at North Road, Darlington in 1863. After amalgamation with the NER in the same year, the Darlington workshops became a major location for the NER. Over the next decades, Darlington Works expanded at the expense of the NER's earlier works at Gateshead and constructed and repaired large numbers of locomotives for that company. The NER had a near-monopoly of the territory suggested by its name for which it required large numbers of engines specially to shift the enormous quantities of coal which it handled.

The railway became a major presence in the town which became noted not only for locomotive building and repair, mostly at what became the NER's works, but also some smaller private companies involved just in construction. In 1902, the important locomotive-building form of Robert Stephenson & Co. transferred its operations from Newcastle. Darlington also became known for the presence of an important bridge-building business. It was not unknown for a town which developed a reputation for railway heavy engineering to attract other engineering-related companies as noted in the case of Derby.

Just before the First World War, the number of employees at the NER works was around 2,300 and the 1911 Census indicated a minimum of 3,500 directly employed railway workers in a town with a population nearing 56,000. Darlington was entitled to see itself as a railway town.

## Doncaster

This town was known to the Romans as 'Danum' and it became a market town astride the Great North Road; its medieval prosperity being evident in its large parish church. This was burnt down in the nineteenth century but rebuilt along very similar lines and has an imposing tower rising to 170 feet. The town was handily placed between the woollen industries of the West Riding of Yorkshire, the coal pits of South Yorkshire and the fertile agricultural land to the east. The River Don was navigable between the Humber and Sheffield. Before the railway came, Doncaster had manufactured wax lights and stockings and possessed minor iron foundries, was a coaching town and had a racecourse where the famous St Leger was established in 1776. The racecourse was to generate useful traffic for the railways. As early as September 1850, the GNR was advertising special trains from London to Doncaster for the races. These ran via Peterborough, Boston and Lincoln.

The dawn of the railway age posed a serious threat to Doncaster, which was served by a network both of long-distance stagecoaches and local shorter distance services. Many regular heavy road waggons also served the town. Such was the impact of the more successful early railways elsewhere, however, that by 1840 the burghers of the town were anxious to secure a place for it on one, or preferably more, railways. The town was fortunate to have two extremely forceful supporters and advocates in Edmund Denison, a West Riding MP and Robert Baxter, a local solicitor. They were absolutely determined that Doncaster was to get a railway and remain a place of significance. It was growing steadily before railways arrived. In 1801 the town's population was 5,697 which had risen to 10,455 forty years later. The rate of growth was to increase markedly in the second half of the century, during which time the railway became the town's largest employer. In 1891, the population stood at 25,933.

Many schemes were being put forward for a main line joining London to places like Leeds, York and Newcastle-upon-Tyne. They largely envisaged routes passing through the western side of East Anglia, the Lincolnshire Fens then through the ancient and important city of Lincoln and towards South Yorkshire before heading for York and the north. The GNR emerged as the front-runner and built the first component intended to be part of this major eastern trunk line. This was at the comparatively late date of 1848, and it ran from Peterborough via Spalding and Boston to Lincoln. The intention was quickly to extend it via Gainsborough to Doncaster jointly with the Great Eastern Railway.

The GNR decided to locate its first locomotive and engineering works at Boston, but it was widely thought that once the company had built its line from London to Peterborough, these facilities would be transferred to the latter city. In 1846, the citizens of Doncaster approached the GNR directors asking them to locate the company's new works at Doncaster, only to be rebuffed. In May 1851, the company decided that Peterborough would have the works but, shortly afterwards, they abruptly changed their minds and decided on Doncaster after all. This was a momentous event for the town which may have been in danger of stagnating but the promised railway of the GNR was going to put it on the railway map and as a bonus it would gain an engineering works and become an industrial town. In retrospect we can see that, without these developments, Doncaster would probably have remained a smallish market town like Retford or Newark-on-Trent, further south.

The decision having been made, the GNR wasted no time in building and equipping what was now its main locomotive works. Much of the Boston workforce transferred to Doncaster and by 1853 about 950 men were employed in the works. The population of the town surged with inward migration. The GNR did not commit itself to the extent of town-planning that could by that time be seen at Swindon or Wolverton, for example. However, it did provide some housing and a school for employees' children and contributed to the cost of building a new Anglican church of St James's in the district close to the railway station.

The GNR was an ambitious, entrepreneurial company but it never grew to match the size of companies like the GWR, the L&NWR and the MR which were the product of mergers and ruthless takeovers. On the other hand, not having engaged in the predatory hunt for companies to absorb into its own operations, it did not have a legacy of duplicate assets with which they had to deal such as several locomotive and rolling stock works. All its major construction, repair and maintenance facilities for locomotives, carriages and wagons were concentrated at Doncaster in what came to be known as 'The Plant'. A very large locomotive depot was opened just south of the station and extensive sidings were provided so the railway had a major physical presence in the town which had grown to a population of about 40,000 by 1901 at which time The Plant alone employed 3,000 workers.

Doncaster provides a fine example of the influence that railways could have in an urban community. Not only was the railway the major employer but its workers' efforts generated much of the town's wealth. The GNR was the largest single ratepayer. The company assisted the development of elementary education and, through the Mechanics' Institute, became a provider of technical and liberal education for adults. The GNR provided accommodation for a variety of sports and recreational activities and there was a close link between the company, its workforce and the Doncaster Rovers Football Club which was founded in 1879. Employees of the GNR set up several brass bands and choral societies. As at Derby there was a keen horticultural society which staged shows attracting large crowds. Many of its employees became involved in local politics. Before the First World War, Charles Wightman, a blacksmith and Patrick Stirling, the famous mechanical engineer, served as mayors of the town.

## Oswestry

The company known as Cambrian Railways took itself very seriously and was a hard-working concern. It needed to seize every opportunity it could, given the generally sparsely populated territory it served. Its headquarters were at Oswestry, a small market town of ancient origins with some fine old buildings and scanty remains of a castle. Before the coming of the railway, Oswestry had been a coaching town on the London to Holyhead Road. There was some small-scale malting and textile business in the town and some coal-mining close by. In 1848, before the first railway arrived, the population was approaching 5,000. In that year, the Shrewsbury & Chester Railway opened its short branch from Gobowen.

For a railway company setting out its stall to be Welsh in its title, there was some irony that Oswestry was firmly in Shropshire. There had been controversy around the decision as to where the headquarters should be. Welshpool in the old county of Montgomery had entertained hopes that it would be chosen for the honour. It lay on the main line of the Cambrian from Shrewsbury to Machynlleth and Aberystwyth whereas Oswestry was somewhat out on a limb for the company's operations.

The Cambrian was always financially challenged, and it went bankrupt twice, in 1868 and 1884. It says something for its fortitude, or perhaps for its sheer bloody-mindedness, that it concentrated its administrative and engineering headquarters at the one point, rather like the MR at Derby except, of course, that the MR was immensely bigger and served parts of the country which provided far more generous amounts of traffic.

Oswestry might have found itself on the extremely ambitious Manchester & Milford Railway, intended to connect Manchester to the west coast of Wales. This bold endeavour was never completed. When the Oswestry & Newtown Railway was opened in 1860, Oswestry became a junction. In 1863, the Oswestry, Ellesmere and Whitchurch Railway opened with running powers over the L&NWR to Crewe and Oswestry found itself on a main line, albeit always of a secondary nature. The Cambrian Railways Company was created in 1864 out of several small companies in mid-Wales, including those just mentioned. Deeply rural branch lines were built to Llanfyllin and Llangynog as the town became something of a transport hub. In 1861 Oswestry had a population of 5,400; in 1871 of 7,300 and almost 9,500 in 1901. The choice of Oswestry as the Cambrian's focal point undoubtedly made a major contribution to this growth.

Notwithstanding its impecunious situation, the Cambrian went ahead and built an impressive railway quarter just to the east of the town. An engineering works suited to the size of the company was built and initially employed 450 'skilled artisans', no trifle in a town with a population of only a few thousand. The workforce on the railway fluctuated with the state of the wider economy and the level of company business, the Cambrian seemingly particularly susceptible to vagaries over which it had little control. In 1898, the Cambrian commissioned an enquiry into its business which opined that the works was considerably overmanned.

The population of Oswestry grew steadily, doubling between 1861 and 1911 while the business carried out by the works increased as the Cambrian extended its operations and engaged in various schemes of modernisation. It is likely that the presence of the company's headquarters attracted some inward migration and put money the way of local businesses. There is no evidence that the company provided housing for anyone other than its senior managers. The small but impressive station and its offices, the goods facilities and the works and nearby locomotive depot gave the railway a considerable presence in Oswestry but the town retained its character as the market centre of a predominantly agriculturally-based district. The company did open a Railway Institute just before the First World War and it provided a local eyecatcher with the works chimney which was 150 feet high.

The GWR does not seem to have valued the Cambrian very highly. It always made it clear that it had no intention of finding a way of diverting its London to Chester and Birkenhead trains through the town.

## Ashford

Ashford in Kent had long been a market centre dealing especially in cattle that had been fed on the lush pastures of Romney Marsh. It stood on the South Eastern Railway (SER) at what became a significant junction of lines from London to Dover with others to Maidstone, Canterbury and southwards towards the Dungeness area and also to Hastings. Its first railway opened in 1842 when it gained a direct link with London. The line to Maidstone was owned by the SER's deadly rival, the London, Chatham & Dover Railway (LC&DR) who initially had their own station in Ashford. The SER and the LC&DR amalgamated in 1899 to form the South Eastern & Chatham Railway (SE&CR).

Plenty of land was available just south-east of the town where an engine shed and the works were laid out and a village created for company employees and their families. The accommodation was simple and was grouped around a green and contained community facilities such as a bathhouse, a shop, a pub and, in due course, a school. Extensions were made to this settlement which was given the name 'Alfred Town'.

The works began building locomotives in 1853 and by 1914 had turned out 600 when it had become the main engineering works of the SE&CR dealing also with carriages and wagons. After the amalgamation, the former LC&DR's Longhedge Works at Battersea was run down and much of its activity transferred to Ashford along with accommodation for those workers and their families who chose to move to Kent. By 1914, there were 2,500 employed at the works. The works became the centre of an industrial suburb, somewhat aloof from the town itself and contrasting with its continued role as a market for a predominantly agricultural hinterland. The 1911 Census showed Ashford's population as approaching 17,000, significantly larger than the 3,700 that it had been in 1841. Clearly, while the railway contributed to Ashford's growth and prosperity, it never totally dominated the town. Ashford can reasonably be called a railway town.

## March

March was a small town before the railway age with its centre by the River Nene about a mile south of where the station, opened in 1847, came to be built.

March became a major and exceptionally busy railway junction, the meeting point of lines of the Great Eastern Railway (GER) to Peterborough, Wisbech and King's Lynn and to Ely, and of the Great Northern & Great Eastern Joint to Spalding, Lincoln and the North and to St Ives. Railway operations around the town were dominated by mineral and goods traffic. Advantage was taken of a large area of flat land north of the station to build several wagon sorting yards which eventually were replaced by one the largest marshalling yards in Europe. An extremely large locomotive depot was built to service the yards. The railway became the major employer in March and the better wages available in railway employment drew many countrymen from the surrounding Fens to leave agricultural employment. This angered the farming fraternity who had to increase wages to recruit and retain land workers. Overall, the development of March as a railway centre brought money to the town by increasing the spending power of the local population. Despite its very considerable presence in March, only forty-one company houses were ever built.

Passenger operations played a very secondary role at March and originating passenger traffic was no more than might be expected of a small, although growing, town. The largest volume of traffic handled was coal, arriving over the Joint Line and via Peterborough from the East Midlands and South Yorkshire mining districts. A seemingly endless procession of coal trains arrived, the wagons then being sorted and marshalled into new trains carrying the 'black gold' to the almost insatiable industrial and domestic consumers of London. Another major source of traffic was agricultural produce grown in the Fens on what was perhaps the most fertile land in Britain. Much of this traffic, such as sugar beet, was seasonal.

## Hurlford

This small settlement had iron and fireclay works before the coming of the railways. It was about 3 miles south of Kilmarnock. The Glasgow & South Western Railway (G&SWR) decided to build a locomotive depot, the allocation of which was mostly involved in working mineral trains in the district. The company built a substantial village for incoming workers and their families. They were known as 'The Blocks' and were demolished as railway activity was run down from the 1950s.

Kilmarnock itself was a railway engineering centre. Andrew Barclay, who had been there since 1840, started building locomotives in 1859 when a new arrival, Dick, Kerr & Co, started in the same business. The G&SWR had moved its works from Glasgow in 1855. Hurlford and Kilmarnock between them provided large numbers of railway engineering and operating jobs, having a major presence in the district. The same railway company built a large engine shed at Corkerhill on the rural fringes of Glasgow where they built a model village of 132 dwellings, an institute which doubled as a place of worship, a library and reading room, communal baths and a company shop.

## Wellingborough

Wellingborough was an old country market town before the railway age, trading in wool. By 1800 it was known for the making of boots and shoes produced on a domestic basis. The town was well served by coaches and stood on the River Nene which had been made navigable. However, if the local industry was to expand, the town needed the better form of transport offered by railways.

The first line was that of the London & Birmingham (later L&NWR) on its route from Blisworth and Northampton to Peterborough. This opened in 1845. Its station was rather inconveniently placed for the centre. Soon this railway was being used to move quantities of locally mined iron ore to ironworks elsewhere. The MR opened its station in 1857 on the progenitor of what became the Midland Main Line. This connected the town with Nottingham, Derby, Leicester, Bedford and, at that time, London King's Cross, by running powers over the GNR from Hitchin.

The presence of these railways spurred local production of boots and shoes on an industrial scale. The MR found Wellingborough a handy place for the building of marshalling yards and a large engine shed. Being roughly halfway between London and the pits of the East Midlands, it made sense to use cheap land for sorting and remarshalling the constant procession of loaded coal trains going south and the empties returning north. Close to the station, Butlin's, the firm that mined the local ore, opened a total of four furnaces. The existence of these furnaces and the railway complex provided many jobs. This caused the town to extend eastwards towards the railway with much working-class housing in this quarter. The population of the town rose from 4,700 in 1831 to 6,400 in 1861 and 18,500 in 1901. A late addition to the town's railway network was a short branch of the MR to Higham Ferrers, opened in 1894.

It would be unwise, unequivocally, to describe Wellingborough as a railway town but clearly the railways were a vital factor in contributing to the growth of its industries and in providing much employment. Certainly, a stranger arriving at the ex-MR Wellingborough Midland Road Station from the north in the mid-1950s would have passed great activity in the extensive sidings and seen many steam locomotives on the engine shed and might well have thought they had arrived at a place dominated by the railways. Equally, a visitor by road from the west could have been excused for being unaware of the presence of the railway.

## Rugby

In 1831, Rugby had around 2,500 inhabitants. It was a well set-up market town with an economy largely dependent on agriculture. It was soon to change. In 1833, the L&B received parliamentary sanction. As well as building a line between these two places, including a planned station at Rugby, at Birmingham a connection was envisaged with the Grand Junction Railway which was intended to provide a railway link from Birmingham to Liverpool and Manchester. Rugby was therefore about to find itself located on what then would be the country's main trunk railway. This was an exciting prospect, but these were the early days of railways and there was much trial and error in completing these projects. The Grand Junction opened in July 1837 and the L&B was opened throughout in September.

A second line soon arrived at Rugby. This was the Midland Counties Railway from Leicester, and it opened in July 1840. It was part of a grander project which involved linking various cities in Yorkshire and Derby, Nottingham and Leicester with London through the exercise of running powers over the London & Birmingham to Euston. The Midland Counties and the L&B were soon to be absorbed in two major conglomerates, respectively the MR and the L&NWR and, since their interests were frequently in competition, relations often became distinctly frosty.

Three new lines were soon to be built, all converging on Rugby. They were the Trent Valley main line from Stafford (1847); a line from Peterborough and Market Harborough (1850) and one from Leamington Spa (1851). All these were under the auspices of the L&NWR. Rugby was now a major junction of six routes including the major line to the north which now avoided Birmingham. Most trains on this line at that time changed locomotives at Rugby which now became a major interchange point. Major extensions and improvements were needed at the station, the relative contributions made by the two companies being a source of disagreement. The inadequacies of the station's refreshment room gained notoriety when Charles Dickens wrote a satirical piece titled 'Mugby Junction' in the Christmas 1866 edition of *All the Year Round*. Dickens was a frequent traveller on the railways, and it is thought that he was venting his spleen on refreshment rooms collectively, not simply on that at Rugby, because such facilities were an almost universal butt of sarcasm.

Leaving aside the 'sawdust sandwiches' and 'shrunken oranges' to which Dickens refers, the railway was proving to be a factor encouraging considerable growth in the town itself. Its population was about 7,000 in 1851 and reached 10,000 in 1881. Rugby had been known for its old grammar school which, in the nineteenth century, underwent a transformation into a prototype of the British public school. Now it was also known as a place to change trains. It seems likely that the railway contributed to the growth of the school by making it easily accessible from so many directions. Another addition to Rugby's junction status came with the opening of the line to Northampton in 1881.

The original station was on the fringe of the town which was to grow towards its later replacement with working-class residential streets built either by the L&NWR or by private builders. As Rugby expanded, some new industries were established. Perhaps the only one whose appearance could be ascribed to the railways was a company that repaired wagons. Direct employment on the railway increased and the L&NWR set up a Railway Institute for educational and edifying leisure pursuits. This was made available to non-railway employees and served a very useful purpose in technical instruction as large engineering companies opened in the town around 1900. Rugby developed something of a tradition of valuing adult education both for vocational and non-vocational purposes and some credit should be given to the L&NWR for its early efforts in this direction.

The L&NWR built a large locomotive depot at Rugby with an associated repair workshop. Its allocation was mostly of freight and mixed traffic locomotives. The major industries that developed in Rugby were mostly close to what became the West Coast Main Line and generated considerable business for the railway, although there was never a large marshalling yard at Rugby. In 1903, 1,400 men were employed by the L&NWR, a significant number but one which became a decreasing proportion as new employers took on labour in the period up to 1914. The British Thomson-Houston Company, for example, had a workforce of about 800 when production started in 1902.

We have not finished yet with railway developments at Rugby. Along came the Manchester, Sheffield & Lincolnshire (MS&LR) reinventing itself as the GCR and deciding to join the big boys by building a new, superbly engineered high-speed line from South Yorkshire and the East Midlands to a London terminus of its very own at Marylebone. This approached Rugby from the Leicester direction, crossed the south-eastern end of the L&NWR's station complex and shot off into the depths of the Northamptonshire countryside towards Woodford & Hinton. It loftily disdained any contact with the L&NWR in the Rugby area, although it did deign to provide a station. This was mockingly called 'Rugby Central,' but it was no more central than Rugby's first station had been. It opened in 1899 and did widen the range of places that could be reached by passenger train from Rugby. However, the Great Central was primarily a goods and mineral operation and a seemingly endless procession of such trains thundered across the impressive 'birdcage' viaduct giving the impression that they were far too busy to bother dallying at Rugby, a place merely on the way to somewhere else.

We may or may not want to call Rugby a railway town. However, it was certainly a town whose growth and development before the First World War was strongly influenced by the London & North Western Railway.

## Newton Abbot

From 30 December 1846 when the South Devon Railway from Exeter opened its station as 'Newton', only renamed Newton Abbot in 1877, this always seemed to be a place where the available facilities lagged behind the amount of traffic it was required to handle. Newton Abbot was a small market town, and the station was built to the east of the centre. The historic core of the town remained recognisable but the approach from the station was more modern and urban.

It was as if the railway was always trying to play catch up. The first station was a primitive affair and its enlargement by 1859 was no improvement. A thorough rebuilding in 1861 was an improvement but soon needed further development. The line towards Torquay had been opened in 1848 and was extended to Paignton in 1859 and Kingswear in 1864 but the eastern approach from the Exeter direction bringing the most traffic remained just a single line until 1865. When standard gauge replaced broad gauge in 1892, further improvements were made to the station and the engine shed modernised and enlarged. In 1878, the GWR had absorbed the South Devon Railway. A branch to Moretonhampstead opened in 1866. At the intermediate station of Heathfield, this in turn extruded a branch to Exeter via Chudleigh, which opened in 1882. A marshalling yard at Hackney just to the east, opened in 1911. It was enlarged in 1913 and yet more improvements were made to the station in 1913. After all this bodging, a completely rebuilt station was opened in 1927, more capable of dealing effectively with the traffic flows which reached their peak on holiday summer Saturdays.

The South Devon opened a locomotive works in 1848 and a shop for carriage repairs in 1849. One of the shed's prime functions was to provide pilot locomotives to double-head heavy trains leaving in the Plymouth direction and having to surmount the daunting Dainton incline. In 1914, over 2,000 came to be employed on the railway with its locomotive and carriage and wagon works, its marshalling yard and loco shed as well as the passenger and goods stations. Newton Abbot never grew into a large town, but railways played a major part in developing and sustaining its economic life.

## Carnforth

In 1846, when it gained a station on the newly built Lancaster & Carlisle Railway, Carnforth had a population of fewer than 300 and was situated on the main turnpike road which later became known as the A6. Some writers assert that until 1864 this station was known as Carnforth-Yealand. It was certainly given that name in some editions of *Bradshaw* but never officially. Yealand is a village a few miles north of Carnforth which briefly had a halt on the Lancaster & Carlisle.

In 1857 the Ulverstone [*sic*] & Lancaster Railway arrived at Carnforth forming a junction with the Lancaster & Carlisle. The Ulverston company was absorbed by the Furness Railway in 1862 and the Lancaster & Carlisle by the L&NWR in 1857. In 1867 the MR arrived in Carnforth courtesy of the Furness & Midland Junction Railway from Wennington where it left the MR's line from the West Riding of Yorkshire to Lancaster. Goods traffic was developing rapidly, conveying raw materials to the iron and shipbuilding industries of Barrow-in-Furness and carrying some of Barrow's output to markets in the West Riding, for example. Further traffic developed with the establishment in the early 1860s of the Carnforth Haematite Iron Co Ltd. This works, which expanded considerably over the next decades, was located at Carnforth precisely because of its excellent railway facilities for handling the necessary iron ore and coke traffic. It had good water supplies and limestone could easily be brought in by rail. The works had its own internal standard gauge system. The rise of this works meant that Carnforth came to be dominated by two mutually dependent industries. At its peak it employed about 500 workers. It fell victim to the difficult economic conditions around 1929-31.

The Furness & Midland Junction built a small station of its own to serve Carnforth but this closed in 1880 when a curve was put in to allow trains from the Wennington direction to use the suitably enlarged joint station at Carnforth.

Although co-operating to an extent, the three companies built their own engine sheds and sorting sidings and there was much exchanging of traffic between them. The L&NWR and the MR also built housing for their workers. Much housing for railway workers was, however, provided by private builders. Even here, the railway played a role bringing in substantial quantities of sandstone from Lancaster and the Lune Valley. The ironworks built an industrial village close by for the workers it had to import from elsewhere. None of the companies involved did much to create the supportive social facilities that we have seen elsewhere. Carnforth grew in the nineteenth century but not spectacularly. From 1861 to 1871 its population increased from 393 to 1,091 and peaked at around 3,000 in 1891. Railway employment was a significant factor in its economy.

## Earlestown

Newton-le-Willows was an old market town but with a growing industrial element when railways arrived in the 1830s. The area around became a hub of early main line railway activity including that of the L&MR from 1830. A wagon works was created by the L&NWR close by at Earlestown where a rather undistinguished village composed of 340 workers' dwellings was erected. This settlement took its name from that of Hardman Earle, a director of the L&NWR who was largely responsible for establishing the works. It grew to become a small town with schools, chapels and churches, an institute for education and recreation and a hotel, allotments and sports facilities.

Slightly earlier, in the early 1830s, a private locomotive building concern, the Vulcan Foundry, was established nearby at Newton and it built a small settlement for its workers which became known as Vulcan Village. Although it supplied some domestic customers, it perhaps made its name known through exporting. The settlement that developed can fairly be described as a railway town, its dependence on railways being added to in 1846 when the printing works of McCorquodale opened. This company specialised in the production of printed material for various railway companies, this perhaps being one of the lesser discussed aspects of the business generated by railways.

## Melton Constable

This deeply rural spot in Norfolk was the hub of the Midland & Great Northern Joint Railway system. While growing with the coming of the railway, it remained no more than a village. However, Melton Constable had many of the attributes of railway towns such as Crewe or Swindon, albeit in miniature.

It was a virtually new settlement owing its existence to the Midland & Great Northern which chose to locate its headquarters, well-equipped engineering workshops and main engine shed at the point where four of the company's routes converged. Proceeding to the west was the long cross-country line to South Lynn where there was a branch to Peterborough while the 'main line' continued through Holbeach and Bourne to an end-on junction with the MR at Little Bytham. Northwards, trains ran through Holt to Sheringham and Cromer and southwards to Norwich City. Eastwards a line made for North Walsham and Yarmouth Beach.

Housing had to be built to accommodate the workforce required by the company. The settlement also contained a school and a recreation ground, a mission hall and a railway institute. Melton Constable had its moments on summer Saturdays when the system which centred on the station was occupied to, or beyond, capacity. Nearly all the system was single track and appalling delays could develop as holiday trains particularly to and from the East Midlands made their tortuous way across the undulating Norfolk countryside and the flat Fens of Lincolnshire.

## Grantham

This town derived its medieval wealth from its market and the wool trade and even today the splendid spire of the parish church has a dominating visual presence. It is the fifth tallest in the UK. There was lively business in the hostelries and other activities brought by the Great North Road which passed through the centre of the town.

Modern industrialisation began when Ruston & Hornsby established an engineering works in 1815. The first railway was the Ambergate, Nottingham & Boston & Eastern Junction Railway, not as grand as its title. It opened a line to Colwick Junction just outside Nottingham in 1850. This ran from a point near the canal basin to the west of the present station. The direct 'Towns Route' of the GNR from London King's Cross to York opened in 1851 and Grantham quickly gained importance as a point where express passenger locomotives were changed, and an engine shed was built to provide accommodation and servicing.

A district of working-class terraced housing sprang up around London Road and close to the station. A church was erected to serve this community even before the railway came. Other working-class housing was to be found to the west of the railway. Two further lines built later used a south to east curve at Barkston Junction where they turned northeast towards Honington. At this point, one line went north to Lincoln leaving the other going east to Sleaford and Boston. All the lines came into the GNR's sphere of influence.

Apart from trains on what became known as the East Coast Main Line, the other lines serving Grantham had passenger services of a secondary nature. The line to Colwick and ultimately Nottingham came to carry heavy mineral traffic. Grantham became a very busy junction but without much in the way of originating non-passenger traffic until the High Dyke branch was built to provide access to iron ore deposits. The engine shed never became a large one but, with its allocation of express passenger locomotives, it seemed to be more important than its mere size or allocation would suggest. It might be questionable to designate Grantham a railway town, but the railways provided many jobs, and its presence would have been difficult to ignore in what remained in this period a comparatively small town.

## Shrewsbury

This town has a long history because of its strategic position in the Welsh Marches and as a bridging point on the navigable River Severn. William I recognised the importance of Shrewsbury by building a castle overlooking the river. The town became a market centre for a rich agricultural region and its fine abbey provides evidence of the wealth that could be generated from the wool trade. In the eighteenth century, Shrewsbury became a major coaching town on the road from London to Holyhead. The nineteenth century saw Shrewsbury become a significant railway centre although it did not develop the industrial base that went with many places well served by railways. Its population grew in the nineteenth century but quite modestly and Shrewsbury never developed into a large town.

Shrewsbury's first railway opened on the relatively late date of 12 October 1848 and was the Shrewsbury & Chester, later to become part of the GWR. The second arrival was the line from Stafford leased by the L&NWR and opened on 1 June 1849, closely followed by the Shrewsbury & Birmingham on 12 November 1849. This company shared the tracks from Wellington to Shrewsbury and was later also absorbed by the GWR. In December 1853, a line was opened throughout from Shrewsbury to Hereford. In December 1858, the L&NWR opened its route from Crewe. More lines were to come. In January 1862, the Shrewsbury & Welshpool Railway opened for passenger traffic, the line being jointly operated by the GWR and the L&NWR. In February 1862, the Severn Valley Railway opened to Worcester, this line becoming part of the GWR in 1870. The last new line at Shrewsbury was from a station near the Abbey to Llanymynech largely for access to limestone quarries in that district. This opened in August 1866 but the unremitting hostility of the L&NWR and the GWR caused it to shut down completely in 1880. In 1909 it reopened as the Shropshire & Montgomeryshire Light Railway.

The lines into and out of Shrewsbury can truly be said to have boxed the compass. The main station came to be operated jointly by the L&NWR and the GWR and was one of Britain's more remarkable stations. It stood next to Shrewsbury Gaol straddling the winding River Severn and had a remarkable façade in a loosely Tudor-Jacobean style perhaps intended to complement the ancient fabric of the castle to which it was adjacent. The station became very busy. The two major passenger traffic flows were from Crewe and the north-west to South Wales and the West Country and from Birkenhead and Chester to Birmingham, then to London or the South Coast. At least 100 passenger trains were handled daily and approximately double that number of freight workings. There were three major sets of sorting sidings. A sizeable number of locomotives was allocated to the shed at Coleham, jointly operated by the L&NWR and the GWR.

Despite being such an important nodal point on the railways and providing considerable employment, Shrewsbury is not regarded as a railway town. This indicates that the possession of many routes, busy round-the-clock activity and trains to a wealth of destinations are not themselves sufficient to merit such categorisation.

Something similar might be said about Salisbury. Another ancient centre of communications, it too became a major railway hub, in this case with lines radiating in five directions, the first arriving in 1847 from Bishopstoke (later Eastleigh) and operated by the L&SWR. It became a key interchange point for London, Exeter and the West Country, Bath, Bristol and South Wales, and Portsmouth and Southampton. It was dominated by the L&SWR but the GWR had a significant presence. Many trains changed locomotives there and extensive provision was made for goods traffic. The railways created considerable employment but the city continued, after the railways had arrived, largely to pursue its serene role as an episcopal, market, social and administrative centre. It grew but did not become a large town.

## Wigan and Preston

An old expression tells us that the exception proves the rule. It is impossible to fathom the logic behind this piece of homespun wisdom.

Wigan and Preston are places that have rarely, if ever, been described as railway towns yet they were both served by networks of great complexity, were exceptionally busy traffic centres where the railways occupied vast amounts of land and had a major physical impact on their surroundings. These are facts that cannot be disputed. The usual omission of Wigan and Preston from any list of Britain's top railway towns, if it proves anything, simply emphasises the inexact nature of the concept of what constitutes a railway town.

The Romans called Wigan 'Coccium' and by the Middle Ages the town was an important market centre. In the fifteenth century coal was being mined in the area while cotton manufacturing became an important industry in the nineteenth century. The town was located on the Leeds & Liverpool Canal. It had for long been a focal point of roads and in the nineteenth century it became the centre of an extremely complex tangle of railway lines which by 1914 belonged to three companies, the L&NWR, the L&Y and the GCR. Lines converged on Wigan from at least ten directions. Trains to Manchester were operated by the L&Y on two routes as well as by the L&NWR and GCR on their lines. The L&Y and L&NWR competed for traffic to and from Liverpool via Kirkby and St Helens respectively. The West Coast Main Line of the L&NWR thrust its way through the spaghetti of lines and from Bamfurlong Junction in the south to Standish Junction in the north had an avoiding line well used by a heavy stream of freight traffic. The same company jointly with the L&Y had a line leaving the route to Preston and the north at Boar's Head and directed to Chorley and Blackburn. Even the L&Y had an avoiding line skirting around the south side of Wigan from Hindley to near Pemberton.

The L&NWR's Wigan North Western and the L&Y's Wigan Wallgate stations were close to each other and ideally placed for the town centre. The GCR as the late arrival had to make do with a somewhat less convenient site designated 'Central'. The line going northwards out of the L&NWR station was on a very conspicuous embankment while Wallgate was tucked away in a cutting. A very wide range of destinations could be reached by through trains from these stations. Each of the three companies had their own engine sheds which were concerned mostly with providing locomotives for mineral and goods traffic. The three companies also had their own facilities for handling and sorting general freight traffic.

Preston, a few miles north of Wigan, was also occupied by the Romans and was likewise a market town in medieval England. It also developed as an important cotton-manufacturing town but lacked the collieries which were a feature of Wigan. Although its network of lines was not as complicated as that of Wigan, it was arguably a more important railway centre. A tramway connecting the two sections of the Lancaster Canal was opened in 1803 running from Walton Summit, south-east of Preston to the canal basin close to what later became Maudlands Junction, north of Preston Station. The first proper railway was the North Union Railway which opened in 1838 and gave the town railway access to London, Birmingham, Liverpool and Manchester.

Preston was perhaps the West Coast Main Line equivalent of York on the East Coast Main Line. Lines jointly owned by the L&NWR and the L&Y to Kirkham & Wesham divided there to provide three approaches to Blackpool. At Poulton, later Poulton-le-Fylde, on the northernmost of these lines there was a junction with the route to Fleetwood, originally the main line through the Wyre Peninsula from Preston. The L&Y had direct lines to Southport via Banks and Liverpool via Ormskirk. At Euxton Junction, south of Preston, a L&Y line to Bolton and Manchester Victoria left the West Coast Main Line. Another L&Y line ran eastwards from Preston to Blackburn, Burnley and eventually the West Riding of Yorkshire. A short and isolated branch line struck north-eastwards from Preston to Longridge.

As with so many other places, Preston's railways grew in a piecemeal fashion which meant that in the 1840s there were no fewer than five passenger stations. However, by 1914 passenger services were concentrated on one station on Fishergate which was convenient for the town. The two parts of this station continued often to be referred to respectively as the 'North Union' and the 'East Lancs'. By this time, the station was being served only by the L&NWR and the L&Y. It was a large, busy and very complex station, one of the main nodal points on Britain's passenger and mail railway system.

There were extensive goods handling facilities at Preston, some a heritage of the companies that had served the town in the past. A short branch descended a very steep incline to the docks. An extremely imposing – if perhaps somewhat ugly – hotel jointly owned by the L&NWR and the L&Y stood close to the southern end of the station overlooking Miller Park and the River Ribble and could be accessed by a bridge and path built for the purpose from the station. Both companies had engine sheds at Preston, the L&NWR establishment on the west side of the main line close to Maudlands Junction and the L&Y some distance south at Lostock Hall.

Given the very substantial presence of the railways in both towns, the quantity of traffic arriving, originating or passing through, the amount of land given over to railway usage and the large number of jobs created by the railways, it is surprising that these two towns are rarely thought of as railway towns per se. Perhaps we should be content to call them 'major railway centres' because that is what they most certainly were.

*Chapter Five*

# Cathedral Cities and Railway Towns

In this chapter, we look at a few places important enough to have been cathedral cities and which were established well before the era of the railways. These did not necessarily have large populations by the standards of the time, but they became railway centres of considerable importance and, even if not absolutely dominated by the presence of railways, their local economies, their appearance and character, were greatly changed once they became part of the growing national network.

## Peterborough

A small market town built around a Benedictine abbey of some magnificence which was lucky, after the Dissolution of the Monasteries in the late 1530s, to be designated a cathedral, Peterborough was a city not because of its size or importance but because it was the seat of a bishopric. It was not an early arrival on the railway system, perhaps because the area around lacked extractable minerals like coal and was already well served by navigable waterways. However, the presence of extremely rich agricultural land in the nearby Fens and South Lincolnshire prompted the L&B to build a line from Blisworth to Peterborough via Northampton, Wellingborough and Oundle. Shortly after this line had received parliamentary sanction, another line to Peterborough was approved. This line, promoted by the Eastern Counties Railway (ECR) came from the Ely direction and made an end-on junction with the London & Birmingham's line using a joint station later known as Peterborough East. The line from Blisworth opened for public services on 2 June 1845. The ECR's line opened to passengers in January 1847.

The Stamford to Peterborough section of the Leicester to Peterborough line of the MR opened autumn 1846. It was completed throughout in 1848. In the same year, the GNR opened its 'Loop Line' from Peterborough through Spalding to Boston and Lincoln with a connecting line to Grimsby by way of Louth. On 7 August 1850, the GNR opened its line from London which was served by a new station on the west side of the city, originally called Peterborough Priestgate, then, in 1911, renamed Peterborough Cowgate and, in 1923, Peterborough North. This was on the site of the present Peterborough Station. In 1852, the GNR opened the 'Towns Line' which was a more direct route to the north than that offered by the 'Loop Line'. It passed through the 'towns', which were Grantham, Newark and Retford, before reaching Doncaster.

The city was now the hub of lines radiating in six directions. The network of lines was not yet complete, however. In 1866, a line which was to come under the joint ownership of the MR and the GNR was opened to Wisbech, Sutton Bridge and eventually Great Yarmouth. Trains on this line ran from the GNR station. A line, promoted by the L&NWR which had subsumed the London & Birmingham, used the same tracks as far as Wansford before branching off at Yarwell Junction towards Market Harborough and Rugby. This opened in 1879, A last piece to be slotted into this network involved the GNR. In 1883, this was a short section from Fletton Junction on its main line to London which linked into the L&NWR's line at Longville Junction and ran, by virtue of running powers, to Drayton Junction. There it turned north on a short spur to Hallaton Junction on the Joint Line of the GNR and the L&NWR. At the lonely Marefield South Junction, trains from Peterborough turned abruptly west to pass along the GNR's line to its inconveniently situated but quite grand terminus at Leicester Belgrave Road. This route opened to passengers in 1883. It provided an alternative to the MR's Peterborough to Leicester line and ran through highly attractive but sparsely populated countryside which offered little originating traffic. It was hopelessly uneconomic and passenger services were withdrawn as early as 1916.

These developments meant that Peterborough became one of Britain's major railway centres. The railways made an indelible stamp on the city without which it might have remained a somnolent market and cathedral city, at least until Peterborough became a designated new town in the second half of the twentieth century and electrification meant that commuting to London became a realistic proposition.

The coming of the railway transformed Peterborough, generating developments which were to change its character forever. The railways did much to dictate the very shape of the city. Relatively little urban development took place to the west except a few streets close to the MR's Spital Bridge engine shed where many of the company's workers lived. East of the railway was a different matter. Here a massive amount of land was given over to sidings belonging to the GNR and mostly related to their traffic in coal. On the eastern margin of this land, housing primarily for railway workers and their families spread from the vicinity of the North Station almost to Walton. It included an entire community of houses, shops, a church and two schools built by the GNR and known as 'New England'. Several streets of company housing for its workers were built and came to be known as 'The Barracks'. Numbering about 220 individual units, the housing accommodation provided by the GNR was of good quality by the standards of the time and enjoyed gas supplied by the company's gas works. Large numbers of men in this district were employed at New England engine shed which was one of the largest in Britain with an allocation of well over 200 locomotives. There were 80 miles of sidings at New England. Maintaining and operating such a large fleet of locomotives was extremely labour-intensive. It was also thirsty work and New England contained a concentration of public houses, a not uncommon feature of such districts elsewhere. When built, New England was in the countryside just north of the city. It had its own single platform station which provided a market day only passenger service to the GNR station. An Anglican church was built and a nonconformist chapel as well as allotments and a recreation ground.

Other enclaves of railway workers' housing were to be found for employees of the L&NWR in the Woodston district and, for the GER's workers, in Fletton. These were built by private companies. All the main companies serving Peterborough had their own engine sheds. By the end of the nineteenth century, 25 per cent of the working population of Peterborough was employed on the railways. This was one of the highest percentages in any settlement that had been in existence before the railways.

Further employment was provided by some private wagon-building companies including the Co-operative Wholesale Society. The GNR had locomotive repair workshops at New England, and it may be that this helped the emergence in later years of a precision engineering tradition in the city as there was a pool of skilled men to draw on. Trackwork was fabricated at Peterborough. The brick industry which became synonymous with Peterborough depended very heavily on the distribution of its output by rail, particularly to London. It was said that at one time a person who climbed up the tower of the cathedral could see more industrial chimneys than could be viewed in any other location in the country.

Peterborough narrowly missed out on becoming the engineering centre of the GNR. In 1850, serious consideration was being given to the transfer of the maintenance facilities from Boston because it was roughly equidistant from London, Doncaster and Grimsby and was a focus of GNR traffic which meant that dead mileage in moving locomotives for servicing and repairs could be minimised. It was not to be and company politics, not least the wishes of the forceful lawyer Edmund Dennison, led to Doncaster being chosen instead.

The GNR's station was a very inadequate facility for the traffic it had to handle, and the layout included notorious 'dogleg' curves which meant that non-stop expresses were forced to pass through the platforms at a greatly reduced speed. Proposals were many for an upgrading of the station, but it had to wait until the twentieth century for effective modernisation to be carried out. The GNR station became a major interchange point but some unfortunate passengers to and from lines served by the GER and L&NWR who wanted to change were faced with a trudge through the city centre to the East Station. Peterborough without doubt was a town in which railways were a major source of employment and a significant contributor to the local economy. Like many such towns, the sound of railway activity was almost incessant. However, from a population of around 8,000 in 1851, it grew to little more than 34,000 in 1914 and remained no more than a place of medium size until more recent times.

## York

York, despite its relatively small size, has always seemed to have a major presence in English history. In the early nineteenth century, although being an ecclesiastical and administrative centre and focus of prestigious social activity, York was somewhat in the doldrums. The railway acted as a fillip to the city's fortunes, and it grew steadily, if unspectacularly, in the period up to 1914. The scale of railway activity in York required a large labour force. The 1851 Census showed over 500 people identified as railway workers but, as usual with censuses, there were some in occupations that did not give a clear indication of whether or not they were railway workers. The 1881 Census gave a figure of 1,148 'clerks in' York. Many of these may have been employed by the railway but exactly how many cannot be established. Most of these designated as railway workers seem to have migrated to York, particularly from other parts of northern England. We can be certain that for much of the time the railway was York's major employer but by 1914 the industrial scale chocolate manufacturers, Terry's and Rowntree's, between them were accounting for a rapidly growing percentage of the working population. York, although still a railway nodal point of great importance, was less of a railway town than before.

This emphasises how difficult it can be to quantify the railway's contribution to the growth of a multi-dimensional place like York. What can be said is that the railway created large numbers of jobs and diversified the range of employment available in the city. Railways also promoted tourist activity which brought money in from visitors and created jobs. Figures indicate footfalls of passengers going up annually from around 570,000 in the 1890s to reach over 650,000 by 1913. What cannot be ascertained with any certainty is how many of these were tourists. York had much to attract visitors and the railways made it easy for them to come to the city.

The original station at York was on an awkward site which had involved the controversial piercing of the ancient city walls for access and required many trains to reverse. It was also increasingly inadequate for the volume of traffic it was being called upon to handle. The NER had gained a monopoly of rail services to the city in 1854 when it was formed from a merger of the Y&NMR, the York, Newcastle & Berwick and the Leeds Northern Railway. The general confusion and frequent accidents caused by operations at York Station put the NER in a poor light, an image it was keen to erase. However, it took its time getting round to building a brand-new station on a site outside the walls and on the western fringe of the city. It was completed in 1877 and, with its curved train shed, it soon became recognised as one of the greatest architectural monuments of the railway age. In the following year, a huge and splendid railway-owned hotel was built adjacent to the station. York was one of the busiest railway centres in Britain.

## Carlisle

Carlisle was known to the Romans, the western end of Hadrian's Wall being nearby. The origins of the cathedral go back to 1093 and there is a castle nearby. Carlisle has always been an important transport hub and its strategic position near the Solway Firth and the Scottish border means that it has had a turbulent history arising out of Anglo-Scottish hostilities and the marauding Border Reivers. By the time railways began to arrive, hostilities, at least officially, between England and Scotland were a thing of the past.

In the early 1830s, Carlisle was a city with a population of around 20,000, a significant regional centre with thriving textile industries. These included what was then the largest cotton mill in England. The first railway arrived in 1836 and Carlisle went on to become a railway centre of great importance and one where the railways had a major presence. By 1876, eight lines converged on Carlisle. These were owned by no fewer than seven companies, three of which were based in Scotland. These companies were the NBR, the CR and the Glasgow & South Western. The English-based contribution was the Maryport & Carlisle, the NER, the MR and the L&NWR. We can say that, after some initial disputes, all these companies were persuaded that it made sense to use just one passenger station. The persuasion came from the CR and the Lancaster & Carlisle Railway, the latter being a component of the future L&NWR. They had reached an agreement to build and operate a joint station for their Anglo-Scottish services. Not so with goods and livestock depots. Each company jealously operated its own depot which meant that the convoluted tangle of lines in the city's immediate neighbourhood saw a constant flow of short distance transfer freight workings between these various depots. Each company maintained their own premises and employed their own staff which led to needless duplication of function and jobs even if it did create much employment. Similar duplication occurred with the engine sheds. The central station, rejoicing in the fabled name 'Carlisle Citadel', was brought into use in 1847 and was conveniently situated for the centre of the city.

The railways assisted the city to become a major industrial city with a diverse base. As well as the textiles already mentioned, several firms had iron foundries and were engaged in either manufacturing machinery for the textile industry or making agricultural implements. Success in one industrial sector often attracts new companies in similar areas of activity. In 1846, for example, Cowans Sheldon began making a wide variety of turntables and heavy cranes. Very different was the biscuit-making company of J.D. Carr. This was a progressive business using what at the time were high levels of automation to produce cheap products of consistent quality. This company made great use of the railways for distribution purposes. Another industry which benefitted from the expansion of the railways involved several clock-making concerns. Time was of the essence for railway operation. Carlisle's industrial development benefitted greatly by the cheap coal and raw materials railways brought to the city.

The city doubled its population between 1841 and 1901 and a large proportion of them would have owed their employment, either directly or indirectly, to the railways. Despite so much land within the city boundaries being owned and used by the various railway companies, none of these companies engaged in serious provision of housing or community facilities. We would have to categorise Carlisle as a major railway centre in which it was difficult to ignore its physical presence and economic impact but, for all that, declare that it cannot really be described as a railway town. Ironically, it may be that the very diversity of the city's industries which the railways helped to bring about that meant that no one industry was ever dominant. Despite its relatively early transformation along industrial lines, Carlisle never grew into a large city.

## Chester

Chester ticks all the boxes so far as being an ancient settlement, a regional centre, a cathedral city and a major railway hub. Interestingly, however, it is rarely considered as a railway town.

The main station, which became known as Chester General, was a joint establishment served primarily by what became the L&NWR and the GWR. L&NWR lines approached Chester from Holyhead and the North Wales coast, from Mold and Denbigh and from Crewe and Whitchurch; the GWR arrived from Wrexham and Shrewsbury and the Birkenhead Joint from Birkenhead and Warrington. Passenger trains on these lines were handled in what became a massive and very busy station. The GWR and the L&NWR had goods and motive power depots.

Chester Northgate, very much the minor player, was a sleepy two-platform terminus station served by Great Central trains from Wrexham and Bidston and Seacombe and Cheshire Lines trains from Manchester Central. A small goods depot and engine shed were close to the station.

Large quantities of land were owned by the railways which were a considerable employer in Chester but they cannot be said to have shaped the economic life of the city as they did in York or Peterborough, for example. However, very close to Chester and just inside Wales there was a thoroughgoing railway community around Saltney and Mold Junction and this will be dealt with elsewhere.

*Chapter Six*

# Railway Industrial Districts in Provincial Cities

## Gorton and Openshaw

What was for long and rather imprecisely described as 'Gorton', is a district on the southeast side of Manchester. It is now an inner-city suburb but, before the railways arrived, it was little more than several scattered settlements containing less than 2,000 inhabitants. Many were engaged in hat manufacture. The railways totally changed the nature of the place.

The district was penetrated by two canals opened in 1796 and 1797. Canals were able to bring in the requisite coal and raw materials and carry away the products of the cotton mills that were beginning to appear.

The first railway at Gorton was the Sheffield, Ashton-under-Lyne and Manchester Railway which opened in 1842. In 1847 it became part of the MS&LR. Richard Peacock who was the company's Locomotive Superintendent, was tasked with identifying a location for a new locomotive works and chose a site at Gorton in the Openshaw area, about 2 miles east of Manchester where land was considerably cheaper than anywhere nearer the centre of Manchester. The canals could bring in fuel and the necessary raw materials. A works was built in 1846 which quickly became known as 'Gorton Tank' and several streets of housing and various social facilities were built nearby for workers and their families. Adjacent to the works was a locomotive depot which grew to be one of the largest in Britain. Just before the First World War, it had an allocation of around 175 locomotives.

The role of Gorton in the early years was largely the repair of locomotives and rolling stock which had been built by outside contractors. Only in 1857 did actual locomotive building start at Gorton.

Richard Peacock was a thrusting entrepreneur who played a leading role in turning the Gorton and Openshaw district into a major centre of engineering, especially that concerned with railways. He helped to establish the Ashbury Carriage and Wagon Works and then the Whitworth Engineering Company close by. In 1854, he entered a partnership with Charles Beyer and opened a locomotive works on the opposite side of the MS&LR line to Gorton Tank. The Beyer-Peacock works became known as Gorton Foundry.

The population growth of the district was remarkable. About 5,000 inhabitants in 1841 had become almost 33,000 in 1871. Most of the population had at least one wage-earner in the family employed in the local engineering plants including Crossley Brothers who built gas and oil engines. The two railway works were major employers but other employment included chemical and rubber works, several ironworks and a horseshoe factory. The MS&LR with enlightened self-interest built a school for the children of its employees which opened in 1855. This was one way to ensure a supply of labour for the future. The company does not, however, seem to have engaged in other forms of social engineering such as the provision of housing and places of worship.

In 1871, the MR opened an engine shed close to Gorton Foundry. This was in addition to the enormous shed being developed by the MS&LR which went on to become the largest depot of the later GCR. Sizeable wagon repair workshops were situated close to this shed. By 1900, Gorton Tank was outgrowing its site and with no space to expand, the GCR decided to establish a new carriage and wagon works close by at Dukinfield. This opened in 1906 but did not diminish Gorton's position as a mechanical engineering hub because the skills that had developed in the district attracted further engineering incomers. For example, Vickers & Armstrong Whitworth opened a sizeable factory just west of Gorton Tank. This became involved, among other activities, in building locomotives particularly after it had taken over the nearby works, Ashbury's.

Gorton became the archetypal railway engineering district. Beyer Peacock was an extraordinarily successful business which, by January 1907 had produced 5,000 locomotives. The company was particularly involved in the export of its products. At its peak, Gorton Tank had a workforce of over 2,000. Despite the amount of employment and wealth created by the various engineering works, the fruits of success were not shared very equitably. Gorton was a hellhole of chronic atmospheric pollution being noisy, overcrowded, smoky and unhealthy for its almost totally working-class population. The shareholders and senior and middle managements of the local companies made certain that they did not reside in the district.

## Springburn

Scotland had a long history of the manufacturing of locomotives. Glasgow was the centre of such activity. In 1831, the small company of Murdoch, Aitken & Co built a few engines for the Monkland & Kirkintilloch Railway. Some other minor companies emerged, building the occasional locomotive alongside other mechanical engineering ventures but in 1843 Neilson & Co started building locomotives on a larger scale and the industry became established. Its first premises were in Hydepark Street, Anderston but in 1861 a move was made to a new site in Springburn just to the north-east of Glasgow. This district went on to become Europe's largest railway engineering centre. Two main line railway companies were involved; the CR at St Rollox and the North British at Cowlairs. Additionally, there were the private company railway builders. Neilson, Reid & Co and the Atlas Works of Sharp, Stewart & Co. In 1903 these combined with Dübs & Co. to form the world-famous North British Locomotive Company. This company developed the capacity to turn out about 400 new locomotives annually. It built extensively for the domestic market but perhaps was best-known for its exports. These went in huge numbers to countries in the British Empire which, to some extent, were a captive market, but also to a wide range of other countries across the world.

By the end of the nineteenth century an extraordinary industrial enclave had developed in this hilly area, most premises having rail access. The North British Locomotive Company had its Hyde Park [*sic*] and Atlas Works on either side of the North British line from Sighthill East Junction and the City of Glasgow Union Railway which came together just to the north at Cowlairs Junction. The CR's St Rollox Works lay about three-quarters of a mile to the south and the NBR's Cowlairs Works only about a quarter of a mile to the west. Around a mile north was the very large Eastfield locomotive depot of the NBR while the CR's St Rollox engine shed, then generally known as 'Balornock', stood about three-quarters of a mile to the east of the Hyde Park Works. Very close to St Rollox Works was the extensive Sighthill Goods Depot of the NBR. A mile south-east of the Hyde Park premises was Provan Gas Works which in turn had a near neighbour in the form of an iron works. On either side of the NBR's line into Glasgow Queen Street were Pinkston Power Station and Tennant's chemical works which suffused the entire district with malodorous stenches. Atmospheric pollution was inescapable. Every building had a patina of soot. The main lines into Queen Street and Buchanan Street stations penetrated the area and there were various connecting lines. It was impossible to move around the area and be unaware of the presence of railways.

The St Rollox Works of the CR founded in 1854 and greatly extended in the 1880s, at its height employed several thousand men. It constructed and repaired the company's locomotives and rolling stock and was a superbly equipped facility. Like the workshops of other large companies, it attempted to be largely self-sufficient. Cowlairs Works was opened by the Edinburgh & Glasgow Railway in 1842. This company was ambitious and decided to have a facility to build its own locomotives rather than, as was the general practice at the time, to have them built by outside contractors. The NBR took over in

1865 and greatly expanded its capacity, including carriage and wagon construction. Somehow St Rollox and its products stole the glamour but over the years Cowlairs produced large numbers of solid, workaday locomotives in an unusual dark brown livery with red and yellow lining.

The Edinburgh & Glasgow was well to the fore in providing housing for its employees and their families. In 1863 it built 'the Blocks'. These were imposing terraces on the slopes of Springburn Hill. Far from utilitarian in appearance they were in a miniaturised Scottish baronial style with turrets and crowstepped gables. Built of grey sandstone, they had rich red sandstone embellishments, were well fitted out and among the best housing for ordinary grade railway staff anywhere in Britain.

Springburn was transformed into a heavily urbanised industrial suburb and densely populated working-class residential district much of which consisted of Glasgow's typical tenement blocks. It was evidence of the self-help community spirit that developed that some NBR men set up the Cowlairs Co-operative Society whose shops and services, over the years, came to have an almost ubiquitous presence in the Springburn district. In the same spirit, the community developed various cultural activities such as organ recitals, band competitions, adult education courses and public lectures on a rich variety of subjects.

By the mid-1890s, Springburn was a teeming, lively place with a population of about 27,000. It was predominantly working class in social composition and an overwhelming part of its working population was employed directly by railway companies or by companies working on contracts associated with the railway industry.

## Shields Road, Glasgow

Just south of the River Clyde in Glasgow's South Side there accumulated a concentration of railways of quite extraordinary complexity. It was in a district which developed rapidly in the nineteenth century with all manner of industries, often highly polluting, interspersed with densely packed, largely working-class housing, much of which consisted of tenements. The area was bounded by Shields Junction no.2 and

Bellahouston in the west, Strathbungo in the south-west, Pollokshields East in the south, Gushetfaulds Junction in the south-east, and Gorbals Junction and Bridge Street Junction in the north. It embraced parts of such districts as Kinning Park, Tradeston, Laurieston, Gorbals and Govanhill.

The almost chaotic spaghetti of lines in this area had its origins in the unbridled competition between the Caledonian and the Glasgow & South Western Railways. For much of the nineteenth century, when government policy was one of minimal intervention in business activity, competition was encouraged even though it often led to needless duplication of facilities as it certainly did around Shields Road. Various early railway companies serving this area had been absorbed into either the G&SWR or the CR, but the legacy of their earlier competition lived on and little had been done to rationalise services by 1914. There were, for example, three Shields Road stations, almost side by side. Several of the lines threw out connections even to those of their rival's lines and the local network was further complicated by the existence within it of several goods stations.

The district around Shields Road must have provided considerable railway employment but jobs on the railways are likely to have taken a definite second place behind the myriad industrial, commercial and other workplaces. Anyone moving around the area could not but have been aware of the presence of railways and their associated activities. It did not constitute a railway suburb in the same sense as Springburn, but it needed to be included in any attempt to examine towns or other areas of settlement in which railways had a major presence.

## Hunslet

Leeds was a pioneer of steam railway locomotive building. In 1812, Matthew Murray produced what many people consider to be the first commercially successful steam locomotive. This was *The Salamanca* which saw the light of day at the Round Foundry at Holbeck in Leeds, very close to Hunslet which was to become a major centre of private locomotive construction. Previously the district was known for the manufacture of pottery. The Round Foundry was short-lived, closing in 1843. Fifty-three locomotives were built there including twenty splendid single-driver broad gauge locomotives of the 'Firefly' class for the GWR. At a time when the railway system was expanding enormously, most companies were going to private contractors for their locomotives and other rolling stock rather than producing in-house.

E.B. Wilson & Co of Pearson Street was on the scene early but went bankrupt in 1858 whereupon much of its stock-in-trade was taken over by near-neighbour Manning, Wardle & Co of the Boyne Engine Works which had been established in 1840. This became well-known for the widely varying types of locomotives it built. It produced contractors' locomotives used in railway construction, industrial locomotives for customers with their own sidings or systems, narrow gauge locomotives of all kinds, 'one-offs' and highly specialised small batches. Its products were widely exported. By the time it had closed in 1927, it had built more than 2,000 steam locomotives.

When Manning, Wardle and Company closed, what was left of its business was taken over by Kitson's. This company traced its ancestry to 1835 when James Kitson established the Airedale Foundry which built no less than 5,400 locomotives in its working life of 101 years. These included examples for some major British companies such as the MR and L&Y and many international customers, particularly in countries that were part of the then British Empire. Some of these were very large and powerful locomotives and the company had the capacity to handle such contracts that were beyond many other locomotive builders.

Hudswell, Clarke occupied the Railway Foundry, formerly the location of E.B. Wilson & Co. They were prepared to build locomotives, even single examples, to meet the specific requirements of customers. They were also involved in many other aspects of mechanical engineering. In an advert of 1891, they said: 'Makers of greatly improved locomotive engines on four or more wheels ... Specially designed for contractors, collieries, iron works, docks, quarries and short branch railways: engines specially built for any gauge of railway, weight of rail, steep gradients or sharp curves'. Among the company's many successes was supplying locomotives used in association with the building of the Manchester Ship Canal and then chunky 0-6-0Ts for operating the Canal's ongoing extensive railway system.

The Hunslet Engine Company dated back to 1864 and specialised in industrial locomotives. These included 0-6-0 saddle tanks and, much later 0-6-0 diesel shunters. The narrow-gauge railways of North Wales bought many of Hunslet's products including highly specialised machines for the demanding conditions in which many of these railways operated. Perhaps the most extraordinary products of the Hunslet Engine Company were three locomotives for the Heath Robinson-like Listowel & Ballybunion monorail in Ireland, in 1888. When Hunslet ceased production in 1961, another piece of Britain's once proud and successful railway engineering industry followed others into oblivion.

The Hunslet district was about a mile south of Leeds city centre and was a densely packed enclave of factories and workshops interspersed with lines, goods depots and sidings belonging to the NER, the MR and the GNR. Mixed in with these were streets of terraced houses. Other industries whose discharges added to the general pollution were flax-spinning mills, chemical and glass works and the large brewery of Joseph Tetley & Co.

*Chapter Seven*

# London's Residential Railway Suburbs

London had long had suburbs – two outside the walls of the City come immediately come to mind. They are the district known as Tower Hamlets to the east of the Tower, and Southwark, across the Thames, which was outside the jurisdiction of the City authorities and became notorious as a place of vice, violence and debauchery. Long before the railways, wealthy commuters had travelled to the City and Westminster using water transport or coaches from more distant places such as Greenwich, Chiswick and Richmond.

Before the railways came, towns and cities were very compact by later standards. In 1867, London's continuously built-up area, despite a population of well over three million, stretched only about 4 miles in each direction from Charing Cross. In 1901, its population having more than doubled, London had spread across an area ten times as large although this included a few areas with little building development. Many who could afford to do so had left the metropolis, with its noise, dirt, general bustle and its sometimes threatening air, for quieter, more salubrious surroundings in the capital's growing suburbs. Similar processes took place in provincial cities. Manchester manufacturers and men of commerce moved to Altrincham, Wilmslow and Alderley Edge; Liverpool businessmen and shipowners fled to Southport, New Brighton or West Kirby. From Birmingham the flight was to Solihull and Leamington Spa and in Glasgow to Helensburgh, Bearsden and Milngavie. This process was evident as middle-class white collar and better-off skilled manual workers aped those higher up the social scale and moved out of the cities although being constrained by travel and time costs as to how far out it was practical for them to move.

In this chapter, we examine aspects of the growth of some London suburbs and try to determine how far their growth in this period can be attributed to the influence of railways.

The first main line railways to arrive in London initially seemed little interested in providing stations for local services on its approaches. Perhaps the first true suburban railway was the London & Greenwich, opened in 1836. It was not long, however, before companies running into termini south of the Thames began experiencing encouraging levels of short-haul traffic especially for commuters. By 1858, about two-thirds of the trains at London Bridge operated by the SER and the LB&SCR were carrying commuter traffic. The same could be said about Waterloo and Victoria. Many of their trains served existing peripheral towns such as Richmond, Twickenham, Wimbledon, Croydon and Streatham. With regular train provision, these places began to grow, and infilling of intermediate locations led to the opening of more stations on London's southern approaches. As we shall see later, the GER proved to be the company that most vigorously promoted short-haul commuter lines. Such activity may have had a shaping influence on urban development in many parts of eastern London north of the Thames. Whether the shifting of huge numbers of lower-paid commuters on discounted fares made business sense is another matter.

The Southern Railway embarked on a very extensive and successful programme of electrifying passenger services south of the Thames between the two world wars. The 'sparks' effect is well-known for the way in which it encouraged housing development along its routes through such counties as Kent, Surrey and Berkshire. Before 1914, the Metropolitan Railway penetrated parts of Middlesex, Hertfordshire and Buckinghamshire to places like Pinner, Rickmansworth, Aylesbury and Uxbridge. These lines were vigorously marketed after the First World War under the brand of 'Metroland', a phenomenon affectionately satirised by Sir John Betjeman. In both cases it is easy to see how outer-suburban residential growth followed the provision of good services for reasonably affluent commuters who worked in central London but wanted to live in healthier and quieter semi-rural locations. Northwood, Pinner and Ruislip, for example, clearly owed much of their growth to the efforts of the Metropolitan Railway and can fairly be described as 'railway residential suburbs'. It is important to emphasise, however, that such suburban growth was not inevitable and, both north and south of the river, there were cases where the provision of a station and a good train service did not lead to a quick burst of residential development and the creation of a suburb. Before 1914, the period covered in this work, it is sometimes problematical to decide whether a particular district outside central London deserves to be called a 'railway suburb'.

By 1900, Greater London consisted of an almost continuously built-up area housing a population of about six million. The outward spread of London in the nineteenth century was remarkable but suburbs were not a new phenomenon. It is the nature of suburbs to start as appendages to the parent city and then, as the city grows, themselves to be absorbed in it. In due course, the former suburbs themselves extrude extensions in the form of new suburbs, and so it goes on. Holborn, for example, was once part of extramural London although very close to the City of London. Dulwich, Greenwich and Highgate are examples of villages that were peripheral to London but even when there were green fields separating them from London, they increasingly came under its thrall. London crept out and gradually engulfed them and, while they retained some of their former village character, they evolved into suburbs and came to constitute part of Greater London.

'Commuting' is a phrase which initially refers to the act of travelling to and from work by public transport and doing so regularly enough to earn a 'commutation' on the fare in the form of a discounted season ticket. Commuting, if it simply means travelling some distance between home and work, predates the railways. Central London offered much employment and people living in outlying villages such as Islington and Camberwell would walk to and from their places of work well before

Victorian times. These villages were then what might be called 'walking suburbs'. Some better-off 'commuters' might use short-haul coaches or horse buses. The affluent would probably use their own carriages. Most of those working in central London lived close enough to their work not to need public transport and would probably not have been able to afford it anyway. This situation changed dramatically during the nineteenth century and railways played a significant role in the growth of the commuting habit. The desire to put a distance between the home and the workplace was an entirely understandable aspiration for those Victorians who could afford it. London was filthy, smelly, disease-ridden, noisy and parts of it were extremely menacing.

The London & Greenwich Railway was opened in 1836 and was quickly followed by two other short lines, the London & Blackwall and the London & Croydon. They immediately attracted some commuter traffic. Other longer lines not of an inter-city character followed. The North Kent Railway, for example, opened in 1849 and ran out via Lewisham, Blackheath and Woolwich and eventually to the Medway towns. Lewisham and Blackheath were already highly desirable locations with many large houses. Lewisham began to take on a more working-class character with the new residential development that occurred after the opening of the line. Blackheath remained more fashionable although enclaves of working-class housing appeared. Some of the new residents of both commuted by train the short distance to London Bridge. Horse buses appeared, feeding passengers onto the railway at Blackheath from neighbouring but still very rural villages such as Eltham. The North Kent Railway contributed to the growth of these places, but they would not normally be considered as railway suburbs.

In the 1870s, horse trams started to appear in parts of London. The use of iron rails allowed horses to pull a passenger car with a bigger payload than a horse bus. Horse trams and their electric tram successors were the archetypal form of transport for the urban working class. Their fares were lower than the railways and they ran more frequently and had more stops. A network of routes operated initially by several different companies began serving areas of dense working-class housing in the inner suburbs. Where the trams passed through hitherto sparsely populated districts, housing usually followed and the trams played a role in relieving the overcrowded housing in central London by allowing working-class people to live a few miles out but, using their cheap fares, to commute to and from work in the central areas. These electric trams provided serious competition for stations serving inner-suburban districts but, ironically, they then gave a boost to the railways as many of their better-off inhabitants decided that they would prefer to live further out of town. Trams thrived in areas of densely packed industry and working-class housing. They were not viable in less populated semi-rural areas further out where railways were likely to retain the advantage.

Many of the early railway companies had little initial interest in providing services at what might be regarded as the lower end of the market. The GWR, for example, loftily refused to use the word 'suburban' in its timetables until well into the 1860s. However, events were to force the hands of the railway companies as we shall see.

The North London Railway was the first company required by law to make some provision for those made homeless because of the demolition needed for the building of a new line. Much substandard housing was pulled down to prepare the site for their Broad Street terminus opened in 1865. They were instructed to put on special workmen's trains with low fares for working people which perhaps included some of those displaced when Broad Street was built. A similar requirement was demanded of the GER when it was clearing the site for its Liverpool Street Station to replace the Bishopsgate terminus. Such arrangements were codified in 1883 when the Cheap Train's Act was passed, requiring companies whose activities had included large-scale demolition of housing to provide special rates for 'workmen' travelling early in the morning. From 1903, the London County Council published a regular return of all cheap rail and tram fares. In 1914 this publication listed 460 stations at which cheap early morning rail fares were available into central London. Within a radius of 6 to 8 miles from the centre, as many as 40 per cent of suburban rail travellers were travelling at workmen's rates.

What might be thought of as a beneficial piece of social legislation did not please everyone. Some of those who were displaced were able to move a few miles out and find new accommodation. While they might take advantage of the workmen's tickets, their presence could 'lower the tone' of the districts to which they moved. The result was that we find the middle-class residents of such suburbs as Stamford Hill, Tottenham and Edmonton scurrying further out of London in their mission to escape having proletarian neighbours. The railways played a part in a kind of decanting process whereby much of central London experienced marked depopulation. Among the effects was an emphasising of social and class distinctions. Many inner suburbs gained a strongly working-class character. Places further out might experience growth of a more middle-class nature only then later themselves to decline in social status as London continued its seemingly unstoppable outward expansion.

Some suburbs based around existing settlements grew large enough to become towns and take on an economic and social life of their own. They might still be very dependent on the proximity of London but even if they were largely residential in character, they could provide considerable employment opportunities. Wealthy suburbs would contain large houses that required hordes of domestic servants. They were poorly paid and those that did not live in would need homes nearby. These suburbs, whether served by railways or not, might take on a mixed character. Former villages such as Hampstead and Highgate which were already fashionable before the railway age continued to be desirable residential districts but also developed contrasting pockets of deprivation. Hampstead is particularly interesting as an example of a former village that became subsumed in London's continuously built-up area but grew without the agency of direct or convenient railway access to central London until the opening of what later became the

Northern Line tube in 1907. It therefore developed a somewhat self-contained character, still recognisably that of a village.

Between 1861 and 1891 among the fastest growing districts in England and Wales were suburbs of London such as Croydon, Hackney, Hammersmith, Islington, Lewisham, Poplar, Leyton, Tottenham, West Ham, Enfield, Hornsey, Fulham, Willesden, Wimbledon and Woolwich. It would be unwise to ascribe these developments entirely to the growth of the suburban railway network, but this was certainly a significant contributor to the process.

## Surbiton

The London & Southampton Railway, renamed the L&SWR in 1839, opened its first London Terminus at Nine Elms, Battersea in 1838. Stations were provided just outside London at Wandsworth, Wimbledon and 'Kingston'. This station was close to the ancient and important town of Kingston-upon-Thames where influential people were initially hostile to the idea of a railway. The company obviously hoped that by calling this station 'Kingston' they would generate traffic to and from the nearby town of that name. The original Kingston Station opened in 1838 and was replaced by a second station nearby in 1845 also called 'Kingston'. This was renamed 'Kingston Junction' in 1852 although it was the junction not for Kingston but for the branch to Hampton Court which opened in 1849. To add further confusion, Kingston Junction was renamed 'Surbiton and Kingston' in 1863 only to be renamed 'Surbiton' in 1867. This strange saga has a point to it. An affluent settlement developed around 'Kingston' Station of wealthy people who liked its rural ambience but wanted to work in central London. Some of these people had clout and they had been horrified when rumours started that the station was to be renamed 'Kingston-on-Railway'.

Awareness of class is a very pervasive theme in British history and this prosaic and even ugly-sounding contrived name would simply not do and so, almost miraculously, 'Surbiton', an old name for the neighbourhood, was rediscovered, dusted down and bestowed on what its inhabitants were intent on keeping as a socially exclusive neighbourhood owing its modern existence to the railway but not too keen to advertise the fact. Surbiton has been described as 'the oldest suburb in Europe, perhaps in the world, that was called into being by a railway'. (Simmons, 1986: 63-4).

Interestingly, such was the perceived importance of Kingston-upon-Thames that in the early days of the planning of the London & Bristol Railway, later the GWR, Brunel gave serious consideration for aligning the railway to serve the town, although it was eventually built several miles north through Ealing and Southall.

Kingston-upon-Thames eventually gained its own place on the railway system but had to be content with an intermediate station on a section of south-west London's suburban network. Although this made quick access to long-distance trains a little difficult, this did not seem to inhibit Kingston's growth in the period up to 1914.

## Croydon

Croydon was a substantial market town with a population of about 12,500 before the railways arrived. It stood on the main road from London to Brighton and was served by long-distance and short-haul stagecoaches, some use being made of these by well-to-do commuters to and from London. Some of its residents were well-heeled retired folk who had made their money in trade and commerce and were spending their later years in Croydon's relative tranquillity. Croydon gained its first lines through the stations that respectively came to be known as West Croydon in 1839, and East Croydon in 1841. The LB&SCR had a monopoly of services at these two and the other six stations built within its boundaries and enjoyed very frequent services into no fewer than five major stations in London and southwards towards Brighton. Croydon developed a character that was both urban as it grew into a large town, important enough to generate its own inward commuter traffic, and suburban because it became a district favoured by middle-class commuters for being the right distance from London's bustle and grime. Croydon cannot be described as a pure railway town. It was not the creation of the railway, but railways contributed greatly to its rapid growth. In the 1860s, for example, it saw a rise from 30,000 to 56,000 in its population. It developed its own railway quarter around Selhurst when rolling stock maintenance facilities were opened in 1911 close to a complex series of junctions where lines towards Clapham Junction and London Bridge respectively, intersected. Railways were a significant factor in Croydon's growth into a large town.

## West and North London

Four main line railway companies, or five if the belated Great Central Railway is included, ran out of London in a northerly or western direction. They were the GWR, the GCR, the L&NWR, the MR and the GNR. They operated out of Paddington, Marylebone, Euston, St Pancras and King's Cross respectively. Leaving the GCR, the other companies seemed initially to be interested mainly in long distance traffic. Those few stations opened in the early years within 20 miles of London generally had infrequent services.

The GWR opened a station at Ealing in 1838. It was an established village and considered a desirable place in which to live with many elegant large houses whose owners liked its rural seclusion along with its proximity to London. The arrival of the railway did not initiate much population growth or railway business. These both had to wait had to wait until the 1860s and 1870s when largescale residential development started and Ealing became known as the 'Queen of the Suburbs', famed for its healthy environment, high quality housing and its amenities which included good rail access to London, at least after the opening of an extension of the District Line of the Underground in 1879. This seems to have encouraged a bout of speculative building and Ealing was set to become a dormitory suburb, the growth of which owed much to the railways. Ealing was still a good place to live but one that was less socially exclusive.

The L&NWR showed little interesting in providing stations close to London that would encourage speculative housing and suburban development. Likewise, the MR did little to promote residential development on its route into St Pancras although, in conjunction with the Great Eastern Railway, it built the peripheral Tottenham and Hampstead line and opened stations such as Crouch Hill and South Tottenham & Stamford Hill in 1871. This provided a useful west to east service through growing working- and middle-class suburbs but there is little evidence that that the railway contributed to residential development along the line.

The GNR had different ideas. This saw the potential for residential development that could follow the building of lines into the salubrious so-called 'Northern Heights'. In 1867, a line was built from Finsbury Park to the rural fastnesses of the Mill Hill area, extruding a branch to High Barnet opened in 1872. A further branch connected Highgate to Alexandra Palace. This opened in 1873 to serve the building which was intended to be North London's rival to the Crystal Palace. A line was also built from Wood Green (Alexandra Park) to Enfield, opening in 1871. There was an element of imperialism because the GNR wanted to establish itself firmly in these districts to deter other companies. The GER was already established at Enfield and the GNR wanted to give it a run for its money. In the case of the Alexandra Palace branch, there was the hope that busy leisure traffic would develop as well as expectations that residential development would follow the opening of a station at Muswell Hill. In this respect, the GNR was badly disappointed, housing being slow to follow the coming of the railway. The lines to Mill Hill and to High Barnet penetrated what were still predominantly rural areas which developed slowly but steadily as residential dormitory suburbs owing much of their growth to the railway. Palmers Green and Winchmore Hill on the line to Enfield were very small settlements before the railway arrived. Growth was slow at first, some landowners being reluctant to sell for housing purposes, but a momentum developed and these stations came to serve well-populated railway suburbs.

## North-East London

The growth of London's north-eastern suburbs in this period was remarkable. Railways played a very large part in that growth.

Dalston, Hackney, Clapton and Enfield were all old-established settlements in the countryside which, by the nineteenth century, had become desirable residential locations for well-to-do people who owned carriages and commuted into London to make their money. The Lea Valley was a natural transport artery and a line built by the ECR from its Bishopsgate terminus towards Broxbourne opened in 1840. A branch to Edmonton and Enfield from this line opened in 1849. Another early ECR branch was to Loughton. Trains started running in 1856. These lines all penetrated very rural districts with scattered villages and small towns. When built, they offered frugal financial returns except perhaps in the built-up areas closest to London. The ECR perhaps thought that urban development would follow the provision of passenger services, or it was trying to establish a position in this area which no later railway company would be able to challenge.

The ECR became the GER in 1862. This company quickly found itself acting as a facilitating agent of social change. Landowners and speculative builders scented rich pickings from housing development in the still semi-rural areas to the north-east of London. At the same time, but from a completely different angle, concern was expressed about what their squalid, overcrowded housing conditions were doing for the poorer residents of central London and its fringes. They saw in the railways a means of improving the living conditions of working people by clearing slums and building new housing in more salubrious surroundings. It was hoped that by doing this, improvements could be made in what was considered as their depressed physical and moral condition.

A key line was that opened in 1870 as far as Walthamstow, extended to Chingford in 1873. New housing, predominantly for working-class families, sprang up in the Walthamstow area. Considerable additional growth for somewhat better-off residents took place further north. Walthamstow grew spectacularly from around 11,000 in 1871 to 95,131 in 1901 and took on a very working-class character. The previous well-heeled inhabitants fled further out of London to still green environs while many of the new residents took advantage of discounted workmen's fares to get to their work in central London. Trains to and from London were cheap even without the discount and were also very frequent on the network of intensively operated lines terminating at Liverpool Street. The ECR therefore contributed to tackling central London's housing problems by providing the means of transport whereby lower-paid, but not the lowest-paid, workers could move to densely packed but certainly somewhat healthier surroundings. These took on a very distinctive character. They were built to conform to the basic standards of the Public Health Act of 1875. With only the most minimal of gardens, these houses were crammed tightly at up to forty per acre. Although well-built, they were derided in some circles as being monotonous. Tottenham, Walthamstow, Leyton and parts of Wood Green were working-class railway suburbs.

A journey out of London, particularly one where the line was elevated on a viaduct, took on the appearance of a layer-cake. Generally, districts became greener and more spacious the further out from London the train travelled. At their outer ends, the lines might even pass through some open countryside before finally leaving London behind. It was likely that the stations beyond the continuously built-up area would attract some housing nearby and generate traffic to and from central London. This was not, however, an iron law. The GER was to get its fingers burned with the Churchbury Loop. This opened in 1891 and ran from Edmonton to Cheshunt. It was expected to attract speculative housebuilders able to offer the inducement of a convenient train service to and from London for the middle-class clientele they were hoping to attract. It seemed as if the GER was somewhat lukewarm about this line, and it put on a poor service which succumbed to closure in 1909 after cheap and frequent electric trams started running along the road parallel to the line. The Churchbury Loop was reopened in 1915 only to close again in 1919. It eventually reopened with electric trains in 1960, this time successfully.

A similar disappointment for promoters could be found south of the Thames. The SER opened lines to Hayes in 1882 and Bexleyheath in 1895. Serious suburban development did not take place until the 1920s and 1930s again indicating that the provision of services was no guarantee that housing would quickly follow.

## Reflections

Some caution is needed when probing the idea of 'railway suburbs'. In the period under review, few districts on the periphery of central London owed their existence entirely to the railway. Generally, railways developed and accelerated social tendencies already apparent in the districts where they built stations. This meant that they rarely exercised a determining influence on how a settlement developed. When a new line was opened through an area becoming built up, a station was likely to be opened and, if possible, it would be located close to what was emerging as its business and shopping centre. However, the specific topography might not allow this, as at Eltham, for example, and the station might be placed inconveniently for the centre of the developing settlement.

One problem with the more affluent railway-served suburbs is to determine the extent to which they justify being called 'commuter suburbs'. When well-heeled families decamped from central London, they would still need armies of servants. Some would move with them, others be recruited near the new domiciles of their employers. This meant that a substantial part of the population of these growing districts consisted of people who had little need to use railways on an everyday basis. Servants were generally low-paid and many lived on the premises,

A speculative depiction of a train on the Liverpool & Manchester Railway at Newton-le-Willows. This was published in 1825, five years before the line opened so the artist has had to exercise his imagination somewhat. Newton and its neighbour Earlestown became railway settlements of some importance. (Authors' collection).

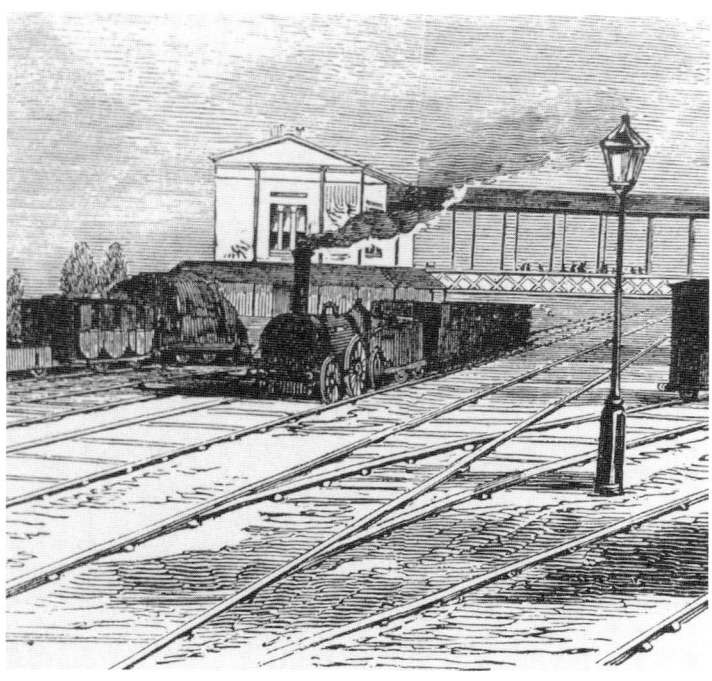

An early impression of Swindon Station. (Authors' collection).

Mixed gauge at Swindon. This gives some idea of the complicated trackwork necessary to facilitate the GWR running trains on standard and broad gauge rails at a complex railway hub like Swindon. (Authors' collection).

The surgery, dispensary and baths at Swindon indicates the contribution the GWR made to the social life of the town. (Authors' collection).

Queenstown Bridge in Swindon shows that the built environment of New Swindon took on an appearance like that of other industrial towns across the country. (Authors' collection).

The 'other' station at Swindon. This is Swindon town in the 1880s, the headquarters of the cross-country Midland & South Western Junction Railway which, although never posing a serious challenge, had a presence which was greatly resented by the GWR who felt that they 'owned' the town. (N. Marlow).

The Rifleman's Arms in Swindon. Typical of pubs in densely-populated urban areas with its street corner site, this was an unashamedly basic working-class boozer whose clientele, very largely male, would have been almost exclusively railway workers. (Authors' collection).

The erection of the 'Euston Arch'. This grandiloquent structure built for the London & Birmingham Railway symbolised the gateway to the North and the Midlands and was evidence of the optimism and belief in the future which was a progressive feature of Britain's rise to world domination in the middle of the nineteenth century. (Authors' collection).

An early view of Crewe Station. (Authors' collection).

Francis Webb was a talented and resourceful engineer who had a dominating influence in the town of Crewe. He was a martinet who treated the L&NWR's workforce as servants, but he did much to establish Crewe Works as a centre of excellence and contributed to good causes in the town. (Authors' collection).

L&NWR housing in Crewe. As can be seen, this is quite impressive housing and would have been occupied by staff who would now be described as supervisory or middle management. The rule of thumb in Crewe was that the higher up the company hierarchy an employee was, the further away he lived from those places where the railway made most noise. (Authors' collection).

The enginemen's hostel in Gresty Lane, Crewe. Many footplate workers had to perform duties which required them to lodge away from home between shifts. Some stayed in private homes perhaps occupied by the widows of railway workers and where the conditions could vary from good to absolutely appalling. Hostels such as this were basic and austere but the fact that they were nicknamed 'barracks' suggests how they were viewed by those who had to use them. (S. Williams).

The erection of an early locomotive in the workshops at Wolverton before Crewe took over as the centre of locomotive building and maintenance for what became the L&NWR. (Authors' collection).

A school built at Wolverton which was available not only to the children of railway workers but also non-railway workers. (Authors' collection).

The Railway Institute at Wolverton. Through establishments like this, the railway companies played an important part not only in providing recreational facilities but also encouraging education and self-help among their employees. (Authors' collection).

The rather curious little saddle tank built by Bagnall's of Stafford hauling two impressive double-deck tramcars on the line between Wolverton and Stony Stratford. The locomotive had to have its motion covered because the line ran along the side of the public highway. (Authors' collection).

The approach to Riccarton Junction from the east. This gives some idea of the bleak surroundings of this railway village which owed its existence to the North British Railway. (Authors' collection).

A postcard view of Hellifield showing railway housing and a place of worship. (Authors' collection).

Rowsley shed of the Midland Railway before it was rebuilt in 1879. On display are several of the company's typical small locomotives engaged in banking, shunting and local freight work. (Authors' collection).

An impression of Normanton, 'the Crewe of the Coalfields', which became an early nodal point owing its modern development to the railways. (Authors' collection).

An example of railway housing at Normanton. This substantially built house was probably occupied by a supervisor and his family. (S. Williams).

A distant view of Inverurie showing the presence of the Great North of Scotland Railway's engineering works in what had been a very small settlement in rural surroundings. (Authors' collection).

A depiction claiming to be that of the early station of the Midland Counties Railway in Derby. (Authors' collection).

Although the Midland Railway was the dominant company serving Derby, its station was inconvenient for the town and in terms of its location it was upstaged by the Great Northern Railway which had a station much better placed for the town. The GNR indelibly stamped its presence on Derby with this bridge over Friargate. In terms of volume of traffic, however, the GNR's line was a backwater. (Authors' collection).

Oswestry Station in early GWR days, scarcely changed from its ownership by the Cambrian Railways. In the bay platform note the Gobowen shuttle train which provided connections to the GWR's main line from Shrewsbury to Chester. (Authors' collection).

The housing provided by the Glasgow & South Western Railway at Corkerhill near Glasgow. When the company established its engine shed there, Corkerhill was largely rural and the housing was provided for workers migrating into the area. (S. Williams).

The southern end of the L&NWR station at Wigan. Not normally thought of as a railway town, Wigan nevertheless was the centre of a web of lines of extraordinary complexity. This image graphically shows how detailed the route knowledge of an engine driver had to be if he was to work his trains safely. We can only admire the skill of such men and feel that they did not necessarily receive an adequate reward for their efforts. (N. Marlow).

Preston was another town with a massive railway presence but which, again, is rarely considered to be a railway town. This is the Fishergate entrance to the L&NWR's part of the station. (Authors' collection).

Housing erected by the GNR in the New England district of Peterborough for workers employed nearby at the enormous engine shed and marshalling yards. Although much of this housing has disappeared, these terraces in Lincoln Road are still occupied. (Authors' collection).

No fewer than seven railway companies served the frontier city of Carlisle and the unregulated competition of Victorian times meant that there was considerable duplication of facilities. Perhaps the smallest presence was that of the Maryport & Carlisle Railway and here one of its local passenger trains is approaching Carlisle Citadel Station. (Authors' collection).

An image of the frontage of Chester's main station which the GWR and L&NWR came to dominate. A very fine building designed by Francis Thompson, the artist has, however, been somewhat carried away and has stretched the length of his subject. (Authors' collection).

The erecting shop at Gorton Works in Manchester in the 1920s. This gives some idea of the scale of activity at what had been the major engineering facility of the Great Central Railway. A 'J39' 0-6-0 and an ex-GCR '8A' 0-8-0 can be seen receiving attention. (Authors' collection).

Distant view of the viaduct carrying the London & Greenwich Railway. The surroundings appear rustic, even idyllic, but the area it crossed became intensively developed and the viaduct, much of which was greatly widened, came to divide rather than bring together the districts through which it passed. Viaducts in many other places, particularly in packed suburbs close to town or city centres had the same effect (Authors' collection).

Part of the same viaduct showing use being made of some of the arches. Some originally had homes built in them but, not surprisingly, these were not very successful because of noise and vibration. Such arches, especially around London, did become the location of myriad small businesses and could cast something of a blight on their surroundings. (Authors' collection).

The railways assisted those who could afford to do so to make their money in commercial and industrial districts but live in suburban areas well away from grimy, overcrowded surroundings. Most cities and large towns developed leafy suburbs containing often architecturally eclectic villas of the sort shown. (Authors' collection).

The early terminus of the London & Southampton Railway at Nine Elms, some distance from central London but accessible by boat or cabs. It was replaced by the more convenient Waterloo Station of the L&SWR. (Authors' collection).

Cartoon satirising the 'respectable' suburbs so sought after by the Pooters, affectionately portrayed in George and Weedon Grossmith's understated classic *Diary of a Nobody*. (Authors' collection).

The French artist Gustav Dore spent much time in London in the second half of the nineteenth century closely observing and recording aspects of London life, especially those of what some would now call the underclass. Here he shows railway arches providing shelter for the indigent homeless. (Authors' collection).

Stratford in East London owed much of its nineteenth century growth to the presence of what became the Great Eastern Railway which created a railway district around its main station, various sorting yards and an engineering works. The GER was always strapped for cash, but it managed to produce some fine locomotives at Stratford such as Claud Hamilton, a 4-4-0 designed for express passenger work. (Authors' collection).

An aerial view of Barrow-in-Furness showing the juxtaposition of town centre, railways and Buccleuch Dock. It also gives an idea of the environmental pollution of so many industrial towns until manufacturing declined and clean air legislation was enacted in the decades following the Second World War. (Authors' collection).

Although this is not the best of images, it gives some idea of the symbiosis of railways and the brewing industry in Burton-upon-Trent. Pictured is part of the Worthington Brewery. (Authors' collection).

The vaults under St Pancras Station which housed the mass supplies of beer which the Midland Railway despatched from Burton-on-Trent for the thirsty topers of the Metropolis. (Authors' collection).

An early depiction of the first station at Coventry. This shows the famous three spires in the background. (Authors' collection).

Alderley Edge showing the Queen's Hotel in the background just before the First World War. A swish hotel in a posh suburb which was pampered by the L&NWR. (Authors' collection).

A Chester Corporation tram in the 1900s at the Saltney terminus of the route from Chester General Station. The bridge carries the Chester to Shrewsbury line of the Great Western Railway. (Authors' collection).

Coal for export! The coal sidings at Goole on the Lancashire & Yorkshire Railway. Note the carefully graded coal in the wagons. Goole was established as a minor port before the railways arrived but owed much of its subsequent growth to the L&Y. (Authors' collection).

Coal awaiting shipping at Cardiff Docks. Note the private owner wagons. No wonder Cardiff was the world's largest coal exporting port. (Authors' collection).

The coal sidings at Cadoxton near Barry. Coal was the economic lifeblood of the South Wales Valleys and the mining communities in those valleys owed so much to the railways for distributing the 'black gold'. (Authors' collection).

Distant view of Neyland. Note the housing on the hilltop. Most of these dwellings were occupied by railway workers and their families in the heyday of Neyland's role as a packet station and fishing port. (Authors' collection).

A Great Western mixed-gauge train approaching Bath through Sydney Gardens. The elegant bridges and retaining walls indicate the GWR's wish to flatter the influential burghers of the spa town by making a nod to its Georgian architectural heritage. (Authors' collection).

The classical frontage of Ashby-de-la-Zouch Station. It was hoped that Ashby would become a fashionable spa so an impressive station was built to handle the hoped-for crowds. It did not happen. (Authors' collection).

A Highland Railway train at Strathpeffer. A very commodious station for a very small town. Short lived high hopes were entertained for tourist traffic but the town never 'grew up'. (Authors' collection).

A bird's eye view of Brighton engine shed of the LB&SCR. We must presume the picture was taken on a Sunday given the crammed locomotive yard. (Authors' collection).

London Road viaduct on the LB&SCR's line to Lewes and points east. This shows that a place did not have to be a railway town in order to be dominated by a railway. (Authors' collection).

Donkey rides on Silloth Sands. A minor English seaside resort which owed much of its admittedly modest growth to the North British, a Scottish Railway Company. (Authors' collection).

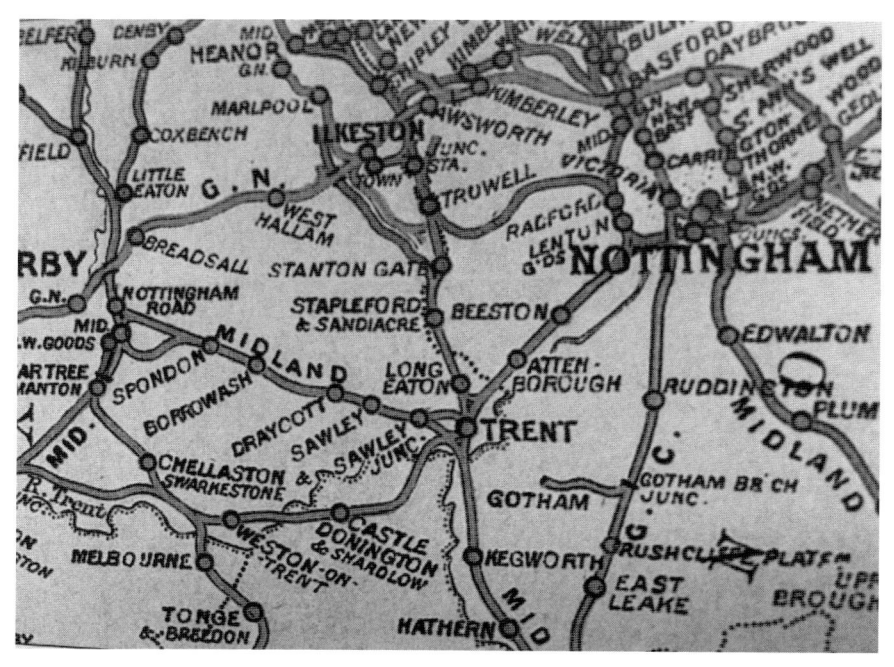

A map showing the location of Trent. (Authors' collection).

A Midland Railway express calling at Trent in the 1900s. (Authors' collection).

A GWR express leaving Didcot in a westerly direction. (Authors' collection).

The massive provender store of the GWR at Didcot. Didcot was a small railway town where much of the population was dependent on railway employment. (Authors' collection).

Grange-over-Sands Station on the Furness Railway. The Furness assisted the growth of Grange as a modest and genteel seaside watering place. There was a promenade between the sea and the railway and in those days the seawall was washed by the sea at high tide. (Authors' collection).

A navvy mission hall erected when the London Extension of the Great Central Railway was built in the late 1890s. Intended to save the souls of the navvies, it was an uphill struggle to keep them on the path of righteousness. (Authors' collection).

Two views of Stockport Viaduct. This viaduct has continued absolutely to dominate the valley of the River Mersey and Stockport town centre. The railway installations at Stockport were extensive although the railway did not contribute greatly to the town's growth in the nineteenth century. It is, however, impossible to think of Stockport without taking account of this monumental structure. (Authors' collection).

A later view of Stockport Viaduct. Work on its construction started in March 1839 and the first passenger trains ran across on 10 May 1842. It continues to be a monument to the heroic early days of the railways'. (Authors' collection).

The gas works at Lincoln. In the days of town gas, almost all settlements of any size had their own gasworks using coal most often brought in by rail. To that extent, they were all railway towns. (Authors' collection).

a trip by train being a special event in their lives. Nor were the wealthy womenfolk necessarily likely to make frequent use of the local train services. It might be the male head of the family who alone used the train regularly as a commuter. What he wanted was a semi-rural, quiet dwelling in a respectable neighbourhood and which was within easy travelling time of his place of work in central London. Clearly, much of the money he earned would be spent locally on groceries and other necessities and be disbursed in wages to those he employed. This money, more likely than not garnered from employment in central London, therefore stimulated the local economy. The railway's part in all this was perhaps to act as the facilitator of this new set of relationships. As Kellett (1969-70) said:

> The relatively exclusive first-class daily travellers ... though relatively small in numbers, were able to release great potentialities for expansion in the undeveloped rural districts around London ... Most of the products required by the family and servants in the mid-Victorian outer suburb were produced locally ... The money spent with local tradesmen ... in turn stimulated the growth of local service industry.

The railway companies were somewhat ambivalent about workmen's cheap fares. For the GER particularly, they generated an enormous amount of traffic for poor financial reward. Another bugbear was that the use of discounted tickets by the working-class travelling public tended to drive away the more profitable middle-class passengers. Given that workmen's trains tied up rolling stock that was mainly used only at peak periods, it is hardly surprising that some companies went through the motions and especially those which served the western and north-western fringes of London showed little enthusiasm. It was the GER that took the concept of cheap fares on trains serving the working-class suburbs most seriously. It became remarkably efficient in handling peak hour traffic and had refined its operations to the extent that in 1904 it admitted that it was making money out of the 2d fare charged for 'workmen' from Enfield to Liverpool Street.

The last quarter of the nineteenth saw a general rise in real incomes and this, combined with a large increase in middle-class administrative and clerical jobs, facilitated an overall growth in spending power. This led many people to raise their social aspirations and to express this by renting homes in more 'desirable' districts. Social differentiation was emphasised where people were judged by their address and very subtle distinctions could accrue in neighbourhoods where the inhabitants of one side of the street might look down on those who lived across the way. It was a dynamic situation. A much sought-after district might find its desirability and snob value eclipsed almost inexplicably by the rise of another district elsewhere.

Other forms of transport, especially the electric tram, assisted the process of London's outward spread but the expensive infrastructure needed for tramway construction and operation was generally best suited to the more densely built-up parts of suburbia close to central London. Trams were somewhat disadvantaged by effectively being banned from the streets of the City, the West End and Westminster whereas these districts could be penetrated by underground and tube trains. None of London's surface railway termini was ideally situated for the centre of the metropolis. Weary commuters working in one part of the centre often had some travail to put up with before grabbing a place on the train whisking them off to their bijou dwellings in Sidcup, Teddington, Highams Park or Finchley.

*Chapter Eight*

# London's Railway Districts

Having considered the relationship between railways and suburbs, we now move on to look at what for convenience we can call 'railway districts'.

The railways had an enormous physical impact on London. Whereas some of the earlier main line termini such as Nine Elms and Bishopsgate lay on the periphery of the built-up area or outside it, later stations of this sort tended to penetrate further into the core of central London. They approached over viaducts or in cuttings and tunnels. Inevitably this involved great disturbance of existing property and had a major impact on the landscape. Tunnels involved the least visible disturbance, but viaducts and cuttings could radically alter the nature of the districts on which they imposed their presence. They could create highly divisive barriers permanently altering the integrity of established communities. The example perhaps cited most often was that of the viaduct of the London & Greenwich Railway which carved a swathe through parts of Southwark and Bermondsey. As rail traffic into London Bridge built up, this viaduct was widened several times. While roads passed under it, the viaduct acted as a barrier to communication between the northern and the southern parts of what was now a divided community.

It was quickly realised that the building of a railway on a viaduct or in a cutting could change the nature of the area through which it passed, frequently to harmful effect. The L&SWR proposed to build a line on a viaduct from Waterloo to the Thames at Bankside. This line would have crossed Waterloo Road, Blackfriars Road and Southwark Bridge Road and it was recognised at the time that it would constitute a formidable brick barrier cutting off much of Southwark, Lambeth and Kennington from the Thames and London north of the river. Opposition was such that the line was not built. Nearby, the L&SWR's wide viaduct into Waterloo, completed in 1848, was seen to have closed off streets, destroyed the integrity of the area and caused its social decline. The underneath of the viaduct's arches attracted all manner of urban low life.

Two nineteenth-century writers jointly described the approach to London over this set of viaducts:

> What an odd notion the stranger must acquire of the Metropolis, as he enters it by the South-Western Railway! How curious is the flash of the passing Vauxhall Gardens, dreary with their big black trees, and the huge theatrical-looking summer house, built for the orchestra and half-tumbling to decay; and the momentary glimpse of the Tartarus-like gas-works, with their tall minaret chimneys, and the red mouth of some open retort there glowing like the crater of a burning volcano; and the sudden whisking by the Lambeth potteries, with their show of sample chimney-pots, and earthen pans, and tubing, ranged along the walls and the minute afterwards, the glance at the black rack-like sheds, spotted all over with the snowy ends of lumps of whiting, thrust at intervals through the apertures; and then the sickening stench of the bone-boilers, leaking in through every crevice of the carriage; and the dreary-looking attics of houses as the roofs fly past.

A railway district about 2 miles square close to central London developed around the major termini serving the main lines from the north belonging to the L&NWR, the MR and the GNR companies. From west to east these lines ran into Euston, St Pancras and King's Cross respectively. Along the southern edge of this conglomeration ran the Metropolitan underground line while the North London Railway provided a west to east boundary in the north. This district which included Somers Town and Agar Town was already blighted but appealed to the railway companies because the land was cheap. Charles Dickens was fascinated and, in *Dombey and Son* (1869) provides a vivid description:

> Every garden has its nuisance but every nuisance was of a distinct and peculiar character. In one a dung-heap, in the next a cinder-heap, in the third, which belonged to the cottage of a costermonger, was a pile of whelk and periwinkle shells, some rotten cabbages and a donkey; and the garden of another ... had become a pond of thick green water.

Where the railways forced their way through the inner-city built-up areas, they used their compulsory purchase powers to buy up land and then usually cleared existing buildings to make way for the infrastructure they needed for their operations. Dickens alludes above to what the railway companies could expect to find in the districts they bought for these purposes. They contained some appalling slum housing which would be cleared, the impact being to worsen the housing situation in neighbouring districts as the wretched occupants would simply be cascaded into neighbouring slums, already overcrowded. Legal requirements brought in during the second half of the century requiring railway companies to provide housing for at least some of those people displaced were never fully effective. Railway building did involve some incidental slum clearance but the periphery of most of the lines into central London exhibited continuing blight of the built environment.

## Industrial Railway Districts

London is not normally thought of as the hub of Britain's Industrial Revolution. However, its sheer size, the accumulated wealth of its diverse citizenry and the many functions it undertook created a huge demand for manufactured products. In 1861, 15 per cent of manufacturing jobs in England and Wales were in London. Traditionally, most of the productive units were small. They came in an infinite variety of trades and produced mostly, and some exclusively, for the London market. Before the age of the railway, the raw materials needed by these industries came in by road, sea and inland waterways. From the 1840s, the railways gained a large share but never a monopoly of handling the raw materials needed by London's industries.

Among the industries which developed in London during the nineteenth century was that of building railway locomotives and rolling stock. Four major railway companies had factories engaged in this activity. They were the L&SWR at Nine Elms, opened in 1839; the Eastern Counties (later the GER) at Stratford in 1847-48; the North London Railway at Bow (1853) and the LC&DR at Longhedge (Battersea) in 1862.

By far the largest of these establishments was Stratford Works where the Great Eastern built nearly all its locomotives and other rolling stock. Like other large railway companies, the GER tried to produce many of the consumable items it needed in-house and so its works had many departments other than engineering. At Stratford, the company produced virtually all the printed matter it needed, for example. The complex at Stratford included a strange, isolated railway settlement, originally called Hudson Town after George Hudson who had once been Chairman of the ECR. It had housing and other social facilities for railway workers and their families who had migrated there after leaving agricultural work in East Anglia and Lincolnshire.

Bow Works was close to Stratford but, while being much smaller, it gained an enviable reputation for the quality of its work. The works was the centre of a tightly knit community with a social centre, the Bow Institute, which became a popular place of entertainment in the East End. The Nine Elms works of the L&SWR outgrew its site and its activities were progressively transferred to Eastleigh in Hampshire between 1891 and 1910. This was particularly significant because the closure of the Nine Elms facility epitomised the decline of Battersea's sizeable industrial quarter. It was the last heavy engineering factory so close to central London. Longhedge, close to Nine Elms, was never very large and closed in 1911 when the work was transferred to Ashford in Kent.

Some private locomotive manufacturers were also to be found in London. Early on the scene were Messrs Braithwaite and Ericcson who entered their locomotive *Novelty* in the Rainhill Trials on the L&MR in 1829. It failed to complete all the tests but for all that appears to be the first locomotive to have been reliably timed as running a mile in less than a minute. They were a small-scale manufacturer whose output including some for export, but they closed in 1841. The largest of the other companies was George England's Hatcham Ironworks at New Cross. Between 1840 and 1872 they built about 250 locomotives, but their closure marked the end of private locomotive building in London. Many private companies continued to supply the railway industry with such things as signalling equipment. Of these, Saxby & Farmer of Kilburn was a nationally known company. The Westinghouse Brake Company had its British factory at King's Cross. Other London-based firms supplied items as diverse as lifts, carriage fittings, water closets and printed ephemera. Substantial numbers of workers and their families depended on railway-associated employment.

There were other districts in London, not necessarily involved in manufacturing but which were dominated by the physical and the economic presence of the railway industry. That around Euston, St Pancras and King's Cross has already been mentioned. Stratford and Bow with their works was another. Three others come quickly to mind: Old Oak and Willesden Junction; Battersea and Clapham Junction and Bricklayers Arms and New Cross. All had large locomotive and rolling stock servicing facilities and goods yards and depots. These produced a constant cacophony of noise; they generated road congestion and various other kinds of environmental pollution. They took up vast swathes of land and, since most railway work was highly labour-intensive, they offered large numbers of jobs. Railway work was not particularly well-paid and so many employees and their families needed to live close by. Districts like those mentioned are not thought of as railway towns but a very large proportion of their workforces and of the wages that were earned and spent in the locality were the result of the railways' presence.

Let us consider the tangle of lines in the Bermondsey and New Cross area. The origin of these lay with the London & Croydon Railway which opened in 1839. This took over parts of the former Croydon Canal but then used part of the viaduct of the London & Greenwich Railway on its way to and from London Bridge. When it turned south, it passed through the station then called New Cross and, much later, New Cross Gate. Between New Cross and Croydon, an extra line was put in running under the atmospheric system. Opened in January 1847, it was clearly unsuccessful because it was shut down in May of the same year by which time the London & Croydon and the London & Brighton Railway had amalgamated as the LB&SCR.

A tunnel, the first in the world under a river, had been built by Marc Brunel and opened in 1843. It was not successful as a foot tunnel and in 1866 it was bought by the East London Railway who opened it in 1869 to complete a link between the networks of lines south and north of the Thames which stretched out to the east of central London. In 1870, this line came under the management of the LB&SCR although it was co-owned by the GER, the South-Eastern & Chatham, the Metropolitan and the Metropolitan District Railways. The East London terminated trains at what had become the LB&SCR's New Cross Station while, confusingly, it also ran trains to terminate at another station called New Cross close by. The LB&SCR built an engine shed also called New Cross.

In 1844, the Croydon Railway and the SER opened a new terminus close to the Old Kent Road which took its name 'Bricklayers Arms' from a noted nearby hostelry. A reason given by the companies was that the approaches to London Bridge were becoming increasingly congested, especially with freight traffic but it is likely that there was a covert but more pertinent explanation. From 1842, the London & Greenwich was demanding a substantial toll on traffic other than its own that was travelling to and from London Bridge and these companies of course had to pass this on through the fares they charged.

With breath-taking insouciance, this station was referred to in company information as 'The Grand West End Terminus'. The only justification for this name was that the Bricklayers Arms had once been a stop for coaches heading out of London in the direction of places like Dover. About half of the SER's trains and an hourly service on the Croydon line used Bricklayers Arms. This had been a ruse on the part of the two companies. With its income from tolls falling, the London & Greenwich relented, and the two companies began to run increasing numbers of their trains into London Bridge. In 1852, the inconveniently placed Bricklayers Arms passenger station closed, by which time the SER had taken out a lease of the Greenwich company. The SER opened a large goods depot at Bricklayers Arms and a sizeable locomotive depot and extensive carriage sidings at Rotherhithe Road. The LB&SCR opened a goods depot at Willow Walk close by.

In 1849, the LB&SCR opened its Deptford Road branch from Old Kent Road Junction. This line, little known because it never carried a regular passenger service, was, however, of great importance to the LB&SCR because it provided their main link with the water traffic on the Thames. Large quantities of coal, timber and stone were handled. In 1899, a branch was extruded to the City Corporation's Foreign Cattle Market at Deptford which provided the unusual sight of a full-size railway train running along the middle of a public road. Another branch which proved unsuccessful was built into the Surrey Commercial Docks.

The South London Line of the LB&SCR, opened throughout in 1867, ran in an arc between London Bridge and Victoria. This left the lines into London Bridge close to Corbet's Lane Junction and then turned first south and then west through districts such as Peckham and Brixton in which predominantly working-class housing development was rapidly taking place. This had stations in the New Cross area at South Bermondsey, originally Rotherhithe, and Old Kent Road. It was electrified in 1909 on the overhead system by the LB&SCR attempting to counter the competition from electric trams.

Cutting across the south of the contorted tangle of lines around New Cross was the curious short branch line of the SER from Nunhead to Greenwich Park. This venture was never a success and it closed in 1917.

New Cross and Bricklayers Arms have been used as an example of what for convenience can be called 'railway district'. Such districts had characteristics in common. One was that the railways owned immense amounts of land but created plots within their complex networks of lines which were too small to find any practical use, not being readily accessible. Anyone living in railway districts when steam locomotives provided the major form of railway motive could not but have had their lives affected by their noise and atmospheric pollution. The goods depots that were often a feature of these districts generated a great deal of road traffic. In the case particularly of New Cross, the innumerable railway viaducts, when built through established districts, could effectively destroy the social coherence of a neighbourhood and create all manner of social problems.

## Brentford

Brentford was an interesting case. By the 1850s the GWR had a large goods depot at Paddington. A serious problem facing the company was its use of broad-gauge track. This meant that expensive and time-consuming transhipment was involved where goods had to be interchanged with the wagons of other railway companies. Some had pre-empted the GWR by gaining early access to London's docks. They were not interested in assisting the GWR to reach the docks along mixed-gauge lines.

The GWR came up with a solution. It promoted a subsidiary company, the Great Western & Brentford Railway, from Southall on its main line into Paddington to the Thames at Brentford. The line was only about 3 miles long and was opened in 1859, a custom-built dock at

Brentford following shortly after. Using the dock at Brentford allowed the GWR to tranship goods into river barges and send them down the Thames avoiding London's crowded rail and road network. This also allowed the GWR to avoid the need to negotiate access to the docks along the tracks of another railway or to build its own independent line. Downstream from London Bridge the goods could be transhipped into larger vessels or delivered to customers by road. Among the merchandise handled through Brentford Dock was animal feed, coal, food produce, timber and iron and steel.

Brentford had long been a place of some importance, located on the main road out of London to the west, where there was a bridge across the Brent, a tributary of the Thames, and ferries were available to the Surrey side of the Thames. The Grand Union Canal from the Midlands joined the Thames nearby. The coming of the railway considerably assisted its transformation into a perhaps rather unexpected industrial and working-class enclave on the fringe of London. The excellent communication by river and railway encouraged more industrial development which may entitle Brentford to be described as a railway suburb. It has a very different in character from Kew and Richmond on the other side of the Thames.

*Chapter Nine*

# Major Industrial Towns

The factors that come together to influence the nature of urban settlements are many, varied and unique to each specific location. We are examining a wide range of places on which the railways impacted as we probe around the theme of railway towns. Here we look at some industrial centres which owe much of their growth to the railways but are not normally thought of as railway towns.

## Middlesbrough

Middlesbrough grew from the site of scattered farms to a vigorously expanding industrial town in the space of a few decades. The original purpose of the S&DR, opened in 1825, was to convey coal from pits located to the west of Darlington down to the River Tees at Stockton where the coal was discharged into vessels on the river. The Tees was not easy to navigate for anything other than small craft so an extension of the railway was planned along the south bank of the Tees to a greenfield site where a new port could be developed. From there a deep channel would be created to allow access for larger vessels to the sea. The line to what became known as Middlesbrough opened in December 1830. A planned town was created from scratch. It owed its origin to the decision of the railway company to build this line from Stockton.

It became a boom town! The original parish housed no more than 400 souls when the railway arrived but ten years later it had 5,700 people. It was doing brisk business as a port and a dock was being built. Several brickworks had started operations and ironworks quickly followed. A bonus came with the discovery and exploitation of iron ore close by. The rate of growth was quite extraordinary. In 1851 the population stood at about 8,000 but rose to 56,000 in 1881 and 105,000 in 1911.

The railways not only provided a vital means of transport for Middlesbrough's burgeoning businesses, but the S&DR bought the dock in 1849 and in 1874 the NER, its successor, rebuilt and greatly enlarged it. It also built a station worthy of this fine, ultra-modern town which it had played such a large part in creating. Further business from which the railways benefitted began when a line was built which enabled high-grade haematite ore for the Teeside iron industry to be conveyed across the Pennines from the Furness area with return business in the form of Durham coke.

## Barrow-in-Furness

Like Middlesbrough, Barrow was a product of the nineteenth century, a port and a centre of iron-production. It had the natural disadvantage of relative isolation. Traditionally, the approach from Lancashire was across the notoriously dangerous shifting sands of Morecambe Bay. Before the coming of the railways, local slate and ore was despatched from a facility close by. Barrow owed a great debt to the railways for facilitating its industrial growth by providing the local transport infrastructure it needed and the longer-distance links to the rest of the railway system, markets and sources of raw materials. Just as the NER had a monopoly of railway operation around Teeside so the much smaller Furness Railway Company (FR), also with a monopolistic position, needs recognition for its crucial role in Barrow's development.

Barrow would have found itself close to a major trunk route had proposals gone ahead for a main line up the west coast from Lancashire to Scotland. This would have been a major undertaking with an embankment across Morecambe Bay and then an alignment skirting the western edge of the Lake District massif on its way to Carlisle. Such an enterprise would have given some true meaning to the phrase 'West Coast Main Line'.

Vast deposits of iron ore had been discovered in the hinterland in the eighteenth century and buyers were found away from the area. The only practical way of moving it was by sea and a jetty was built at Barrow Island in 1782, being close to the tiny settlement of Barrow. The output of ore increased from 7,500 to 40,000 tons between 1825 and 1840 but production was hampered by the inadequacy of the local roads. What was needed was a tramway or railway linking the mines with the shipping points. A railway line was opened in 1846 and immediately provided a great boost for the iron and slate mining industries. This line was the nucleus of the FR which had been incorporated in 1844.

The mineral rights in the area were in the hands of the Duke of Buccleuch and the future Duke of Devonshire both of whom were keen for developments to take place by which they could further enrich themselves. In 1849, the Whitehaven & Furness Junction Railway district was opened along the coast towards Whitehaven, but the Barrow area remained largely isolated from the wider railway system until a line built by the FR, opened in 1857, connected it with the West Coast Main Line at Carnforth. A later short connection at Carnforth, built in conjunction with the MR, provided access to a cross-country line to Leeds and Bradford.

Barrow became a company town, monopolising all railway movements and taking over the dock facilities. It also built and totally dominated the town. Labour was needed and so housing and social facilities were provided. The FR had an exceptionally energetic manager in James Ramsden who supervised the development of a town which, although not particularly distinguished architecturally, offered a better environment than many contemporary industrial settlements. Particularly striking were blocks of four-storey tenements which, outwardly at least, had a certain elegance.

Barrow boomed. Using local supplies of high-quality haematite iron, ideal for the Bessemer process, Henry Schneider established a steel works which went into production between 1857 and 1859. In 1863, the FR was instrumental in establishing the Barrow Steel Company, mostly involved in the manufacture of steel rails. It merged with Schneider's in 1866, creating the Barrow Haematite Steel Company and the result was the largest steel works in Britain at that time. Much of the steel went away by sea and the FR was involved in a continuous process of expanding and improving the town's docks. Temporarily they were Britain's largest docks after London and Liverpool. Passenger steamers plied to and from Belfast and the Isle of Man. However, the town's isolated position thwarted its desire to become a major passenger port. The line to Carnforth along the north side of Morecambe Bay was not built to handle fast passenger traffic.

In 1851 Barrow had a population of 700, over 3,000 in 1861, but in the 1870s it had reached about 47,000 after which expansion continued but at a much slower rate. The FR's fortunes reflected this slowdown. The town was hit by the national economic downturn from the mid-1870s, but it recovered and the railway network and the town it served remained buoyant, a medium-sized, heavily industrialised manufacturing town and port unexpectedly located close to the Cumbrian massif.

## Burton-upon-Trent

Burton was a market and cloth-making town in the Middle Ages which, so the story goes, diversified when the head of the local monastery realised that the water in aquafers under the town was particularly suited to the making of light beers. He would have known all about this since most monastic establishments of any size had breweries whose output was consumed by the brethren, this being one of the perks of the job.

Brewing on an industrial scale began in the 1770s with the opening of the Trent and Mersey Canal which, along with the Trent itself, allowed fuel to be brought in and Burton's produce to be taken away to the consumer. The first railway at Burton was the Birmingham & Derby Junction in 1839. This became a major component of the MR in 1844 and that company was then to dominate the railways in the town although the L&NWR, the North Staffordshire and the GNR obtained access to the town by means of running powers.

Early on, several large-scale brewers such as Bass, Allsopp and Worthington established themselves in the town on a variety of sites and they made full use of railways to provide the transport for inward raw materials and fuel and to take their heavy and bulky products to the MR's sidings for outward despatch. The town centre became dominated not just by the imposing buildings of the breweries but also by a dense network of private lines crossing streets and causing infuriating road congestion as little trains, usually of no more than three or four wagons, made their way from one part of the system to another hauled by diminutive but immaculate shunting engines, seemingly all 0-4-0s with the short wheelbase necessary for dealing with the sharp curves that were a feature of the system. There were about thirty of these level crossings. The brewery buildings, the smell of brewing and the seemingly ubiquitous presence of these irksome little trains defined Burton's town centre. Plans to build a line around the periphery of the town to eliminate or at least reduce the disruption in the town never came to anything. Meanwhile the economy of the town went from strength to strength. In 1869, with a population of about 25,000, Burton had 26 breweries with 5,000 employees. By 1900 the network of brewery railways amounted to 40 miles, and it continued to grow as did the complaints from those trying to move around the centre. Burton's economy depended on the brewing industry. This meant that the movement of these trains had priority.

Stories abounded of engine crews on the internal brewery railways being in a more-or-less permanent state of intoxication while at work owing to the cordial relationships that they enjoyed with their colleagues who were on the production side.

The MR was fully aware of the economic advantages it enjoyed as the dominant railway provider in Burton and it contributed to the upgrading of an important road bridge and, following constant complaints about the inconvenient siting of the station, rebuilt it on a new site, again not actually very convenient, in 1883.

Burton was absolutely dominated by brewing and associated industries and is considered being in this time Britain's premier brewing centre. It is not considered as a railway town, but it is unlikely that it would have gained, never mind maintained, its leading position had it not been for the service provided by the railways.

## Coventry

In 1400, Coventry ranked with Bristol, York and Plymouth as one of the four leading provincial centres of England. Becoming a city in the fourteenth century, part of its wealth came from cloth and thread, dyed blue by a special process which kept the colour from fading. Over the following 200 years, clock-making and the weaving of ribbons became Coventry's main industries until imports of silk from France and watches from Switzerland brought about a severe slump in both. The city went into the doldrums and lost population until new industries established themselves. These were cycle-making, engineering and car manufacturing. Daimler in 1896 became the first motor firm in the town.

When the L&B was being planned, the local business community was largely indifferent. They were well served by road coaches and a very lucrative canal bringing in cheap coal supplies. With its industries making very light artefacts, no clear advantage of a railway was then perceived. In turn, the railway company seemed to lack interest in the town and built a station which irritated the locals by being situated very inconveniently. A better-sited station replaced it but relations between the city and the successor company, the L&NWR, remained icy.

The L&NWR monopolised the provision of Coventry's railways, even after new lines were built to Leamington and Nuneaton. As the economic and social advantages of railways became increasingly obvious, the unfriendly monopoly of the L&NWR became increasingly resented and feelers were put out in 1865 for a Coventry & Great Western Junction Railway and, in 1898, to the GCR to build an alternative line from Rugby to Birmingham. Nothing resulted from these schemes and the nearest thing to the breaking of the L&NWR's monopoly came with the granting of running powers to the MR for goods traffic only, over the line from Nuneaton.

The L&NWR ascribed no great value to Coventry's potential source of valuable traffic – and it showed. Only from 1900 when the town was growing rapidly did it enlarge the station and upgrade the goods-handling facilities. The lesson perhaps to be drawn was that a company that had a virtual monopoly of railway provision in a town or city might become rather complacent about the service it provided where no other company offered competition. Coventry's example also showed that the size of a population was not necessarily crucial in influencing the extent of the provision made by the local railway company or companies. Coventry had become a large city by 1914 but the industries for which it was noted were mainly not of the kind for which rail traffic was particularly suited at that time. A populous city, a major manufacturing centre – these realities were not enough to make it a large railway focus. The influence of the railway in Coventry's development was less than that in many much smaller places.

## Bradford

If there can be said to be a large manufacturing city in the UK which never progressed beyond the stage of being something of a railway backwater, it must be Bradford. It was the only such city never to be situated on a through line. It had two major railway termini, Forster Square and Exchange, which were effectively at the end of secondary lines from nearby Leeds, and various other minor routes. The limited service of direct trains to and from London by the MR and GNR seem to have been almost an afterthought. Admittedly the L&Y provided services to two other northern industrial powerhouses, Liverpool and Manchester, but these were not very fast services and they traversed secondary main lines. It certainly did not help Bradford that it was so close to Leeds.

The early years of railway development passed Bradford by despite the town having a growing population, many earning their living in the local ironworks and in the developing woollen worsted industry.

By 1840, Bradford was Britain's biggest town without a railway and its continued expansion as an industrial town was being hampered by its poor transport links. Unsuccessful efforts were made to persuade George Hudson to build a branch to Bradford from his North Midland Railway. However, in 1846 the Leeds & Bradford Railway opened, running its trains on a very circuitous line from Leeds into its Market Street Station at Bradford. This was later replaced by Forster Square Station. The Leeds & Bradford was fully absorbed by the MR in 1851.

The next arrival on Bradford's railway scene was the Lancashire & Yorkshire which opened its Drake Street terminus in May 1850. This was on a branch from the company's main line between Manchester and Leeds. Bradford now had two stations separated by a few hundred yards. That short distance could be said to have had consequences for Bradford ever since. Many schemes were proposed over the years to link the two stations by viaduct or by tunnel, but they all came to nothing.

In 1854, the Leeds, Bradford & Halifax Junction opened an inconveniently sited terminus at Adolphus Street which gave Bradford a shorter route to Leeds. This company was absorbed by the GNR in 1865 and in 1867 its passenger trains were diverted into the L&Y's Drake Street Station which now came under joint ownership and was renamed 'Exchange'.

Quite a complicated network of additional lines was added to Bradford's railways over the following years, but none materially changed the perception that Bradford missed some of the opportunities that could have come had a line connecting Exchange and Forster Square been built. We are left to speculate fruitlessly how Bradford might have fared had its railway history been different. As it was, Bradford's halcyon days as an industrial centre occurred despite being poorly served by main line railways.

## Kingston-upon-Hull

Hull was another large industrial town which, although it had an extremely complicated railway system, has always suffered, and not just from the railway point of view, from its relative geographical isolation. This has condemned it to being away from any major Anglo-Scottish railway and has meant that, at least until comparatively recently, it has had to put up with poor through services to London. People travelling to Hull from various other parts of Britain have frequently needed to change at Doncaster, Leeds or perhaps York. Hull was once disparagingly referred to as a 'fish dock at the end of a railway siding'.

It would be easy to see the railways serving Hull as primarily designed for the conveyance of minerals, fish and a wide variety of merchandise and passenger operations as a secondary consideration. Although the railways had a large presence in Hull, even an infuriatingly intrusive one given the number of level crossings it once had, the place is not generally thought of as a railway town. For much of the period up to 1914 the NER had a near monopoly of Hull's railways and this was the cause of some resentment among the local citizenry. The Hull & Barnsley Railway arrived in 1885 primarily as a coal-carrying enterprise but was unable to challenge the NER's dominance. An amusing aside is that Hull was penetrated by a third railway. This was the MS&LR which served the station called Hull Corporation Pier. This was indeed a remarkable, although not quite unique, station in that it possessed all the facilities expected of a railway station except platforms, tracks and trains. It opened in 1849 to serve the MS&LR-owned ferries which plied across the Humber to New Holland Pier where they connected with trains to Grimsby.

A bewildering range of imports came through Hull's docks, some of them being processed before being carried elsewhere by railway. Fresh fish was conveyed to markets elsewhere on an industrial scale. Hull also dealt with large amounts of inward coal, fuel for its land-based industries but also for its steam-powered commercial shipping fleets and the vast number of steam trawlers operating out of the port. In the period we are reviewing, railways provided the transportation service which was vital to Hull's prosperity. The railways even owned Hull's docks. There were vast reception sidings on the western side of

Hull and a huge engine shed at Dairycoates. All this meant that the railway was a major employer in Hull. Over the years there were many passenger stations but Paragon, once possessing a total of fourteen platforms, was truly a station of which Hull could be proud and which bore comparison with the best elsewhere.

Hull had a long history and enjoyed prosperity from the Middle Ages until, at the end of the eighteenth century, it ranked fourth among British ports behind the much larger towns of London, Liverpool and Bristol. Its fortunes continued to grow with the rise of the whaling trade and the woollen industry in the West Riding of Yorkshire. Smuggling, although part of the black economy, contributed to the town's prosperity. Hull had a diverse economic base and may not have been a railway town in the generally understood sense of the word, but the railways helped to sustain its prosperity in the rapidly changing circumstances of the nineteenth century.

## Consett

The first half of the nineteenth century was a time of rapidly rising demand for iron to serve the needs of Britain's growing heavy industries. The railways themselves were a major factor in stimulating demand for the products of the iron industry as well as providing the means of moving the raw materials it needed and taking its products to the consumers.

In 1837, ironstone was found high on the moors of south-west Durham around what became the town of Consett. In 1840, iron production began in this remote spot. Coal was available nearby. The Derwent Iron Company established blast furnaces and rolling mills at Consett. Renamed the Consett Iron Company in 1864, business was good and the population of Consett quickly grew to over 20,000 from virtually nothing in 1801. The quality and availability of the local iron ore supplies deteriorated in the 1850s and a network of railways was used to bring in alternative supplies, from Teeside and West Cumberland, for example. Steel production developed in the 1880s and Consett became a real boom town. It was a company town much in the way that Crewe or Horwich was but here it was the Consett Iron Company that dominated. Workers had had to be brought to this inhospitable district and it was thought that the Consett Iron Company and its predecessors built around 2,700 houses. They also built the physical infrastructure required for a viable social community. Increasingly Consett came to need imported ore from places like Spain. Much of this was brought into Tyne Dock near South Shields and hauled and pulled and pushed by rail up ferocious gradients to Consett. It was its isolation and the need to bring in raw materials which meant that Consett was an expensive works to operate.

Consett epitomises the symbiotic relationship between heavy industry and the railways in this period. With poor roads and an absence of navigable water anywhere close by, Consett could only function and prosper by enjoying the services of the railway. Company town certainly. Was it made by the railway?

*Chapter Ten*

# Railways and Suburbs in Provincial Cities

Here we consider how some of the larger provincial cities developed passenger lines into their hinterlands and to what extent the railways contributed to the development of their suburbs.

Newcastle, perhaps surprisingly, was the first provincial city to open a line which attracted suburban development. In 1839, the Newcastle & North Shields Railway opened, providing a service to North Shields, an established settlement 7 miles away on the coast. The part of the coast north of the Tyne had long been popular with people from Newcastle and on high days and holidays there had been a busy traffic to the seaside settlements in that area by pleasure steamers. The line was extended to Tynemouth in 1847 and further extended up the coast to the closely connected settlements of Cullercoats, Whitley Bay and Monkseaton. A good railway service encouraged both residential development and the provision of leisure facilities in these places and Tynemouth was provided by the NER with an impressive station designed to handle large holiday crowds. A new line was added running south-west closer to the Tyne and providing an alternative route to and from Newcastle. It approached the city from the north and encouraged further suburban residential development. Commuter and leisure traffic built up so encouragingly that the North Tyneside system was electrified by the NER in 1904.

Before these lines were electrified, large amounts of passenger traffic had been lost to electric trams, but it was steadily regained and the system became extremely busy carrying commuters to their suburban homes and coastal villas, workmen to docks and shipyards and holidaymakers and trippers to the seaside. While we cannot quantify the exact contribution of the North Tyneside electric trains to the growth of the places they served, it is justified to describe them as railway suburbs. They provide an example of how efficient electric railways could influence changing population patterns.

Some other cities were close to the sea and likewise developed nearby seaside places as resorts and desirable residential localities. This happened to Bristol with Portishead, Clevedon and Weston-super-Mare all of which grew, at least partially, because of the opening of lines to and from that city. A railway was opened from Liverpool to Southport in 1850. This encouraged the development of suburbs along the line, generally the more desirable being further north towards Southport. This town was developing as a seaside resort of dual character. It had much expensive housing and high-quality retail facilities in the delightfully laid-out Lord Street. While looking upon itself as rather superior to Blackpool it also developed many facilities attractive to a more working-class clientele. Hull had lines reaching the coast at Withernsea and Hornsea. They opened respectively in 1854 and 1864. The former from the start was intended to be a rail-connected dormitory town. The railway assisted the development of both as destinations for trippers from Hull in which role they were quite successful. However, despite having reasonable railway services, neither developed beyond being small towns and they never attracted significant numbers of visitors from places further away.

Manchester provided several examples of railways that played a significant role in shaping places that became suburbs. The first was a line to Altrincham, a small market town about 8 miles south of Manchester. Much of the line, opened in 1849, ran alongside the Bridgewater Canal and quickly replaced the steam passenger boats that had plied between Manchester and the northern fringe of Altrincham. The latter place and its neighbour Bowdon were already desirable residential districts for affluent men making their money in Manchester. With Sale, an intermediate stop on the line, they developed as well-treed, fashionable suburbs with many fine villas and their growth was greatly encouraged by a good train service. The Cheshire Lines Committee route to Warrington and Liverpool encouraged the development of some affluent housing at Flixton and Urmston. The LNWR's line to Stockport encouraged housing for the moderately well-off at Heaton Chapel, for example. Later, the L&Y line from Manchester Victoria to Bury had as one of its purposes the development of quality suburbs in the hilly area north of Manchester and successfully contributed to the growth of housing around Heaton Park and Prestwich.

Rather different was the line that the Manchester & Birmingham Railway opened in 1842 through Stockport to Crewe. South of Stockport only Wilmslow of intermediate points seemed at this time to offer much in the way of potential passenger traffic. Perhaps unexpectedly, the M&B found some useful business in trippers from Manchester alighting at Alderley, just south of Wilmslow, to enjoy the sylvan pleasures and fresh air of Alderley Edge. In 1843, an excursion train brought no less than 3,000 passengers to Alderley. Philanthropic bodies organised excursions for poor children, employers for their employees and temperance societies for healthy relaxation eschewing the temptations of the demon drink.

This beauty spot then became a favoured suburb for well-off Mancunian businessmen and a small town developed to meet their shopping needs, all this being assisted by a good train service. A luxurious railway-owned hotel was opened. The L&NWR absorbed the M&B in 1846 and, in 1876, renamed the station as Alderley Edge. The L&NWR set out deliberately to encourage commuter traffic at Alderley by providing free passes for travel to and from Manchester for a term of twenty-one years for people prepared to build homes around Alderley. The main local landowners, the de Trafford family, were only too happy to sell land for the right kind of select housing development. The L&NWR derived useful business from Alderley Edge, but the town remained small. The locals preferred it to be thought of as a village. Its population rose from 400 in 1810 to over 3,000 in 1911.

Wilmslow, its close neighbour just to the north, also became a railway suburb. Although it was also a desirable location, it was not as socially exclusive as Alderley Edge and it grew considerably bigger. There was no question of discounted workmen's tickets from either station!

The L&Y vigorously advertised the healthy nature and the social prestige attached to living in what it dubbed the 'Northern Heights' of Manchester. This was the hilly area containing growing suburbs for the middle class such as Crumpsall, Heaton Park, Prestwich and Whitefield which were served by the line from Manchester Victoria to Bury Bolton Street. In 1916, this line was electrified. Residential development in this district had been growing steadily encouraged by a good service of steam trains but the electrification showed dramatically what a quick, clean and frequent service of ultra-modern electric trains could achieve. Passenger receipts apparently increased by 80 per cent in the first two years of electric operation. The existence of such an excellent service encouraged further residential development. The L&Y went to the length of producing a thick booklet called 'The Breezy Northern Heights of Manchester' which extolled in glowing terms the shopping, educational and recreational facilities that were to be found close to each of the stations in 'The Heights'. The cover of this publication showed an electric train descending from 'The Heights', which are suffused in sunlight and a sense of spaciousness, towards Manchester where belching factory chimneys are crammed together in a Stygian gloom. The growth of these northern suburbs of Manchester owed much to the enterprise of the Lancashire & Yorkshire Railway.

The provision of a railway did not necessarily lead to the development of residential districts by speculative builders, even though the railway would provide quick access to the city centre. Nottingham's housing problems were chronic even by nineteenth century standards. Measures were desperately needed to tackle gross overcrowding and the disease and social desperation it created. In 1886, local businessmen launched a project to build the Nottingham Suburban Railway. This was intended to traverse an area of largely empty land to the east of the centre. The projected line would also give access to sources of natural materials suitable for brickmaking. It looked like a win-win situation as it could provide housing and brickmaking jobs and, hopefully, profits for the investors. The line, skirting round the eastern edge of what was then still a large town rather than a city, opened in 1889 and was about 3 miles long. It proved to be a white elephant. The hilly nature of the terrain through which it passed made it very expensive to build. Although some housing development did take place, it did little, if anything, to tackle Nottingham's housing problems. From the start the line faced competition from trams which were more frequent, more direct and cheaper. The line staggered into the twentieth century, but its services were cut before the First World War making it an even less attractive travel option. Passenger services were totally withdrawn in 1916. It may have been called the Nottingham Suburban Railway, but it never created what can be described as railway suburbs.

If the Nottingham Suburban Railway was an almost complete failure, there were other lines that were built to serve areas that looked ripe for building development but were disappointing for their promoters because of the slowness with which that development took place. In 1908, the GWR opened a line from Tyseley, just south of Birmingham, to Stratford-upon-Avon. This was envisaged as part of a through route from the West Midlands to Bristol and the West Country but the distinctly rural country through which it passed on the way to Stratford looked as it could be developed for the building of railway suburbs. Ten stations and halts were opened. The response of speculative builders was lukewarm and little housing appeared until after the First World War. A similar process was to be seen along the Styal Line, south of Manchester. This was intended as a through route avoiding Stockport but seemed to offer the likelihood that residential development would follow the opening of the line to Wilmslow in 1910. It was well into the 1920s and 1930s before this happened to any great extent.

At Sheffield, the MR in the 1880s was looking to build a line to Manchester. Housing was spreading southwards along the valley of the

River Sheaf and a particularly desirable residential area was developing around Dore and Totley. A line was built heading west along Edale with the intention of providing a through route but also in the hope that high-class housing might follow the building of intermediate stations at places like Hathersage, Bamford and Edale. The line opened in 1894 and proved moderately successful in attracting commuter traffic, although the places along the line remained small. A bonus was a considerable traffic in ramblers wanting to enjoy the delights of this beautiful countryside. These places do not warrant the description of railway suburbs, but the railway undoubtedly played a significant role in their development.

## Colwick

A suburb of a very different kind is to be found on the east side of Nottingham. The old settlement of Colwick remains, consisting largely of a hall and church close to the city's racecourse. Modern Colwick is part of what is now an extensive, largely residential district about 3 miles from the centre of Nottingham and including Netherfield, Gedling and Carlton. It was the site of enormous marshalling yards concerned primarily with receiving, sorting and dispatching vast numbers of coal trains and their wagons full of the 'black gold' produced by pits in Nottinghamshire and Derbyshire.

The origins of this extraordinarily complex centre of railway operations can be said to lie with a small but ambitious railway company with an extremely impressive title, the Ambergate, Boston, Nottingham and Eastern Junction Railway. This company had been formed in 1846 from an amalgamation of three companies. These were the Nottingham & Boston and the verbosely titled Nottingham, Erewash Valley & Ambergate and the Nottingham, Vale of Belvoir & Grantham Railways. The Ambergate company's line ran west from Grantham through the Vale of Belvoir and made a junction with the MR in the Netherfield and Colwick area. This line opened in July 1850. It may have seemed a rather insignificant cross-country line, but it soon found itself as something of a pawn in the power games being played by two heavy-duty companies, the GNR and the MR. The Midland Counties Railway, a predecessor of the MR, had opened a line from Derby to Nottingham in 1839. The MR was created in 1844 and it had opened a line from Nottingham to Lincoln in 1846. The MR opened an improved station at Nottingham in May 1848 and by then regarded Nottingham as its fiefdom. It was not favourably inclined towards any other companies with designs on serving Nottingham.

As was only to be expected, the MR took a dim view of the upstart Ambergate company and tried, unsuccessfully, to take it over in 1851. The Ambergate had realised that it possessed strategic importance, placed as it was between George Hudson's ambitious and growing empire based at Derby and the GNR which was bent on building a shorter alternative to its existing line from London and Peterborough to the north via Boston and Lincoln. This new line which came to be known as the 'Towns Route' ran through Grantham, Newark-on-Trent and Retford on its way to Doncaster and York. It opened on 1 August 1852, despite Hudson having fought tooth and nail to prevent it because it posed a direct threat to the routes he controlled joining London to York.

The GNR coveted access to Nottingham and in 1855 leased the Ambergate company. It opened a new line into Nottingham from the junction with the MR and in October 1857 its trains were running into its own station at London Road, just a stone's throw from the MR's station. Nottingham in itself was a desirable target for the GNR, but the company had more ambitious plans. It wanted direct access to the rich seams of coal in the expanding mining districts north and west of Nottingham which the MR was already exploiting to its considerable financial advantage. The GNR intended to build a line around the eastern and northern side of Nottingham providing access to the coalfields in the Leen and Erewash valleys where the MR already had a presence. Although coal traffic was the main objective, the GNR also had its eyes on the business potential of Derby itself, western parts of Derbyshire and even further west to Burton-on-Trent and Stafford. Raw materials and fuel for the breweries of Burton-on-Trent, distribution of the products of its brewing industry and the handling of agricultural produce and milk from the fertile east Staffordshire countryside would generate useful traffic.

This is where Colwick comes in. There was plenty of suitable land available for the GNR to lay down sidings for the anticipated traffic which would travel along what became known as the 'Derbyshire Extension'. To local railway workers, this route skirting round the north of Nottingham was known as 'The Back Line'. Trains began to run on the section to Pinxton in 1875-76, to Derby and beyond in 1878 and towards Newstead in 1882. Sorting sidings and an engine shed were opened at Colwick in 1878 but such was the growth in traffic levels that the yard had to be greatly extended in 1888 to 1891 by which time there were 20 miles of sidings. A heavy flow of coal traffic left the south end of the Colwick complex to travel along the old Ambergate route to Grantham and thence southwards to Peterborough where much of it was re-sorted at New England and then despatched to Ferme Park Yard, London. Another flow used the GN&LNW Joint Line from Saxondale Junction through to Welham Junction and then on to L&NWR metals towards Northampton and London. A short spur between Bottesford West and North Junction gave access to the GNR's extension of the Joint Line to Newark where it joined the main line northwards to Doncaster and York.

The GNR did not engage in a major housebuilding programme at Colwick but started by erecting two rather unimaginatively named blocks called Traffic Terrace and Locomotive Terrace. A Railway Institute opened in 1885 and a lodging house for train crews. The L&NWR gained access to Colwick via the Joint Line and running powers over the GNR and it established a base at Colwick, admittedly much smaller than that of the GNR. Housing for its employees was built and an engine shed opened. The arrangements with the GNR gave the L&NWR access for a share of the coal traffic from the pits north and north-west of Nottingham. Traffic continued to grow and in 1896–97 further sidings were laid down by which time Colwick had the capacity to handle 6,000 wagons, five times its original capacity. The GNR's engine shed had to be enlarged and at one time housed around 230 locomotives. Various workshops serviced wagons and carried out repairs on locomotives.

The activity at Colwick abated somewhat from Saturday afternoons and was usually quiet on Sundays. For the rest of the week, the railway complex produced incessant noise – engine whistles, shunters' whistles and shouts, the clanging of buffers, coal being emptied into locomotive tenders. It was part of Colwick life, as was the filth liberally distributed around the area by the presence of so many working steam locomotives. The supportive infrastructure built by the two railway companies did not constitute that provided in classic railway towns like Crewe or Swindon. The huge workforce required by the railway was largely accommodated in speculative housing close to the west of the complex. In this district of Netherfield, a very large proportion of the growing population would have depended on the railways for their income. Colwick cannot be described as a railway town. With some caution, It is appropriate to call Netherfield a railway suburb.

## Saltney

In pre-railway days, Saltney was not much of a place. It was on the south side of the River Dee, about 2 miles west of Chester. Much of it was marshy. The nineteenth century saw it become an industrialised suburb of Chester, railways playing a major part in this transformation.

Three companies were involved in Saltney's early development as a railway centre. The Shrewsbury & Chester and the Chester & Holyhead Railway companies opened simultaneously on 4 November 1846 on the stretch between Chester and Saltney Junction. The Shrewsbury & Chester ran initially just to Ruabon and then to Shrewsbury in October 1848. The Chester to Holyhead line was completed throughout in March 1850. The third player was the Mold

Railway Company whose 10-mile line from Mold to Saltney Ferry was intended to convey minerals from the rich deposits around Mold. The Mold Railway was absorbed by the Chester & Holyhead which in turn was taken over by the L&NWR in 1859. In 1854, the Shrewsbury & Chester became part of the GWR. Relations between the L&NWR and the GWR were usually marked by mutual animosity and nowhere was this truer than at Chester Station and the short section of shared line out to Saltney Junction.

A settlement was to be created which had two main centres. A passenger station opened under the name Saltney Ferry which was close to Mold Junction where the branch to Mold left the main line to Holyhead. Extensive sidings were laid down at this point with an engine shed adjacent to Saltney Ferry Station. Its allocation was oriented towards shifting goods and mineral traffic. In the 1890s, the L&NWR built a small village on the north side of the Holyhead main line for its employees on a greenfield site. As well as homes, there were shops, a school, a church, two chapels and an engineman's hostel.

The GWR left the L&NWR at Saltney Junction and then laid down extensive sidings with access to various industrial premises on both sides of the Shrewsbury line. At Saltney Dee Junction there was a GWR rolling stock works originally belonging to the Shrewsbury & Chester company and a branch which ran northwards to pass under the Holyhead main line. This divided with a line running westwards parallel with the Dee to further industrial premises. The other line ran in a north-easterly direction alongside the river to a wharf. The Dee, although increasingly afflicted by silting, was still capable of taking seagoing vessels of up to around 170 tons in the mid-century and for many years the wharf handled large amounts of slate from inland Wales.

Although there was some industrial development at Saltney before the railways arrived, much expansion took place over the next seventy or more years and the presence of convenient transportation services offered by the railways must have persuaded businesses that this was a good place in which to start or expand their operations. Among the industries around Saltney were brickmaking, oil refining, chemicals and fertilisers. All these and others would have made use particularly, of the GWR, but also the L&NWR.

Saltney became an industrial area clustered around the GWR line. A railway village developed a short distance away at the isolated spot where the road to Saltney Ferry crossed the Chester to Holyhead line at its junction with the line to Mold. The planning and construction of this village was the work of the L&NWR; and it exhibited that company's typical architectural style, rather like a mini Crewe.

## A Brief Miscellany

Districts with extensive concentrations of railway activity could be found in several other cities and large towns. Examples are Gateshead which was a hub of the NER with a locomotive works and two large engine sheds at Greensfield and Borough Gardens; Edge Lane and Wavertree in Liverpool; the area of Bristol around Temple Meads, Bedminster and St Philip's Marsh. Aston, Washwood Heath, Saltley and Bordesley in Birmingham; Wolverhampton around Dunstall Park, Stafford Road and Bushbury. All these were on the periphery of major urban areas, frequently where land was cheap and they contained goods depots, sorting sidings, engine sheds and often company or private railway engineering works and these all occupied very large amounts of land. Frequently they contained the premises of other industries, often producing noxious emanations among densely packed streets of working-class housing. The railways were likely to be large employers of labour in these districts but in competition with other businesses for manpower. We would hesitate to call these areas railway districts, but the railways would have stamped their presence on such communities, physically, economically, socially and in terms of noise and other forms of pollution.

## Reflections

Thompson (1982) described suburbs as, 'unlovely, sprawling artefacts of which few are particularly fond'. He added:

> There were suburbs long before the nineteenth century in the sense of places beyond the city limits, the outskirts of towns hanging on to the central area physically and economically, for the most part composed of the ramshackle and squalid abodes of the poorest and most wretched of the town's hangers-on and its most noxious trades.

We have considered a range of suburbs, some largely residential, spacious, affluent and prestigious, others desperately overcrowded, polluted cauldrons of filth and disease. While some of the inhabitants of the more desirable suburbs undoubtedly thought highly of their surroundings, the perception of suburbs was a pejorative one from many quarters. In 1876 one critic declared, 'A modern suburb is a place which is neither one thing nor the other; it has neither the advantage of the town nor the open freedom of the country but managed to combine in nice equality of proportion the disadvantages of both'.

Modes of transport had a critical role to play in suburban growth, but we have seen that the provision of railways was not a necessary condition for the appearance and growth of suburbs. Out-of-town building development was not contingent on the opening of railway stations. Frequently the railway lagged behind, waiting for the appearance of sufficient new development that might warrant the opening of new stations or lines. Sometimes the provision of the railway service was speculative, and the hoped-for development did not take place, or, if it did, was much later. Many early railways showed little interest in serving locations on the fringes of big cities, seeing the longer-distance traffic as having more earning potential. These inner suburbs were often within walking distance of the central business district or were better served by horse buses or horse or electric trams. The stations that were opened in inner suburbs did little to encourage the growth of what were often already densely built-over districts. They were frequently among the earliest stations to close their doors permanently, a trend visible before 1914 and which accelerated during the First World War itself.

*Chapter Eleven*

# Railways and Seaports

## Southampton

Southampton had been one of Britain's leading seaports for over 1,000 years before the railways arrived. It had had a somewhat turbulent history as might be expected by its strategic position. It welcomed the arrival of its first railway. This was the London & Southampton (later absorbed into the L&SWR) which arrived in 1840. It did not take long for relations with the L&SWR to become strained partly because the railway company seemed more interested in servicing the docks than the town.

The arrival of this line had an immediately stimulant effect on the town and the business of the port. This encouraged grandiose ideas in Southampton of it handling large amounts of exports from the industrial heartlands of England, especially the Midlands. The L&SWR, however, was a company with no aspirations for extending its system into such areas. The gripe of the local traders was that it looked as if the L&SWR was going to gain a monopoly of railway access to Southampton. It did not seem inclined to work with them and with other railway companies to encourage railway traffic from the industrial areas to the seaport. Complaints were soon heard about the L&SWR's indifference to the needs of Southampton, the charges it made for its services, its intrusive nature in the older parts of the town and, in the genteel suburban areas, the noise and atmospheric pollution it created.

The town never got its trunk line to the industrial heartlands, but it found itself owing a debt to the railways when the L&SWR bought the docks in 1892 and proceeded, with its successor the Southern

Railway, over the following decades to invest heavily in them. This made Southampton into a great international port for ever associated with the magnificent 'greyhounds of the sea', the great liners that raced across the Atlantic to North America. It also handled large quantities of emigrant traffic to North America, South Africa and Australia.

Southampton was not a railway town but its development as a seaport and therefore its growth and prosperity owed much to the L&SWR. This company maintained a monopoly. Two lines were built, involving other companies which could have opened access to Southampton from distant parts. These were Midland & South Western Junction Railway and the Didcot, Newbury & Southampton Railway. The MR had an involvement with the first and the GWR with the second. These were cross-country lines traversing deeply rural districts and certainly not suitable for fast through traffic. The GWR built a secondary main line from Bristol and Bath to Salisbury. The L&SWR, however, jealously guarded its territorial monopoly. It took time for the L&SWR, the dock and local authorities and the citizens of Southampton to bed down happily together. When they reached this happy position, the L&SWR proved to be a benevolent and progressive monopolist.

## Fleetwood

Sir Peter Hesketh Fleetwood owned large amounts of land in Lancashire and the Fylde Peninsula. He early on grasped the great potential of steam power for use on land and sea and he was determined to harness it for his own benefit. MP for Preston between 1832 and 1847, he knew that Lancashire's cotton industry was held back by poor access to port facilities. Somewhat quirkily, he was also interested in the commercial possibilities of the growing fashion for sea-bathing. With considerable vision, he developed the idea of creating a port and seaside watering place on land he owned at the tip of the Fylde where the River Wyre enters the sea. For this project to become a reality, a railway was needed to link up at Preston with the growing network of lines developing in industrial Lancashire.

The outcome was the Preston & Wyre Railway opened in 1840 by which time there were connections not just to the industrial north but also to London. Not known for being self-effacing, he called the growing settlement 'Fleetwood'. Continuing his energetic activities, he employed the well-known architect Decimus Burton to build a hotel at Fleetwood which, deliberately, Hesketh Fleetwood named the *North Euston Hotel*. An elegant, planned seaside watering place was started but which somehow never fully came to fruition.

There was a long-term vision behind all this. When Fleetwood opened for shipping, a ferry service previously operating from Liverpool to Ardrossan transferred to Fleetwood. This provided the quickest and most convenient route from London to Scotland. There were serious doubts whether steam locomotives would be powerful enough to pull trains over the hilly areas between Lancaster and Carlisle, and Carlisle and Glasgow. Hesketh Fleetwood envisaged his rather grand hotel as catering for travellers to and from Scotland. Soon additional steamer services connected Fleetwood to the Furness area of Lancashire and to Belfast.

Perhaps Hesketh Fleetwood overreached himself because things started going wrong. It took a long time to complete the harbour facilities and even longer to get a projected dock built. Great optimism was replaced by financial uncertainty. Engineering progressed and steam locomotives proved capable of climbing Shap and Beattock, obviating the major purpose of the sailings to Ardrossan. Two short branch lines were built from the Preston & Wyre to Blackpool and to Lytham in 1846 but these lines, sold initially to the Manchester & Leeds Railway, came under the joint ownership of the L&Y and the L&NWR in 1849.

Things began to look up slowly with the new owners of the Fylde's railways investing heavily in the port facilities and a growth in ferry services across the Irish Sea and a limited increase in commercial activities in the docks. Certainly, unforeseen by Hesketh Fleetwood was the development of the town as a major fishing port by 1914. There was a healthy traffic in rail borne fish for many years. In 1901, 5,000 tons of fish were landed, by 1909 the catch was 51,000 tons. The town grew from virtually nothing in the 1820s to a modest 13,000 and combined its business as a port with that of a sedate, slightly neglected seaside watering place.

Fleetwood owed the role it assumed to the support it was given by railways even if they did not directly employ large numbers of people in the town. We will stick our necks out and call it a railway town of sorts.

## Goole

One effect of railways was frequently to damage the business being done at river ports. Fleetwood's rise was greatly to the detriment of Lancaster on the Lune, and, to a lesser extent, of Preston on the Ribble. At Boston and King's Lynn the docks were engrossed by railway companies but never became large-scale operations. The port of Yarmouth, with railway assistance, took most of the previous business of Norwich. Avonmouth was a new creation, equipped with railways from the start, to take over most of the business done in the port at Bristol which was becoming increasingly difficult to work because of silting. Gloucester was an established inland port which was served by a canal carrying small ocean-going vessels and it came also to be well provided with railways. Goole was unique as a river port, in being a successful creation of the nineteenth century. Railways played a vital part in that success.

In 1826, the Aire & Calder Navigation completed a new cut to the village of Goole on the River Ouse near where it joined the Trent. Two docks were built in the expectation of good business given Goole's geographical advantage of being nearer to the coalfields and manufacturing towns of Yorkshire's West Riding than any existing rivals. The L&Y opened a line to Goole in 1848, by which time a third dock had been built and the port was prospering. The canal company added another dock. Goole made the most of its potential. The Aire & Calder was a modern, well-equipped inland waterway capable of taking large canal craft, the Ouse was navigable up-river, and the L&Y was an ambitious company benefitting by making Goole the major eastern terminal of its trunk route across from the Pennines from Lancashire.

Goole was not without its problems, however. Navigation up the Ouse from the Trent was tortuous and difficult, but prosper it did. The L&Y bought out the Goole Shipping Company in 1905 and with its other ships based at Fleetwood achieved a larger tonnage of ships than any other railway company. Frequent regular sailings took place to ports across the North Sea. Goole's facilities and its business expanded up to 1914 but it never grew into as large a town or port as Grimsby or Hull with which it was inevitably in competition. The success of Goole as an inland port can be ascribed to the forward-looking Aire & Calder but that success was also sustained by the efforts of the L&Y and by the NER as a later arrival.

## Immingham

Before it became the site of a massive dock complex, Immingham was a tiny, little-known North Lincolnshire village a few miles west of Great Grimsby on the south side of the Humber Estuary. The transformation of Immingham began when the GCR decided that it needed a large new dock facility on the Humber to relieve pressure at congested Grimsby nearby and, hopefully, to boost its share of trade to Europe.

Work started in 1906 on a massive project which was eventually to create about 2½ square miles of docks and a frontage on the Humber which extended for 1½ miles. The depth of water allowed what were then the largest ships in the world to load and unload without necessarily having to enter the enclosed docks. Eventually no fewer than 170 miles of sidings were provided which could accommodate over 9,000 coal wagons and the port was equipped with state-of-the-art infrastructure. The main business was always intended to be the handling of coal and seven massive hoists were erected to handle this traffic. Each could discharge 700 tons into ships' holds in an hour. Other traffic included bulk grain and timber. A special station was built for the use of boat trains connecting with ferry sailings across the North Sea to Antwerp, Hamburg and Rotterdam. The dock complex became fully operational in July 1912. Three major railway routes converged at Barnetby, southwest of Immingham, along which the GCR channelled a mass of traffic from the East Midlands and South Yorkshire in particular. The stretch of line between Barnetby and Brocklesby where the flows to Immingham and to Grimsby and Cleethorpes parted, became exceptionally busy.

Despite the high level of business activity, the presence of a large engine shed and the requirement for manpower, Immingham did not become a settlement of any great size. It benefitted from the provision by the GCR in 1912 of an electric tramway to Grimsby, where most of the workforce lived. A quirky operation, it became affectionately known as 'The Clickety-Clack'. Local passenger trains ran to Barton-on-Humber and to New Holland Pier where there was access to GCR ferries across the Humber to Hull.

Immingham may never have grown into a large town but it owes its modern development almost entirely to the railways.

## Cardiff and Barry

The conveyance of coal from pithead to water was one of the earliest functions competently performed by railways and their primitive ancestors. There was synergy between railways and the coalmining industry. The steam railways were large scale consumers of coal and the revenue many railway companies received from moving coal was a vital part of their income.

Three rivers enter the sea in the vicinity of Cardiff. They are, from the east, the Rhymney, the Taff and the Ely. Crammed between the three were the huge acreage and complex systems of docks and railways which established the commercial greatness of Cardiff.

A sea lock was opened on the Glamorganshire Canal in 1798 at which time Cardiff only had a population of about 1,000. The creation of the railway-served docks, the associated railways and industrial and commercial activities led to explosive population growth so that by

1871 Cardiff was home to almost 60,000 people. Much of the credit for this must go to the 2nd Marquis of Bute who, with his successors, financed, built, owned and managed the docks until just after the First World War. His family enriched themselves enormously by owning much of the land on which Cardiff and its docks were built as well as mineral rights further up into the valleys.

Various railway companies played a vital role primarily in taking away the coal produced by the huge number of mines once operating in the South Wales Valleys. Relations between the dock authorities and the four companies involved were not always particularly cordial. Equally, there was no love lost between the railway companies themselves. The first of these was the Taff Vale Railway opened in 1841. This soon shot Cardiff into a leading position among the coal handling and exporting ports along the South Wales coast. Over the following decades, Cardiff and Barry vied with each other as the largest coal shipping ports in South Wales. The Butes developed a complex internal railway system to serve the docks into which the other companies fed.

An extraordinary collection of lines was built serving the coal-rich valleys north of Cardiff. As well as the Taff Vale, there was the Rhymney, the Barry and the Cardiff Railways all intent on conveying coal to the docks at Cardiff or others nearby such as Penarth and Barry. These companies were all eventually absorbed by the GWR.

Barry was always intended to be a rival as a port to Cardiff where sheer congestion became a serious issue as the nineteenth century wore on. With powerful supporters, the Barry Railway opened its first dock at Barry in 1879. It was then claimed to be the largest enclosed dock in the country and was intended solely for handling coal. This venture was hugely successful. In 1913 Barry Docks handled 11 million of the total 37 million tons of coal exported from South Wales. As many as seventy coal trains might arrive daily at the receiving sidings at Cadoxton. If we take Barry and Cardiff and add in the smaller facility at Penarth, we have what was the greatest coal exporting port in the world.

The Valleys produced some of the best steam coal in the world and the growth of steamships assured a rising demand through much of this period. However, there were problems connected with the 'black gold'. The railways into Cardiff and Barry developed to serve two industries: coal primarily and the metal industries also located in parts of the Valleys. Cardiff and Barry were essentially exporting ports not designed for the handling of imports. From the railway operators' point of view, they handled what was virtually one-way traffic and they were burdened with moving vast numbers of empty wagons back up the Valleys.

The topographical nature of the Valleys north of Cardiff meant that the only effective means of transporting the coal they produced was by railway. Canals, even if more had been built, could not have moved coal in anything like the quantities easily achieved by the railways. They brought down the coal to the docks which, in turn, created jobs and much prosperity in Cardiff. It is not seriously suggested that Cardiff was a railway town because, while railways continued to have a very strong presence, it diversified in the late nineteenth century to become a cultural, commercial and administrative centre and increasingly the de facto capital of Wales.

A stronger case might be made for Barry as a railway town. The docks and their associated railway installations took up vast amounts of land locally and there was a sizeable engine shed and even a small locomotive works. Both would have provided many jobs. Barry was unusual in becoming not only a coal-exporting town but a seaside resort. The coal came by railway from the Valleys as did a very large percentage of its visitors, at least in the early years. By extension we could argue that what became the mining communities up in the Valleys would not have been what they were had it not been for their dependence on the railways to take away the coal on which their economies depended.

The first railway to Barry Island opened in 1896 and immediately the railway companies operating in South Wales identified demand for what we would now call 'leisure travel'. The Barry, the Taff Vale, the Rhymney and the Great Western companies all began to lay on cheap day and half-day excursions to Barry Island from places in the Valleys. This enabled workers, especially miners, and their families, to escape their often blighted workaday surroundings and fill their lungs with the fresh air of the Bristol Channel for a few hours. They did this in such numbers that the preachers in the chapels were left ruefully contemplating row after row of empty pews on fine summer Sundays.

Barry is perhaps unique in combining so successfully its role as a coal-exporting port with that of a trippers' paradise. It owed this happy coincidence to the railways.

## Neyland

Before the railway, Neyland was a small out-of-the-way settlement called Milford Haven on the north side of the huge natural harbour with the same name in West Wales. In 1859, nearby Milford changed its name to Milford Haven whereupon the previous Milford Haven was renamed New Milford. The population was a mere 200. The railway seemed to have a problem with the nomenclature of their new port but for convenience we will call it Neyland which finally became its official name in 1906.

The South Wales Railway, backed by the GWR, was looking in the 1840s to establish a port from which packet services could be operated to and from Ireland. Even before the GWR fully absorbed the South Wales Railway in 1863, Isambard Kingdom Brunel was engaged in finding a suitable location for this port. Goodwick and Fishguard looked to be the leading contenders, but the job became less urgent because of the economic and social problems in Ireland often blamed on the blight affecting the potatoes which were a staple item of diet, and which was at its peak between 1845 and 1849.

Brunel had a vision that the GWR would not only connect London with the West Country, Bristol and South Wales but be even greater by establishing sea routes to Ireland and North America. He therefore needed a deep anchorage for ocean-going ships close to the point of embarkation. He even built a special mooring for the largest of his three steamships, the *Great Eastern,* and this is remembered in Great Eastern Terrace in the town. He chose a suitable, if cramped, site of level ground at New Milford. The preparation of the site involved evicting existing residents and clearing most of the buildings and then creating a new township on the hill overlooking the previous one. The company built eight homes in the High Street and ten in the appropriately named Railway Terrace. As the employment needs of the railway increased, various social amenities and additional housing had to be built.

The South Wales Railway arrived with a broad gauge, single-line branch in April 1856. A floating landing stage was erected and sailings to southern Irish ports began in early 1857. However, the distance to Waterford was somewhat longer than the later crossing from Fishguard to Rosslare as Neyland was to find out to its detriment later. Neyland was to settle down to many years of busy activity handling the export of coal, imports of cattle and other livestock, passengers and their luggage to and from Ireland; also very large quantities of fresh fish. The population grew as jobs increased. What had been no more than a village a century earlier, achieved the status of an urban district in 1900 by which time Neyland was fully qualified to be regarded as a railway town. It even possessed the prestigious *South Wales Hotel* built for the South Wales Railway which sometimes hosted 'celebrities' overnight when travelling to and from Ireland. These were Neyland's halcyon days, and they were to end abruptly in 1906 when the decision was taken to transfer the Irish sailings to Fishguard. It was not the end of Neyland, however, as the handling of fish continued apace, a dedicated market being opened for the purpose in 1908.

## Grangemouth

The Forth and Clyde Canal was opened in 1790 providing a vital link between the two major rivers of Lowland Scotland. At the point where the canal and the River Carron entered the Forth, the canal company had built a port well-placed for developing a busy coastal and foreign trade. It acted as an outlet for coal and the growing output of the industrial region to the south-west. The problem with the canal lay with its restricted dimensions. Not surprisingly, the development of the successful port called Grangemouth was eyed up by railway companies wanting a share of the action. They were pre-empted by the canal company itself which built its own line from the Grahamston area of Falkirk to Grangemouth. Initially it was worked by the Edinburgh and Glasgow Railway and later by the North British. The line opened to goods in 1860 and passengers a year later.

In 1887, the CR bought the canal, the railway to Grangemouth and all the associated businesses but it had to allow the NBR running powers to Grangemouth and access to the whole of the canal network which the CR now possessed. Neither company was entirely happy with this arrangement as they were, of course, sworn enemies but they soon put on co-ordinated passenger services to Glasgow. The CR, for its part, made improvements to the canal, reduced tolls and introduced an icebreaker to ensure that navigation was possible in the winter months. In 1908 a second line of the CR was opened to the docks.

Grangemouth developed into a considerable dock and industrial settlement, both companies being involved although the CR was very much the senior partner. Its prosperity was heavily dependent on the railways feeding traffic to it. However, what was Grangemouth's gain was a loss for Bo'ness just three miles east. This had been a busy port especially trading with France and the Low Countries. It had already been dealt a serious blow with the expansion of Grangemouth. The townsfolk desperately wanted railway connections and got one in 1856 with a company which soon came under the control of the NBR. This company, as stated, now had access to Grangemouth but wanted a port where it was fully in control. Instead, it had to put up with being partners in a Harbour Commission. Over the following years, the NBR did initiate some improvements and made extravagant promises for more projects when the CR started snapping at its heels and making promises about the improvements it would implement if it was only allowed access to Bo'ness. It was a case of sour grapes stemming from the mutual enmity of the two companies. Eventually Bo'ness did get significant improvements courtesy of the NBR, but it was Grangemouth that grew into an important industrial town and major east-facing port for the highly industrialised Monklands area and Clydeside.

## Harwich

Harwich was an ancient seaport which enjoyed a brisk trade to and from various European countries and it had strategic importance as a naval base. It found itself competing with Tilbury which gained a lucrative Royal Mail contract in 1832 damaging Harwich's business.

The town was desperate to get a railway but had to wait until 1854 when the Eastern Union Railway (later part of the GER) built a branch from Manningtree on its main line through Colchester to Ipswich. In 1862 the Eastern Union became part of the GER, an enterprising if somewhat cash-strapped company. It provided the impulse to restore Harwich's role as a significant seaport. In 1863, the GER started weekly sailings to Rotterdam and added a service to Antwerp the next year. It regained the Royal Mail contract. However, there was robust competition for the ferry traffic to Europe from the ships operating out of Dover and Folkestone, for example. The crossing of the North Sea took considerably longer. The GER upgraded its ship and the port facilities and added a state-of-the-art hotel at Harwich.

The problem at Harwich was shortage of space for expansion and so the GER moved to a greenfield site close by. This was drained, protected by a new sea wall and fine new facilities were built. These included a greatly enhanced freight-handling capacity, a new station and hotel and more infrastructure including some housing for company workers. This new port was called Parkeston Quay after the Chairman of the GER from 1874 to 1893. The new facilities functioned from 1883 and proved to be highly successful.

The enterprise of which the GER was capable was shown in 1885 when, in conjunction with other companies, it put on through trains or through carriages from Parkeston Quay to Yorkshire and Lancashire thereby tapping into large population centres and the potential traffic they had to offer. Harwich took on a somewhat reduced role with the rise of its very close neighbour although much of its working population gained a living from activities around Parkston Quay. The role of the GER was decisive in shaping the economic life of this part of the Essex coast.

## Fishing Ports

Britain's outstanding fishing port was unquestionably Grimsby. It has a claim to be regarded as a railway town in the sense that railways played the decisive role in shaping its modern development. Grimsby's first railways opened in 1848 and two companies, the MS&LR, which became the Great Central, and the Great Northern, served the town before the First World War.

Before the railways arrived, Grimsby was a decayed kind of place. The size and grandeur of its parish church was indicative of its importance in medieval times, but it had become little more than a rundown port, unable to compete effectively with Hull across the Humber. Things were to change very rapidly. The powerful local landowners, the Earls of Yarborough, were keen to develop the local economy and thereby further enrich themselves.

The port was in the hands of the decidedly lackadaisical Grimsby Haven Company who had built a dock around 1800 but things started to happen in 1845 when it renamed itself as the Grimsby Docks Company which was soon absorbed by the MS&LR. A programme of dock construction then began and the town's docks underwent enormous extension over the next seventy years. Grimsby developed as a general port bringing in grain and timber and exporting coal, but the pre-eminent trade became fishing. In 1878 Grimsby despatched about one-third of the total of rail-born fish traffic in Britain. The MS&LR was nothing if it was not ambitious and it bought a fleet of steamships and even fishing vessels. Grimsby had prospered thanks to the railway.

It grew from 3,700 inhabitants in 1841 to 75,000 in 1911 but it did not quite manage to take on the civic dignity that might have been expected of a town of that size.

Four deep-sea fishing ports on the east coast owed a debt to the railways for transporting the fish that was landed to the distant inland markets. Other than Grimsby, they were Hull, Yarmouth and Lowestoft. We would hesitate to describe the latter three as railway towns. Except Yarmouth, these ports were all controlled by the railways which developed very sophisticated systems for getting the fish to the market. While all four towns depended very heavily on the distribution services provided by the railways, the others developed a more diverse economic base, and none were so dominated by fishing and its associated businesses as Grimsby. The railways also did well in transporting to the ports the coal the steam-powered trawlers needed, at least from the 1880s. Grimsby had nine steam vessels registered in 1885, 50 in 1890 and 419 by 1899. The corresponding figures for Hull were 10, 79 and 376.

Two other east coast deep-sea fishing ports that depended heavily on the railways were Peterhead and Aberdeen, while on the west coast, Fleetwood, already mentioned, and Milford Haven and Neyland were major fishing ports again dependent on the railways. Not all would be categorised as railway towns. All the fishing ports mentioned in turn owed a great debt to the emergence and rapid spread of the fish and chip trade but that is another story.

Burntisland on the north coast of the Firth of Forth was a settlement which owed a very large debt to the railways. Ferries from Granton, Leith and Newhaven on the south side of the Forth crossed the river and fed into railway lines towards Dundee and Perth before the Forth Bridge was opened in 1890. The small town was the northern terminus of the world's first train ferry which conveyed rolling stock across the Firth from Granton. This started operating in 1850. Long a small fishing port, Burntisland developed into an important coal-exporting port and the NBR moved large quantities of this precious mineral from the major pits in the Fife coalfield. Some shipbuilding took place at Burntisland and the railway brought in fuel and raw materials. With a strong industrial presence, it is perhaps surprising that Burntisland also developed as a quiet seaside resort whose visitors in the early days mostly came and went by train.

*Chapter Twelve*

# Inland Watering Places

Belief in the health-giving properties of certain mineral waters goes back a long time. We know that the Romans valued the waters that came to the surface at Bath and Buxton. Well-to-do people made their way to Tunbridge Wells, Epsom and Scarborough as early as the seventeenth century. The latter is particularly interesting because it not only enjoyed exploiting a natural spring close to the sea, but it later became an important seaside watering place.

Initially what attracted visitors to the inland watering places, let's call them spas, was the supposed health benefits that could be derived from bathing in the waters, drinking them, or both. Such waters existed in large numbers across Britain, often associated with superstitions of a religious kind. However, only a few of them developed into towns that derived significant income as health resorts. Even fewer managed additionally to become prestigious centres of social activity. Of these, Bath was the archetype.

The spas perhaps represent the first commercially organised 'leisure' resorts. Before the railways came, as far as leisure was concerned there were just two significant classes of people, the tiny minority composed of the very rich who lived on unearned income and enjoyed a life of idleness and conspicuous spending, and the rest who did not have the time or money for such activities. Admittedly, in pre-industrial Britain there were many more usually religion-based 'holy days' on which work stopped, giving ordinary people time for relaxation and communal activities, sometimes of a debauched and dissipated nature. Many old towns also had fair days. The purpose of these was buying and selling and the hiring of labour. There was little call for the modern kind of annual holiday because most people did not have the time or the resources for travelling and accommodation.

In a largely agriculture-based society, the economy was able to absorb the disruption involved in numerous days off – people simply worked harder and longer on the days preceding and following the holy days. However, as steam power came to be widely harnessed in manufacturing industry, heavily capitalised businesses needed to have their plant and machinery utilised to the maximum possible extent and their workforces to be highly disciplined. The disruption involved in observing innumerable festivals and fairs had to go. And go they did particularly in the first half of the nineteenth century. The unpleasant experience of factory work and discipline and the blighted working and living environment of many industrial workers cause a demand to build up for a break from work, ideally getting away from workers' usual surroundings. Many were attracted to the idea of visiting the seaside. Seaside resorts were to become the leisure centres of the new industrial age. Although they varied as to the class of clientele they aimed to attract, they were generally more demotic than the spas which they largely displaced.

Here we consider the interaction between the railways and the spa towns. The leisured classes flocked to spas such as Bath, Tunbridge Wells, Harrogate and Buxton. Bearing in mind that the heyday of the British spa was on the wane by the time the railways began to spread across the country, did the latter make any contribution to the fortunes of such places?

## Bath

In 1801, Bath had a population of 33,000 and was the tenth largest provincial town in England. It was 53,000 by 1841. In 1840-41, it found itself on the trunk line of the GWR from London to Bristol. Within a few years it had good rail links to the Midlands and North, through the Severn Tunnel to South Wales, through Bristol to the West Country and southwards to such places as Salisbury and Portsmouth. These links made travel to the city much easier. Did Bath therefore owe the surge in its growth to railways?

Its population continued to hover around the 50,000 figure right through to 1914. Alone of all English towns with a population of around 50,000 when Victoria ascended the throne, Bath experienced no significant growth. Here was the premier inland spa, the place the lesser ones envied and imitated, stagnating in terms of its population despite its good position on the railway network.

Bath's boom days had been in the eighteenth century when the country's supposed social elite regarded it almost as mandatory to spend the 'season' at Bath. Those who could afford to do so would maintain a domicile there in addition, perhaps, to a house in London and a country seat elsewhere. Large numbers of those who made their way to Bath did so supposedly for medical reasons. Even if they drank and ate excessively and took little exercise for the rest of the year, they could fool themselves that a few weeks under a strict regime at Bath would 'detoxify' them. Others went to Bath during the season purely to see and be seen. Some descended on the town hoping to make an advantageous marriage. Quacks, charlatans and shysters of all kinds found innumerable ways of parting rich fools from their money.

By the time the railways had started to appear on the scene, Bath's halcyon days as the resort of choice for the idle rich were largely over. Such people are notoriously capricious. Many abandoned Bath for other British spas or for watering places by the sea. In increasing numbers, they now flocked to European spas and other resorts on the Continent. They always wanted to keep one jump ahead of what they saw as the tendency for the 'tone' of a favoured place to deteriorate over time. This tendency applied to Bath which, having once stood at the apogee of social desirability, by the early nineteenth century was showing distinct signs of becoming shabby genteel. Many of the attractions which had once brought in the well-heeled remained, if now somewhat down-at-heel. Ornamental gardens, promenades, winter gardens, pump rooms and elegant surroundings could still be enjoyed by a new class of residents. Many liked to see themselves as genteel but tended to fall into the category of 'gentlefolk', a euphemism for those we might now call 'economically challenged' but anxious to keep up appearances.

The railways undoubtedly made travel to and from Bath easier but contributed little to the local economy. Although Bath had two major stations, the original one of the GWR, and the later station served by both the MR and the Somerset & Dorset Joint Railway (S&DJR), the city did not have the industries nor the expanding population to attract serious interest from other companies. The city became known for having a sizeable and somewhat aged and sedentary residential population who created little demand for travel. The GWR certainly stamped its presence on Bath, running through the elegant Sydney Gardens and on viaducts to the south of the centre. Bath gained railway connections at an early stage but remained an example of an established town whose economic and social fortunes were not boosted by the presence of railways.

## Cheltenham

Cheltenham had attracted visitors to sample its waters and other delights before railways happened on the scene and there had been much building and landscaping work to provide the facilities and sense of place required by those who frequented the inland resorts. A tramroad was already open to Gloucester to bring coal and general merchandise from the docks there. The town was keen to become linked to an important part of the growing railway system, experiencing a bad moment when it appeared that the Birmingham & Gloucester's main line might bypass the town and favour it only with a short branch line. All was well however, with the Birmingham & Gloucester, soon to become part of the MR's growing empire, arriving in 1840 at the station later known as Cheltenham Lansdown. In 1841, the Cheltenham & Great Western Union Railway, soon to be absorbed by the GWR, opened its line from Swindon to Cirencester. In 1845 the northern end of the Cheltenham & Great Western Union was opened. This used the Birmingham & Gloucester's metals to Standish Junction, south of Gloucester, from whence it went south-eastwards to join the Swindon to Cirencester line at Kemble thereby enabling access to London. In 1847 the GWR opened its own station, later to be replaced by another that, in 1908, gained the name 'Cheltenham St James'. This was the most convenient of Cheltenham's many stations for access to the town centre. It became a terminus for GWR trains from what became Gloucester Central and London.

Bath was clearly losing its leading position as an inland spa and Cheltenham was a pretender to that role. It had a dynamic that was slipping away from Bath. It possessed a wealth of new and handsome building of a Regency and early Victorian character which contrasted with Bath and its earlier buildings which were now becoming disparaged as 'old hat'. In 1838 the *Queen's Hotel* had opened in the town, being recognised at the time as the finest purpose-built hotel in the country. Affluent newcomers were taking up residence in the town and local businesses were being set up to make the most of their spending power. Before the railway arrived, Cheltenham was gaining a name for stylish shops. The place appeared fresh and fashionable when compared with ever so slightly tatty Bath.

The burghers of the town were aware of the threat presented by the Continental spas and set out vigorously to counter this. They formed a committee which may have been the first example of an English town deliberately using the media to promote what it seemed best able to offer. This was a healthy, clean town in fine natural surroundings with plenty of open space, greenery, handsome buildings, good shops and a lively and a rather exclusive social scene. A bonus occurred when expensive private schools began to appear in the town. In 1841, Cheltenham College for boys opened followed in 1854 by a female equivalent in Cheltenham Ladies' College and, soon after, a training college for teachers. Cheltenham had slipped almost seamlessly into the role of an educational centre as well as that of a spa, a centre of fashionable retailing and a desirable residential town. However, like many towns with sizeable numbers of very affluent residents and visitors, there was a darker side to Cheltenham. The rich needed what seem to us like armies of servants. They tended to be poorly paid and live in real or near-poverty in housing conditions which contrasted starkly with the opulent surroundings of their employers. This led an observer to comment in 1902 that there were slums in Cheltenham as bad as anything that could be found in London or New York.

The schools which became prominent in the town were part of the wave of new establishments known misleadingly as 'public schools' when, of course, they were anything but public. They were designed to be socially exclusive and to inculcate in their male pupils the values and attitudes that would equip them for leadership roles in British society and, crucially, in administering the non-white parts of the British Empire which was approaching the peak of its extent at this time. The ladies' college prepared its pupils for the subordinate but supportive role expected of its alumni. The presence of these schools in the town then spawned the opening of other establishments preparing younger children for the rough and tumble of life in the public schools.

The two public schools at Cheltenham were unusual for being situated in a sizeable town. The tendency was for similar schools to be found in more rural settings. They were also unusual in taking day as well as boarding pupils. This meant that many parents moved to live in Cheltenham to be close to their offspring. Mostly well-heeled, these new residents added to the already exclusive social milieu of the town and the facilities it provided. The railways at Cheltenham served a useful purpose in making the town easily accessible at the beginning and end of terms and for the parents who wished to visit at weekends during termtime. Railways were also the ideal medium at the time for handling the trunks and other paraphernalia required to support life at a boarding school. The town's stations groaned under the weight of these items at the beginning and end of each academic year.

Cheltenham enjoyed a mid-century boom, its population of 40,000 in 1861 being almost three times that of 1831. The town had become an early example of a place dominated by the tertiary or service sector of the economy. After 1860, the pace of growth slackened but some spa towns elsewhere prospered. They often shared the role of Cheltenham as being places less for taking the waters and more for shopping, living and socialising with the right kind of people in genteel and attractive surroundings. Examples were Buxton, Harrogate, Royal Leamington Spa and Tunbridge Wells.

Cheltenham became the focus of lines from five directions. As well as those already mentioned, the GWR built a secondary main line from Birmingham and Stratford-upon-Avon and a delectable cross-country line through the Cotswolds to Kingham and Banbury. It was also served by the Midland & South Western Junction Railway, a line which promised much but ended up delivering little. This meandered through largely empty countryside to Swindon and Andover, leaving the GWR's Kingham line at Andoversford. The wealth of travel opportunities offered by the railways must have helped to shape the direction that the town chose to take in the years up to 1914.

Cheltenham could never be described as a railway town, but it was very interesting for the railway historian because it had an extraordinary number of stations for a place of its size. Lansdown and St James's have already been mentioned. On the old Birmingham & Gloucester line, Cheltenham Tewkesbury Road Station opened in 1862, was renamed Cheltenham High Street shortly afterwards and closed in 1910. Confusion was invited when the GWR opened Cheltenham High Street Halt in 1908 only for it to close in 1917. Cheltenham South & Leckhampton was a GWR station on the line to Kingham. Cheltenham Malvern Road was opened by the GWR in 1908 as a through station serving the Stratford line. We can stretch the point a bit and include a seventh station. This was Cheltenham Racecourse, used only on race days. Clearly Cheltenham was held in high esteem by the GWR which flattered it with later prestigious services such as the 'Cheltenham Flyer'. The railway was a facilitator of Cheltenham's growth, but it never had an intrusive presence in the town nor was it a major employer.

## Harrogate

The use of mineral springs at Harrogate went back centuries but by the 1830s the somewhat scattered population was only around 3,000. However, with pump rooms, baths, hotels and lowly inns, the place catered for about 9,000 annual visitors. Harrogate had not yet taken on anything of a fashionable character and the town of Knaresborough, 3 miles away, was more important with its attractive riverside walks and an established linen-making industry.

Most places of any substance wanted to be served by railways, but Harrogate was not seen by early railway promoters as a place likely to generate useful traffic. It was therefore not until 1843-44 that local people became aware that consideration was being given to building a line or lines to the town. This news was guardedly welcomed so long as the railway's presence was not too intrusive. Two lines had arrived in the vicinity by the end of 1849. One ran to a terminus at Brunswick close to the famous Stray, the priceless open area of land south of what became the town centre. This line ran towards Church Fenton providing access to southern parts of Yorkshire. The other, from Leeds, rather curiously avoided Harrogate but had a station at Starbeck, to the east of the town. This line then forged northwards towards Ripon. In 1851, a third line arrived in the vicinity. This was from York and Knaresborough to Starbeck. Although this station was inconvenient for Harrogate itself, the three lines between them had stimulated a considerable increase in the number of people visiting the town.

The town fathers were now thoroughly won over to the benefits of railway access and approached the NER which had by now absorbed the lines mentioned to ask them to build a line into the town from Starbeck. The NER responded favourably and proposed a link from the Leeds line to join the line from Church Fenton and pass through the Stray to a new station close to the centre of what was the growing town of Harrogate. Leaving this station, the line would then shortly divide with a north-facing curve to join the existing line to Ripon and a curve to the east bringing trains into the existing Starbeck Station. Some concerns were expressed about the penetration of the Stray, but the NER got the parliamentary approval it required. The line passed through the Stray in a shallow and inconspicuous cutting which assuaged the environmental concerns. The new links were all completed by the end of 1862. The well-placed station stimulated Harrogate as a shopping and tourist centre and encouraged the building of high-quality housing, some of which was occupied by families whose breadwinner commuted to business in Leeds or Bradford. The centre of gravity of the developing retail quarter of the town tended to move closer to the station, a development by no means uncommon in Britain.

Harrogate took on the character of a spa town to which people repaired to take the waters, but it also became a dormitory town, a place for shopping and for visiting given its attractive layout, open spaces and delightful ornamental gardens. It benefitted by being something of a healthy 'bolt hole' for trippers from the grimy industrial towns of West Yorkshire who could now be deposited in the centre of the growing settlement rather than having to make their way from Starbeck. It could be described as an outlier of Leeds and Bradford, just as Buxton had a similar relationship with Manchester and Tunbridge Wells with London. Harrogate and these towns continued to grow through the rest of the century whereas Bath and Cheltenham went into something of a torpor. It did not help that they did not have such large centres of population in their hinterland.

## Smaller Spa Resorts

Llandrindod Wells, Builth Wells, Llangammarch Wells and Llanwrtyd Wells were tiny settlements in Central Wales where medicinal springs had been discovered in the eighteenth century. They could be reached, with difficulty because of their remoteness, by road, but this greatly limited the numbers of visitors they were likely to receive. They were thrown a lifeline in 1865 when the L&NWR, eager as ever to extend its empire, built the Central Wales Line. All four places had stations served by this line. The last three remained no more than small villages, but the railway brought visitors in sufficient numbers for them to be able to sustain themselves as mini spas. Ironically, Llandrindod Wells had been the smallest of the quartet before the railway opened but grew, not spectacularly, into a small but rather grandiose town with a population approaching 3,000 in 1911. It became fashionable and the L&NWR put on through carriages from London although it was a somewhat wearisome, roundabout journey via Stafford, Wellington and Shrewsbury. Manchester and Liverpool had through coaches. It is unlikely that the three smaller ones at least would have survived into the twentieth century had the Central Wales Line not been built.

The MR opened its Ashby-de-la-Zouch Station in 1849 although it was then merely 'Ashby'. It was built in an impressive neo-classical style to provide the 'gateway' into a town that the local burghers were determined would, with the aid of the new railway, become a fashionable and prosperous spa. This quaintly named place was thought to have had medicinal springs in ancient times, but little was known of them. Their modern renaissance accidentally occurred when coal mining was taking place nearby and clear water with a distinctly saline content was discovered. Here was the natural elixir which could make Ashby a boom town! Hastily, the Ivanhoe Baths were opened with an accompanying commodious hotel. While there was a pleasing element of serendipity about this, hopes were rapidly dashed when further mining activity greatly restricted the flow. The flow of visitors also declined, and Ashby henceforth had to content itself with the role of a country market town. The small but grand station never played the part hoped for it.

Strathpeffer is a tiny spa town located in glorious Scottish scenery which missed out on being served by a major railway route because of the opposition of an influential local landowner. Instead, a station somewhat misleadingly called 'Strathpeffer' was opened at Achterneed in August 1870. This was located on the line from Dingwall which eventually reached Kyle of Lochalsh in 1897. When the landowner died, the Highland Railway moved to build a short branch line from Fodderty Junction on the Dingwall to Strome Ferry Line. Strathpeffer joined the railway system in 1885. The railway was notoriously strapped for cash and it had high hopes that it would develop lucrative tourist traffic. The company built a luxury hotel intended for the rich and prestigious visitors who would most likely be of the hunting, shooting and fishing type.

Strathpeffer was not a creation of the railways. The therapeutic merits of its waters had been known for some time before the Countess of Cromartie began to spend money on developing what she hoped would be a continental-style spa. The railway, however, proved for a couple of decades to be the main means by which visitors came and went. More opulent hotels were built along with high-quality shops, ornamental gardens and golf courses.

During the brief height of the town's popularity, there were even through sleeping carriages from places far to the south. The 'Strathpeffer Spa Express', introduced in 1911, was a once-weekly train from Aviemore where it connected with a train from Perth. The First World War dealt Strathpeffer a blow from which it never recovered and its days as a spa ended early in the very different conditions of inter-war Britain.

*Chapter Thirteen*

# Some Major Seaside Resorts

Seaside watering places existed long before the railway age. People had always liked to have a dip in the sea, especially in warm weather, but a fashion developed in the eighteenth century as certain doctors and self-appointed 'experts' began to advocate sea-bathing as a curative process for people with real or imagined ailments. Others advocated not only dipping in the briny but drinking copious quantities of seawater. Extravagant claims were made for the therapeutic effects of imbibing sea water. It was said to cure gout and even restore lost carnal urges. The growth of the habit is therefore entirely understandable.

The idea of seaside pleasure resorts combining bathing with various other amenities was very much a nineteenth-century development and their growth depended on the existence of relatively cheap transport to bring the hoped-for crowds from places way inland. However, the residents, the business community and the local government bodies of most seaside resorts faced a dilemma. Did they set out to attract the maximum number of visitors which meant a working-class clientele, or should they aim for reduced numbers but social exclusivity? Their geographical situation could dictate the matter. A resort might simply be too far from the heavily populated industrial districts to attract large numbers of working-class visitors. In the larger resorts there was often a compromise. At Blackpool, for example, the northern end of the seafront had some very grand hotels for well-off visitors which were, nevertheless, close to the unashamed brashness of what became 'The Golden Mile'. The level of railway provision was a factor in deciding the dominant social character of individual Victorian seaside resorts.

It is possible to identify three categories of Victorian seaside resorts. There were those that went all-out to attract working-class visitors in huge numbers. They include Barry, Blackpool, Bridlington, Brighton, Clacton, Cleethorpes, Great Yarmouth, Margate, Morecambe, New Brighton, Ramsgate, Rhyl, Scarborough, Skegness, Southend, Southport and Weston-super-Mare. They all had what might be described as cheap and cheerful attractions and amenities but most also had some pretensions to catering for a better-off and perhaps more genteel class of patron. The respective quarters of such towns might be very clearly demarcated, consciousness of class being such a potent factor in the narrative of British society. Some of these places developed into large towns.

Secondly, there were resorts that self-consciously set out to be more select and succeeded to a greater or lesser extent. These would include Bournemouth, Eastbourne, Torquay and Worthing, all of which became sizeable towns. Smaller examples could be Sidmouth, Lyme Regis and Grange-over-Sands.

Thirdly, there was a medley of other places such as Silloth, Hunstanton, Cromer and Sheringham, Saltburn, Tenby, St Ives and Aberystwyth. They were located close to the sea, attracted visitors although in smaller numbers, and were served by railways. However, they were somewhat distant from major concentrations of population and never developed into sizeable towns.

Before the spread of railways, the difficulties associated with internal travelling meant that the watering places that then existed largely drew their patrons from their surrounding regions. As new spas and seaside resorts came to do business, we can see something of a North-South divide. Generally, it appears that both northerners and southerners liked to stick with what was familiar and were happy to patronise the resorts in their respective parts of the country where the culture, the accents, the dialect and even the food were familiar. Folk from the West Riding headed for Scarborough and Bridlington and people from Sheffield went to Cleethorpes. While Nottingham and Leicester folk made their way to Skegness, those from Birmingham and the Black Country looked to the North Wales resorts, Blackpool and perhaps Weston-super-Mare. Most of the south coast resorts at least as far west as Hampshire drew on people from the southern part of the country and especially, London. On the Essex coast, London provided huge numbers of visitors to Clacton and, above all, Southend. The railways played a vital role making journeys to these places possible whether for day excursions or for longer stays.

The major seaside resorts were industrial towns every bit as much as Birmingham was for small metallic products or Dewsbury for heavy woollens. They provided a specialised product, an opportunity for recreation and recuperation, a temporary escape for their inhabitants from the blighted living and working environments that were so characteristic of the days of Britain's industrial pre-eminence. They acted as a safety valve helping to reduce the tensions experienced by Britain's industrial proletariat. The railways facilitated this process.

Railways made it much easier to go to the seaside and return in the day so what a coastal town needed along with its beach and other attractions was a reasonable railway service to and from not too distant inland centres of population. Trips by pleasure craft predated the railways, a favourite being that from London to Gravesend, but the day trip really opened up with the coming of the railways and cheap fares to encourage excursionists.

Some rather more enlightened employers were quick to realise that they could hire trains for their employees and families and treat them to a day at the seaside. Such an example of enlightened self-interest could work wonders in industrial relations by encouraging loyalty among employees. As early as 1845 and 1846 we hear of employers in the Lancashire cotton industry chartering special trains to Fleetwood.

Some seaside resorts were close enough to allow well-to-do residents to enjoy the pleasures of seaside life while commuting to the places where they made their money. So there were commuters from Brighton and Hove, for example, to London; from Llandudno to Liverpool and

Manchester; from Morecambe to Leeds and Bradford and Southport, Blackpool or Lytham and St Anne's to Manchester.

Given that the places mentioned had railways as a common factor, we will consider how the railways impacted on some of them and whether it is possible to describe any of them as railway towns. Were the railways a decisive factor in how they developed in the period from the 1830s to the First World War?

## Blackpool

Blackpool was the archetype of the large seaside resort devoted wholeheartedly to giving working-class visitors boisterous, bawdy fun and a short, utterly hedonistic escape from the tedium of their everyday surroundings and work. Blackpool was not for those wanting peace and quiet. Nor was it for the faint-hearted!

Since time immemorial, people had sat and watched the waves and the more daring elements had ventured into the water. This was common practice for those who lived by the sea long before medical men and quacks were extolling the benefits supposedly obtained by drinking seawater or immersing in it. Many of those from inland were likely never to have seen the sea, constrained by the difficulties and expense of travelling to places that were beyond walking distance. It seems that the numbers who did make it to the seaside at what became Blackpool increased throughout the eighteenth century and one or two small inns and boarding houses provided some basic accommodation. The visitors would mostly have arrived by stagecoach or their own horse-drawn conveyances and were therefore likely to be reasonably well-off. Blackpool, incidentally, got its name from a 'black pool' where water, coloured by peat, drained into the sea where the Central Pier now stands.

The first railway to reach the northern end of the Fylde Peninsular was built by the Preston & Wyre Railway and it opened to Fleetwood in 1840. This was evidence of the perceived relative importance of the two places at that time. The opening of this line led to a marked increase in visitors to Blackpool who mostly alighted at Poulton which was only 4 miles from Blackpool. The same company opened a branch from Poulton to Blackpool in 1846, attracted by what it saw as the previously unsuspected potential revenue from the leisure market. The railway obviously made travel to Blackpool easier but initially the town aimed at attracting a select clientele. In 1851, the population was 2,500, almost 13,000 by 1881. In the 1900s the population reached 50,000 residents.

A few early excursion trains had underlined Blackpool's business potential and encouraged entrepreneurs, mostly from Lancashire, to buy up land for the building of guest houses and the provision of a range of recreational facilities such as a promenade, two piers, assembly rooms and a theatre. The main thrust became one of catering for large numbers of lower-middle and working-class visitors who may not have had much spending power individually but plenty if viewed as a mass. Before the railway came, there had been some 'carriage folk' who came to Blackpool and even when the town had committed itself to catering for the masses, part of the front, the North Shore, had facilities for more prosperous visitors. There was also a conscious decision to attract comfortably off residents and away from the seafront some highly desirable residential districts were built. It was in these districts and Lytham and St Anne's just down the coast that the well-to-do commuters who used the later 'Club' trains to Manchester were to be found.

Things are never just right for some people. In 1860, a visitor wrote a querulous letter to the editor of a Manchester newspaper rather indignantly saying that he had just paid his first visit to Blackpool and was disappointed by the lack of things to do. He eventually decided to go for a walk on the pier where his gaze happened to chance on what he described as 'young factory girls' cavorting around on the sand with their skirts flying in all directions. His complaint was that in doing so they were revealing far more of their ankles and lower legs than was seemly. Instead of hurrying away in disgust, he rather naively wrote that he dallied for an hour watching them and pondering sadly on the immodesty of young girls and how they knowingly or unwittingly incited men to salacious thoughts.

Blackpool was on a roll. In the early 1880s over 1 million pleasure-seeking visitors per annum were arriving by train and in the 1900s that figure had increased to 3 million. Catering for, accommodating and entertaining numbers of this sort was big business and nowhere else did the business better than Blackpool. Other resorts tried to emulate it, but none was as successful. The famous Tower was opened in 1894. There is little doubt that the railways did much to facilitate Blackpool's success by providing the means of mass transportation to shift vast numbers of Lancashire and West Riding working-class folk to the Fylde Coast. They came on day excursions, half-day trips and for weekends before holidays with pay became the norm. Some who were impoverished wanted Blackpool so much that they would walk there, starting out on Friday after work and arriving on Saturday morning. A few might manage the railway fare back but the poorest would start their trudge home around noon on the Sunday, having probably found somewhere free but unofficial to grab some sleep on the Saturday night.

While the job done by the railways in transporting the hordes of visitors must be acknowledged, it has been suggested that the railways could have done much more to contribute to the town's success, particularly before the 1870s and 1880s. The two companies owning the lines into the Fylde were the Lancashire & Yorkshire and the L&NWR. More should have been done earlier, it has been argued, to enhance track capacity on the approaches to Blackpool and to tackle the notorious congestion at Preston, a major railway centre through which all Blackpool traffic had to pass. This apparent reluctance to make the most of the business opportunities offered by Blackpool may therefore have slowed the growth of the town. It was certainly a source of aggravation for the Town Council. It is not surprising that they wanted to encourage other railway companies to challenge the existing duopoly.

A ray of hope occurred in 1882 when the West Lancashire Railway (WLR) opened its line from Southport to Preston. It had the backing of the MS&LR which wanted to extend its existing line from Manchester to Wigan and join up with the WLR to build a new line through the Fylde to Blackpool. Although the WLR obtained parliamentary sanction for such a route in 1884, the powers were allowed to lapse. The line was never built.

Perhaps it had been the threat posed by this possibility that shook the L&Y and the L&NWR out of their seeming apathy. Between 1888 and 1903 a new short and direct approach was built from Kirkham and Blackpool's two terminus stations were greatly enlarged, both having many extra platforms reserved for excursion traffic. Large amounts of land close to the centre of the town had to be bought for these extensions and to house a mass of carriage sidings providing temporary accommodation for the rolling stock used for the excursion trains. Improvements were also made to the layout at Preston to alleviate some of the conflicting train movements involved where Blackpool traffic somehow had to filter into or cross the already busy tracks of the Crewe to Carlisle section of the West Coast Main Line. What was needed was a Preston avoiding line, a major project first mooted in 1899 but one for which the resources were never found.

A problem for all the railway companies that came to serve major seaside resorts was not dissimilar to that posed by commuter traffic. It involved having to make provision for enormous fluctuations in traffic levels. Rolling stock had to be available to meet peak demand but was underused at other times and had to be accommodated in sidings occupying large amounts of land. Expensive non-revenue-generating movements might be needed to get rolling stock to where it was required. Equally, staff had to be rostered in a way that made them available when and where they were most needed which might mean they were underemployed at other times. This created costs for the railway companies which might not be met fully even by intense peaks of traffic with grossly overcrowded trains. The expense involved in the provision of seasonal holiday traffic was one of the problems that

Dr Beeching identified in the 1960s and which he was determined to eliminate when proposing a reshaping of Britain's railway operations.

The L&Y and the L&NWR do appear to have been somewhat slow in responding to the demand for leisure travel to and from Blackpool, but this traffic built up steadily throughout the period up to 1900. Large numbers of working people and their families were enjoying enhanced real incomes on account of significant falls in the cost of many basic food items, for example, and had extra money to spend for the pursuit of pleasure. Whatever these companies did or did not do, the fact remains that it was the railways that delivered the consumers of Blackpool's attractions and services in vast numbers. In just one day, 3 August 1911, no fewer than 210 regularly scheduled trains and excursions passed through Kirkham heading for Blackpool. Even this was trifling compared with the 425 that passed Kirkham one day in 1936 when the town's popularity was probably at its greatest. A masterstroke in 1912 was the decision of the local council to prolong the season by staging illuminations.

It is inconceivable that the town would have grown into the place it became had it not been for the role played by the railways. Blackpool became an industrial town every bit as much as the textile manufacturing towns of Lancashire or the West Riding from which it drew so many of its visitors. Its industry was the provision of an escape from the everyday reality of uncongenial work and grimy surroundings, and it provided this service on an industrial scale. Blackpool deserves to be considered a railway town of a specialised kind even if it was not a major junction, did not possess engineering works associated with railways, large marshalling yards or even had a sizeable percentage of its workforce employed on the railways.

Blackpool is always thought of as a brash seaside resort. It is less known for being a desirable place to live but just as the railway brought so many of the visitors and carried them back, so the L&Y also assisted the development of Blackpool as a favoured residential town. Blackpool and its near neighbours Lytham and St Anne's were close enough to Manchester as the regional industrial and commercial centre for those who wanted to live in and enjoy the fresh air of the coast and get away from the grime of the place where they made their money. The L&Y identified a lucrative if limited niche in catering for such a clientele.

Local men who wanted and were able to pay for a premium service formed the Lytham St Anne's and Blackpool Travelling Club. They wanted to be guaranteed a seat on both legs of their journey to and from work and to be able to travel in the exclusive company of those they regarded as their peers. The outcome was that the L&Y added a carriage, just for them, to a fast train to Manchester. The members would pay both a first-class fare and a supplement. Such was the success of this venture that a second and then a third carriage were added. Only paying members could use these 'club' carriages and the seats were allocated to specific members. An attendant rode with them to ensure they were fed and watered in what was truly a gentleman's club on wheels.

## Southport

George III may be said to have unconsciously initiated the sea-bathing craze after he plunged into the briny at Weymouth in 1798. What he did was, of course, immediately copied enthusiastically by those with an unoriginal mindset. The sea-bathing age had arrived, and many existing and often very small seaside settlements were to be transformed over the next 100 years. Southport or, as it was previously known, South Hawes, was one such place. The seashore north of Liverpool has long stretches of sandy beach and, in many places, sand dunes, a natural playground. Southport is located about fifteen miles north of Liverpool and around 1800 it began to develop the facilities that came to be expected of a seaside watering place. Much of the development which occurred over the next fifty years was on land reclaimed from the sand dunes.

Even before the coming of the railway, Southport was growing, its population doubling in the 1820s, but it was the arrival of the first railway which really put the town on the map. This was the Liverpool, Crosby and Southport Railway which opened in June 1848. This ran into a very basic station which was replaced by another, rather better one, at Chapel Street in August 1851. This company was absorbed into the L&Y in 1855. Also in 1855, a line was opened from Wigan into a station close to Chapel Street but known as London Street. This line which also provided connections with Manchester, was also soon subsumed into the ambitious L&Y.

Southport was clearly viewed as a growing town with considerable traffic potential. A pier was opened in 1860. It was notable for being only the second such structure in Britain, but it was more noted because of its length, shorter only than that at Southend. Its length was needed to reach water deep enough to allow steamers to berth. Starting at 3,600 feet, it was extended to 4,380 feet by 1868.

Yet another railway company arrived in this part of the town when the WLR arrived from Preston at Windsor Road Station in 1878. This rather basic facility was closed and replaced by a better station at Ash Street. The WLR became part of the L&Y in 1897. The services on all these lines became concentrated on Chapel Street Station which was a fine and capacious place equipped with ten platforms under an overall roof. With an intensive service to and from Liverpool Exchange which was electrified in 1904, direct evidence of its business potential, and even an electrified service to the suburb of Crossens on the Preston line, Chapel Street was very busy and the LYR had a major presence in Southport taking up much land with the station, goods facilities, motive power depot and extensive carriage sidings. Through carriages were laid on to London Euston via Edge Hill at Liverpool and there were other through services to many of the large Lancashire towns and to the West Riding of Yorkshire.

Late on the Southport scene was the Cheshire Lines Railway with a roundabout route to Warrington and Manchester Central. This opened in September 1884 and belated though its appearance may have been, the Cheshire Lines company was determined to make an impression.

It opened a grandiose station on Lord Street, the town's most prestigious thoroughfare. It approached Southport from the south hugging much of the attractive coast from Ainsdale. The line was a dubious economic venture, however, the route simply unable to compete effectively with its rivals.

Southport grew rapidly and in 1890 had a population twice as large as that of Blackpool. It marketed itself as the shopping destination of the North West and Lord Street not only had up-market shops and fancy arcades but also a sense of greenery from its gardens and their floral displays. It had the seaside attractions that would attract large numbers of working-class visitors but somehow it managed to keep a more refined air than Blackpool. It also developed the role of dormitory town for Liverpool and Manchester businessmen and many of its suburbs became characterised by sumptuous villas and fine examples of eclectic Victorian domestic architectural styles.

For decades the railways brought visitors to the town in large numbers and, although this was not a railway town, at Southport as with many other seaside resorts, the railways played a formative role in shaping the town's economic, social and cultural character in the years leading up to the First World War. Some have said that perhaps Southport did not quite know what role to play. Did it want to be a sedate residential and retail town, a bit superior or should it go all-out to attract the masses? It carved out a niche for itself and had much for which to thank the railways.

## Bournemouth

Conflicts of interest were common at seaside resorts. The early resorts were places that usually enjoyed the patronage in limited numbers of 'respectable' and reasonably well-off visitors of the sort sometimes called 'carriage-folk'. Such people liked surroundings with what they would describe as a peaceful and seemly nature. This meant that they did not wish their enjoyment to be spoiled by having to share it with too many of the commonalty whose behaviour might be loud and vulgar.

The better-off local people and businesses might agree with this view, wanting the place to keep its genteel character.

Railways could be seen as a threat. With their ability to transport large numbers of visitors cheaply, even the arrival of one or two trainloads of trippers could quickly lower the tone. This could upset the delicate balance of factors attracting the more desirable visitors and cause them to drift away to other places not yet 'polluted' by the masses. The people of influence in the small, genteel settlement of Weston-super-Mare in Somerset made it quite clear that they did not want the main line of the Bristol & Exeter Railway to approach the town too closely. When a station was opened in 1841, they were happy that it was placed on a short branch line. This may have seemed a good idea at the time but as visiting the seaside became a more demotic pleasure partly enabled by the spread of railways, the townsfolk of Weston began to feel that they were missing out. They ruminated sadly on this reality, and it was as late as 1884 that their branch line was converted to a through loop off what was by then the GWR's main line to the west.

Prejudices and tensions raised by issues of class were very evident at Bournemouth. The site of what was to become a large town was, in the late eighteenth century, an almost empty littoral which, as late as 1851, still only had a population of 695, which had grown to 60,000 by 1901. Bournemouth, as it was to become, had a mild climate, sandy beaches, an attractive pine-clad valley through which the Bourne stream makes its way to the sea and several chines or deep ravines that open out to the sea. Its potential for development became obvious to Sir George Trapps-Davis, a local landowner who, in 1837, set about cautiously creating some of the amenities expected of a high-class resort for the wealthy. The kind of clientele he wanted started flocking there in large numbers and many of them so much liked what they saw that they wanted to stay. They created a demand for exclusive housing developments. The growing town was very much defined by the word 'exclusive'.

Exclusive, that is, until the railway arrived at the relatively late date of 1870. The question of a railway presence had been controversial for many years. Acrimonious confrontations occurred between those wishing to maintain exclusivity and others who wanted maximum numbers to use the town's superb natural attractions. These and various additional facilities of the sort appearing in the growing number of seaside resorts would appeal to a much wider range of visitors who could be delivered to the town by rail. Arrayed against them was a coalition of wealthy retirees who liked Bournemouth precisely because it was peaceful and they were surrounded by their social peers, affluent visitors who did not want the place to change and local businesspeople who liked catering for the rich.

The line between Southampton and Dorchester, 'Castleman's Corkscrew', built by the L&SWR and opened in 1847, made its way several miles to the north via Ringwood and Wimborne. The L&SWR won assent for a line from Southampton and Brockenhurst which provoked fury in Bournemouth and, when opened in 1862, it petered out at Christchurch, 4 miles to the east. There was a sense that, although the L&SWR wanted the railway to get there, much of Bournemouth did not want it at all. For all that, it was inevitable that Bournemouth would join the railway map which it did in 1870 with a station tucked away discreetly but rather inconveniently in the east of the town. In 1874, the L&SWR arrived from the west with a line from Poole in which it was involved with the S&DJR and connected with the 'Corkscrew'. This ran into a station even more inconveniently located to the west of the town. Its connection to the S&DJR, however, was very useful as it gave Bournemouth railway connections to Bath and via the metals of the MR to many parts of the country. Soon the two Bournemouth stations were linked. The station in the east was replaced in 1899 by a new and quite grandiose station, designated 'Central' although this was something of a misnomer. The conservative element among the citizens had lost the battle against the railway but they succeeded in preventing it from penetrating the centre of the town.

By 1914, Bournemouth, despite the aversion of some of the populace to railways, was well served by them. As well as the S&DJR in a northerly direction, the L&SWR ran westwards to Dorchester and exercised running powers over the GWR to Weymouth. Castleman's Corkscrew still provided a roundabout route to Southampton which could be reached more directly via Christchurch and Brockenhurst and several long-distance cross-country trains gave direct through services to places like Manchester, Birmingham, Birkenhead, Sheffield and Nottingham. London's Waterloo was served directly.

Apart from the hostility of influential local citizens, one of the reasons for Bournemouth's slow and late blossoming as a major resort was its relative remoteness from large urban areas and, of course, its poor railway connections. As these improved, so Bournemouth was able to attract visitors from across the country but although it became a popular resort, it always managed to maintain some style. It did not become unduly brash, it appealed to visitors who liked its scenic delights, and it developed high-class shopping facilities. Many people who visited were well-off and some liked it so much that, when they retired, they went to live there. Their spending power helped to keep the town the way many of its people liked it. Although cheap excursion trains were laid on to the town and brought working-class trippers in large numbers, somehow the town managed to retain that which made it distinctive, a place popular but classy at the same time. Some trippers, having been there once, described it as boring, vowing that going there once was enough. Bournemouth did not mind.

Because of its location, visitors had to make an effort to reach Bournemouth. The railways played a crucial part in bringing them there and encouraging the general growth of the town. As would be expected of a large town largely dependent on the service sector of the economy, Bournemouth developed its working-class districts, but it was possible to be a visitor or even a resident and be largely unaware of their existence. Bournemouth vigorously pursued policies that encouraged it to be seen as a seaside resort that was a 'cut above' most of the others. In 1870 when the railway arrived, the population was about 6,000. In 1881 it was approaching 16,900 and over 78,000 by 1911. Railways did not 'make' Bournemouth but they greatly contributed to its success.

## Torquay

Originally called Tor Quay, Torquay was Bournemouth's main rival among the larger south coast resorts of the West Country. Torquay also had a scenic situation, one rivalling that of Bournemouth while being very different. A local landowner had spent a fortune on the place creating the nucleus of a fashionable watering place and desirable seaside retirement location which seemed to appeal particularly to retired senior naval officers. It had started developing as a seaside resort much earlier than Bournemouth and was growing before the railway came. Being even further from major centres of population meant that, apart from relatively local people who liked to dip in the briny, its patrons were well-to-do and were likely to have come this far by stagecoach or their own carriages. This, of course, meant that it was socially exclusive and it became a select resort for the well-off with the kind of amenities that they came to expect of such places.

The South Devon Railway arrived in 1848 with a branch from Newton Abbot. The South Devon was always in the thrall of the GWR and was fully absorbed by it in 1878. The town's growth was not markedly accelerated by the coming of the railway and Bournemouth, despite it having emerged later as a resort, was twice the size of Torquay in 1911. Both places had mild winter climates, moderate rainfall and long hours of sunshine which tempted well-off retirees to take up residence. They wanted sedate surroundings where they could mix with their social peers. Acceptable visitors of the more discerning sort could also enjoy the spectacular coastal scenery at places like Anstey's Cove and Babbacombe. For those who wanted long stretches of golden sand and rather more in the way of popular entertainments, Paignton, next door, was the part of Torbay designed to cater for them in very large numbers. The well-off residents were happy enough to see the hoi polloi make their way to Paignton.

Between them, Torquay and Paignton owed much to the railways. They were, of course, even more distant from large centres of population than Bournemouth but the GWR was extremely active in promoting leisure travel in the many parts of its system which possessed scenic delights and/or seaside pleasures. Especially at holiday times, the branch from Newton Abbot was extremely busy with direct trains bringing holiday makers from the Midlands and even as far as the West Riding of Yorkshire. Trains bringing day-trippers were less common because of the Torbay's relative remoteness but there were excursions from Plymouth, the largest city relatively nearby.

The GWR excelled in the publicity it produced to attract holiday traffic to the West Country. In 1902 the poet Harold Edward Boulton had penned a verse referring to 'Devon, Glorious Devon'! Much was made of this phrase in later GWR publicity.

## Brighton

In 1700, Brighthelmstone was a simple fishing village, but dramatic change was about to happen. In the middle of the eighteenth century, it found itself propelled to fame after the publication by Dr Richard Russell of his 'Dissertations concerning the use of sea water in the diseases of the glands'. Although this was hardly a snappy title, it proved to be highly popular with hypochondriacs of whom there has always been a disproportionate number among the idle rich. In this tome Russell held forth about the healthy virtues of sea-bathing and drinking seawater particularly for those who suffered from dyspepsia. He particularly recommended Brighton, as it was becoming known, for a place to dip into and imbibe seawater. It was fashionable before the railways came partly, at least, because it came to be greatly favoured by the Prince Regent and his hangers-on. Many of them were dyspeptic and dissipated hypochondriacs.

Visitors came in growing numbers by stagecoach or their own private coaches and Brighton benefitted by being only 50 miles from London. While many people went there for the seawater 'cure', Brighton attracted many who went to participate in the raffish delights for which it became renowned. As well as becoming a somewhat louche resort, it was on its way to becoming a substantial residential town. Its population had risen from 7,000 in 1801 to 47,000 in 1841 before the railway had made any significant impact on the locality.

Brighton was eyed greedily by railway promoters, but it was the London & Brighton, predecessor of the LB&SCR, that arrived there first: in 1840. By this time its popularity with the rich and powerful was in decline. This decline accelerated after Queen Victoria declared in 1845 that she hated the place and would never go there again. Her turning her back on the town owed much to the fact that cheap excursion trains from London were bringing hordes of brash Cockneys and although she wanted her subjects to pay obeisance to her, she did not want to hobnob with them. The railways were able to bring trippers en masse which inevitably brought changes in the nature of the town and its business life. Excursions became big business. They ran mainly on Sundays and might bring as many as 100,000 visitors, mostly Londoners, in one day. The Metropolitan Police are alleged to have breathed a sigh of relief on such days as petty crime left the streets of London and bobbed up in Brighton instead.

The good railway communication with London had another effect. This was to boost its population of well-to-do residents. Brighton became almost an extension of London. Many families moved to Brighton and Hove, next door, to enjoy the pleasures of seaside living. The breadwinner might commute by train daily to London for business or, in some cases, he would stay in London from Monday to Thursday night. The woman might enjoy the seaside life while being able to take advantage of the train by popping up to London for a spot of shopping. The LB&SCR encouraged this traffic by providing cheap first-class tickets. The railway even opened a short branch line which successfully encouraged high-class housing development in the suburb of Kemp Town. Brighton's population had reached 120,000 by 1901.

Brighton became a town with a large population of low-paid workers. The rich needed armies of servants and the expanding businesses around entertainment and hospitality also provided large numbers of jobs. Contrasts between rich and poor were very evident in Brighton and have continued to the present time.

A remarkable development in a town of this kind was the decision of the L&BSCR to close its locomotive works in South London and transfer operations to a new site in Brighton, adjacent to the station. The works opened in 1852 and by 1881 about 600 men were employed at the works which was the only sizeable industrial employer in the town. It was estimated that in 1903 about 6 per cent of Brighton's population depended on railway employment. This made the LB&SCR the largest single employer. It was also the only provider of railways serving the town. Town and railway enjoyed a largely amicable relationship. If not a railway town as such, the railways had an enormous influence on how Brighton developed in the nineteenth century.

## Eastbourne

The substantial residential seaside town and resort of Eastbourne was primarily a creation of the nineteenth century. It consisted of a small settlement called 'Bourne' about a mile from the sea and some fisherfolks' dwellings close to the sea and called 'Eastbourne'. The population in 1801 was less than 2,000 but this was to change very rapidly when large amounts of land in the area were inherited by William Cavendish, later to be the 7th Duke of Devonshire. He shared a vision with another substantial local landowner, John Davies Gilbert, and together they set out to create a town 'built by gentlemen for gentlemen'.

With shrewd heads for business opportunities, they were quick to appreciate the potential of the railways. They set about creating a planned town to combine the functions of a healthy but quiet seaside location with those of a superior seaside resort and select residential town for affluent retirees and well-off commuters who could travel to and from London by the LB&SCR which arrived in 1849. Systematic development began soon after and a town centre was laid out with dignified public buildings, high-quality housing and much greenery and open space. They were successful particularly in attracting the wealthy oldies. The commuter traffic took longer to develop, journeys to and from London being rather slow. In some cases, the breadwinner would travel to London on the Monday morning and return for the weekend. A measure of success could be taken by a 529 per cent growth in the population between 1851 and 1881.

It is difficult to assess the contribution that the railways made to Eastbourne's growth. Eastbourne undoubtedly suffered from an awkward position on the railway network. It was on the end of a branch line from the LB&SCR's route along the South Coast from Hastings to Portsmouth. Trains to London had a somewhat indirect route via Lewes to Wivelsfield where they joined the Brighton to London main line designed for fast traffic. The other route serving Eastbourne was the LB&SCR route to Eridge which encouragingly pointed north in the London direction but was never suitable for fast through traffic. The LB&SCR collaborated with the L&NWR in the provision of through carriages from Liverpool, Manchester and Birmingham. These avoided central London by passing through Kensington Olympia and Clapham Junction. Introduced in 1904, they became well used. Before the railway arrived, there were three stagecoaches a week from London and the journey took over nine hours. The travel options offered by the railways had to be better than that.

## Scarborough

Mrs Tomasin Farrow was walking on the sands at Scarborough in 1628 when she noticed a spring emerging from the cliffside. The water was russet coloured. Perhaps rather boldly, she cupped her hands, sipped speculatively and immediately concluded that this water had medicinal properties. Mrs Farrow's innocent act could be said to have put Scarborough on the map. Some years later, Dr Robert Wittie of Hull was announcing to the world that Scarborough's spring water was efficacious for worms, colic and melancholy. The waters were chalybeate, having traces of iron. Scarborough was on its way to becoming a 'spaw' as it was spelled at the time. The age of the spa was about to begin. It became a craze. Affluent middle-class people took the waters with their social peers. Controlling the supply of the mineral waters and charging for access to them could be a real money-spinner.

Scarborough was to enjoy many years in an almost unique role as a place where those who suffered various maladies, or thought they did, could imbibe the metallic tasting waters of the spa and take a dip in the sea or even swig a cup of Scarborough seawater. The town became prosperous by attracting wealthy visitors, often carriage folk from other parts of Yorkshire and affluent retirees so it gained a reputation for social exclusivity which many of those involved locally in what we would now call the hospitality industry were keen to maintain. Many of Scarborough's townspeople were not initially enthusiastic about the proposal in 1840 to build a railway to the town. They feared that the opening of the line would see undesirable, indolent and feckless common people arriving in large numbers and lowering the social tone. A vocal opponent of the railways was George Knowles who, in a pamphlet published in 1840, said:

> Scarborough has no wish for a greater influx of vagrants and those who have no money to spend. Scarborough is rising daily in the estimation of the public as a fashionable watering place on account of its natural beauty and tranquillity, and in a few years' time, the novelty of not having a railroad will be its greatest recommendation.

In July 1845, the Y&NMR opened its line from York. The indigent did not appear in large numbers, probably because they could not afford the fare. Before long, middle-class and working-class trippers were making their way from towns in the West Riding of Yorkshire but Scarborough managed to retain the patronage of wealthy visitors who were likely to make a more prolonged stay in the town. As the more proletarian elements arrived in growing numbers by train, Scarborough developed into what in effect was two resorts: a genteel one with corresponding shops and hotels in the southern part of the town and, to the north, a cheap and cheerful quarter with a less affluent clientele.

## Morecambe

In 1800, Morecambe did not really exist and the only settlement in the vicinity was Poulton-le-Sands. This stood at the southern end of the extremely hazardous crossing of the sands of Morecambe Bay, the quicksand and fast flowing tides of which had claimed innumerable victims over the centuries.

Poulton gained its first railway on 12 June 1848 as a result of the initiative of the Morecambe Harbour & Railway Company which had amalgamated with the 'Little' North Western Railway in July 1846. The line was 3 miles long and terminated at the station which later became known as Lancaster Green Ayre. The line eastwards from Lancaster to Hellifield and Skipton was completed in stages in the following years. The MR took over the operation of the 'Little' North Western in 1852 and absorbed it fully in 1871.

The name 'Poulton' gradually dropped out of use and 'Morecambe' became the official name of the growing town in 1889. The original temporary station near the jetty called Morecambe Pier was renamed Morecambe Harbour in 1854. A station more central to the town was opened but proved inadequate for the growing traffic. Known as Morecambe Town, it was rebuilt in 1907 becoming Morecambe Promenade in 1924.

The L&NWR arrived in August 1864 with a station initially called Poulton-le-Sands which the company in a flurry of indecision then renamed as Bare Lane in October 1864. This was on a branch from Lancaster Castle on the main line from Crewe and Preston to Carlisle and it was inconveniently placed. The 'Little' North Western and the L&NWR had been unable to agree terms for the latter company to have access to the existing centrally-sited Morecambe Station. In 1886, the

L&NWR opened its own, better-placed, station which, in 1924 after the grouping, became Morecambe Euston Road.

The Morecambe Harbour & Railway Company had intended to build a jetty, and this was completed under the auspices of the Little North Western in 1851. The jetty was an unimpressive structure impeded by the short period in which the tides allowed its use by vessels of a viable size, but it was in use from 1851 to 1904. Early sailings were to Piel, near Barrow-in-Furness, in conjunction with the Furness Railway. The jetty came increasingly under the influence of the MR who built up ferry sailings to Belfast which were in direct competition with those of the L&NWR from Fleetwood. Morecambe was always at something of a disadvantage because the quirks of its tidal regime meant that sailings could not be to a regular schedule. In the summer of 1860, there were five sailings per week to Belfast. MR trains from Leeds connected with the sailings. The MR owned the *North Western* Hotel, later known as the *Midland*. It catered for those whose sailing times required an overnight stay. The MR seemed to lose interest in Morecambe as a port when, on the opening of the Wennington to Carnforth line jointly with the Furness Railway, boat trains were run first to Piel and later to Ramsden Dock, Barrow. A few sailings continued from Morecambe until the opening of Heysham Harbour in 1904. After this the harbour area was used for the purposes of shipbreaking, creating what was probably a fascinating if somewhat macabre spectacle in a place trying to make a name for itself as a seaside resort.

In 1892, however, the MR obtained parliamentary powers for an extension to Heysham to a new dock complex and steamer pier which would benefit from a far greater depth of water than was available at Morecambe, about 3 miles away. The Heysham facility came into full use for boat trains and other commercial traffic on 1 September 1904. Heysham proved to be a success, giving the MR a port of its own on the West Coast and a useful share of the trade to northern parts of Ireland. Through trains were laid on from London St Pancras and in 1905 regular sailings to Douglas on the Isle of Man started operating.

The MR seemed to decide that Morecambe was more of an asset as a seaside resort than as a packet station. It was the MR's only West Coast seaside resort and the company was determined to make the most of it. The place enjoyed spectacular sunsets and wonderful views across the Bay to the Lake District, natural charms which were promoted against those of its obvious nearby rival, Blackpool. The company invested in the town's infrastructure to provide the kind of facilities that would attract more visitors. A sea wall, a grand sweeping promenade, a pier and other attractions were built, and a popular horse tram introduced. A measure of the MR's success may be taken from the need to open a larger station in 1907, as mentioned earlier. Another ploy which benefitted the town was the encouragement of some high-class residential housing aimed at wealthy Leeds and Bradford wool magnates who could live by the sea and journey by fast residential trains to their places of work in the big West Yorkshire cities. A lively business developed in day and half-day excursions particularly from Bradford. Morecambe was sometimes referred to as 'Bradford-on-Sea'.

This was a success story for the MR whose activity was so crucial to the town's developing prosperity in the years up to the First World War. Morecambe could not be called an orthodox railway town as such, any more than Blackpool could, but both towns had their economic life strongly shaped by the investment put into them by the respective railway companies.

*Chapter Fourteen*

# Some Smaller Seaside Resorts

We have seen the crucial support given by the railways to the development and continued success of a few major seaside resorts and have ventured to suggest that Blackpool particularly but perhaps Bournemouth as well can be regarded as examples of a highly specialised kind of railway town. Their main industry was leisure and tourism which proved extremely successful and much of that success must be attributed to the role played by the railways in supplying them with the vast bulk of their patrons.

One of the fascinations of studying history is to identify processes at work which have similar outcomes and then find an example of the same process which leads, at least temporarily, to outcomes totally different. This happened on the north coast of Kent. Being placed where they were, some places had for long enjoyed regular visits, particularly at weekends, from boatloads consisting mostly of working-class Londoners bent on a frequently boisterous and bawdy escape from 'The Smoke'. The first railway arrived at Margate and Ramsgate in 1846. The presence of a mode of transport considerably quicker than pleasure craft might suggest that these places would then have enjoyed even greater patronage. The opposite happened. New railways were opening elsewhere, serving places hitherto largely inaccessible and giving Londoners a much wider range of places to go for pleasure-seeking purposes. However, when the LC&DR opened its line parallel with the Kent coast, competition with the existing lines of the SE&CR meant very cheap fares and trippers began to visit the North Kent resorts in previously unprecedented numbers.

The developments along the coast of North Wales are interesting. The Chester & Holyhead Railway (later L&NWR) was built primarily for serving the crossing to Ireland, always seen as being of strategic importance from a political and administrative point of view. The route from Holyhead provided the shortest sea-crossing. Several small settlements along the south side of the Dee Estuary and the North Wales coast itself attracted some local people and a few better-off visitors for the purpose of sea-bathing. The line opened in 1848 and from the start efforts were made to attract leisure traffic at some of the intermediate stations west of Talacre. Attempts were also made to encourage housebuilding at Abergele, for example, giving local householders discounted tickets. The chairman of the Chester & Holyhead Railway, the well-known railway contractor and entrepreneur Samuel Morton Peto, was involved with developing housing and other facilities at Abergele which, from very little previously, grew by 1861 into a small town with 3,300 inhabitants.

Peto was doing this work mainly in pursuit of his own financial interests but the presence of the line running very close to the coast all the way to Bangor led to the expansion of previous small settlements into seaside resorts of which at this time, Rhyl, Colwyn Bay and Llandudno developed into significant towns. Some of the places served by the line's stations never really grew up but Rhyl developed into a cheap and cheerful resort of the mini-Blackpool sort. Colwyn Bay and Llandudno consciously tried, and largely succeeded, to be more stylish. Colwyn Bay combined the facilities of a serene seaside watering place with that of a desirable residential location. Llandudno was a place with style on a site where the Mostyn family were the major landowners. It was being developed as a planned town before the railways arrived, taking full advantage of the glorious sweep of its bay and wanting to attract well-to-do visitors looking for a bit of style as well as the scenic delights. Like Colwyn Bay, it gained prestigious housing developments and was favoured by wealthy businesspeople who commuted by L&NWR trains to Manchester or Liverpool. The cheeky little North Staffordshire

Railway even ran a similar daily club train to and from the Potteries, using running powers from Crewe. The resorts of the North Wales coast owe an enormous debt to the railways. They might have developed in the nineteenth century as resorts had there been no railways, but their growth would almost certainly have been much slower. They were shaped by the railways because it was the railways that brought the bulk of their visitors with their spending power so crucial to the local economy. Insofar as some of them also became desirable places to live for families whose paterfamilias made their money in the Lancashire cities, the railways provided the means for getting to and from work. The value the L&NWR put on the resorts along the North Wales coast is shown by the size of their stations. That at Llandudno, for instance, was rebuilt with five platforms in 1892, totally out of proportion to the travel needs of the permanent residents. Colwyn Bay and Rhyl also had capacious stations. Even before the First World War most of the line between Chester and Llandudno Junction was quadrupled to handle immense surges of holiday traffic which probably peaked on no more than a dozen summer Saturdays.

Where a railway was opened serving seaside watering places which already attracted some visitors or encouraged other settlements along the route to develop amenities for the leisure industry, no standard pattern seemed to emerge for the places affected. On the North Wales coast Rhyl, Colwyn Bay and Llandudno became medium-sized towns but Abergele and Llanfairfechan, for example, held their own as much smaller resorts perhaps appealing to visitors with different tastes. Elsewhere in North Wales, the Cambrian Railways served Aberystwyth which developed as a popular but quiet seaside resort and eventually as an educational and cultural centre. Aberystwyth gained its first railway in 1864 and efforts were made to attract the tourist trade. The Cambrian described it as the 'Scarborough of Wales' and 'The Queen of the Welsh Watering Places'. If that seems extravagant, it was nothing compared to what was said when it fell into the maw of the GWR. It was then publicised as 'The Biarritz of Wales', situated in the 'British Tyrol'. It remained much the largest of a string of small resorts served by the Cambrian Railways northwards all the way to Pwllheli. These included Barmouth, Porthmadog and Criccieth. These resorts were all a long way from any major centres of population and therefore expensive to reach. They were too remote to be the target of day-trippers. For this reason, they tended to develop as places where people of moderate means could stay and enjoy simple seaside pleasures without much in the way of commercialism. It is likely that they owed their modest growth to the railway. It brought them a limited supply of visitors but in numbers sufficient to sustain their viability as minor resorts. If they had had to rely on their visitors coming by coach, they may well not have developed at all. None of the railway-served seaside resorts in North Wales grew to be a large town.

Ilfracombe on the north coast of Devon had a struggle to gain a railway. By 1850 it had become a fashionable watering place, but its clientele was limited because of the difficulties of access, and it was in danger of stagnation without a railway, the nearest being at Barnstaple, over 10 miles away. Various proposals for the building of a line had been put forward and had aroused much ill-feeling in the town when they fell through. However, in 1874 a line from Barnstaple was opened and absorbed by the L&SWR the following year. The town had been expanding before the coming of the railway, many of its visitors being trippers arriving on pleasure steamers from Bristol and South Wales, but the railway provided the means for far more people to reach the town's delights. The townsfolk wanted the railway and were vindicated because the L&SWR and the GWR both valued the traffic potential that Ilfracombe offered, and they provided the services which brought substantial although never huge numbers of visitors. Through carriages were put on to Waterloo and Paddington respectively and Ilfracombe established itself as the premier seaside resort on the coast between Weston-super-Mare and Land's End. This may well not have happened without the agency of the railway. For all that, the population of was only about 8,500 in 1901.

Some resorts on the south coast of Dorset and Devon, like Budleigh Salterton, Sidmouth, Seaton and Lyme Regis are interesting because they were all located on branch lines connecting with the L&SWR's main line from London and Salisbury to Exeter. Although they had their railways, sometimes opened quite late in the day, and often enjoyed through carriages from London on summer Saturdays, they never grew. They retained a select and sedate air and, while being too far off the beaten track for day trippers, they were evidence that seaside resorts did not grow simply because they were railway-connected.

The Isle of Wight had an extremely complex network of railways given the almost total absence of industry but Shanklin and Sandown, for example, owed a considerable debt to the railways for helping them to establish themselves as small, genteel resorts. It took an effort to reach the island which was not well placed for the mass day-tripper market and its resorts lacked the more boisterous delights of Brighton or Southsea. On high days and holidays, however, the ferries from the mainland and the trains could be exceptionally busy.

Although Cromer had been a commercial and fishing port of some significance in earlier times, by 1801 Cromer was a somewhat decayed small town with a population of less than 700. However, even by this time, the delights of the coast and the nearby countryside had been discovered by well-to-do pleasure seekers who mostly arrived by stagecoach from Norwich but necessarily in limited numbers. Many local residents did not want a railway because it might lower the tone by bringing 'excursionists'. In 1877, the East Norfolk Railway completed its line from Norwich, this company being absorbed by the GER in 1881. Visitor numbers had been rising slowly but grew significantly with the coming of the railway. There were still complaints about the length of time that it took travellers from London, for example, to reach the town along the metals of the GER. Cromer set out to cater for a reasonably well-heeled clientele and people with less money who also wanted sedate surroundings and activities. Several hotels, some large and luxurious, were built as well as a sea wall, a promenade and a pier with a concert pavilion.

In 1887 the Eastern & Midlands Railway, predecessor of the Midland & Great Northern, opened its Cromer Beach Station, much better situated for the town that the GER's Cromer High. This offered a potential approach from London King's Cross to Cromer via Peterborough and South Lynn. Such a journey would have been even more convoluted than that by the GER from Liverpool Street.

A third and late arrival at Cromer was the Norfolk & Suffolk Joint Railway. This was the product of an agreement in 1898 between the GER and the M&GNR. It involved the line from West Runton to North Walsham via Mundesley which opened to Cromer in 1906. Cromer remained primarily a smallish select resort which seems to have been what it wanted, and it probably enjoyed its best days in the Edwardian period. By that time the GER evidently valued the business Cromer generated because in 1907 it gave the name 'The Norfolk Coast Express' to an express from Liverpool Street which completed its journey in about three hours. We would be reluctant to say that the railways 'made' Cromer but before the motoring age they brought most of its visitors.

## Resorts made by the Railways

There were some seaside resorts for the development of which the railways were largely or exclusively responsible. Five examples will suffice. They were Silloth in what is now Cumbria, Cleethorpes and Skegness in Lincolnshire, Saltburn in North Yorkshire and Hunstanton in Norfolk. Cleethorpes and Saltburn could be regarded as suburban developments of existing sizeable towns. Silloth and Skegness were remotely situated.

Silloth became a hybrid sort of place – a commercial port and a seaside watering place, both on a small scale. It could be said that Silloth owed its existence to Carlisle, just over twenty-two miles away. In the middle of the nineteenth century, Carlisle was developing as an industrial city but concerned that its continued growth could be inhibited by its poor access to navigable water, in this case the Solway Firth at Port Carlisle.

It had a canal to the Solway Firth but this was unable to handle vessels with a financially worthwhile capacity. The ports of Whitehaven and Maryport were considerably further away from Carlisle. The idea developed of building a port to the west where the Solway Firth joined the open sea. The Carlisle & Silloth Bay Dock & Railway Company was authorised in 1852, the railway opened in 1856 and a dock followed in 1859. When the railway arrived, Silloth was nothing more than a small, bleak settlement of around 100 souls. According to some jaundiced visitors it didn't get much better. Someone described it as 'little better than a rabbit warren'. This uncomplimentary comment was countered in upbeat fashion by the NBR who gilded the lily when declaring that Silloth was 'the Torquay of the North'. The idea of the watering place and the commercial port did not necessarily mix well especially when a plant processing manure opened and its emanations pervaded the bathing area nearby.

Railways were making an impact across the country, and it was evident that they could provide the means of transporting people to the seaside for pleasure. Several seaside places were already enjoying increased prosperity courtesy of the railways and here was an almost virgin site which could be transformed into a convenient resort for the Carlisle citizenry. This could be combined with the commercial port facilities and perhaps even some residential development and the railway would be the factor allowing all this to happen. Carlisle's industry would benefit. Silloth would become a prosperous community. It was what we would now call a 'win–win' situation.

The Carlisle & Silloth got rather carried away. Among its directors were several builders and they went into something of a feeding frenzy. Railway companies were required to observe the conditions laid down by Parliament in the Act authorising the building of each specific line. In their speculative greed, the directors proceeded to exceed the terms of the Act and bought additional land and built residential property, a hotel and a gasworks. Sand dunes were removed to create a site for a promenade. This was all *ultra vires* under the terms of the company's

Act. A seaside watering place was in the process of being built. Not only was some of it strictly illegal, but it was also very expensive, and it basically bankrupted the Carlisle and Silloth. The railway even built a golf course, again without legal authorisation. It was later sold off.

In 1862, the NBR leased the line, an interesting example of a Scottish based company running a line entirely in England, and the development of Silloth was proceeding well. There was a variety of simple pleasures available for visitors, accommodation for those who wished to prolong their stay, an active commercial port and regular sailings by steamers to Ireland and the Isle of Man. The fortunes of Silloth up to 1914 were mixed. The NBR tried to sell some of the land its predecessor had bought illegally but had little success in doing so. The boom was bottoming out. Various additional amenities were added for visitors, but it was clear that Silloth was never going to become another Blackpool. It was simply too far from major centres of population. It did become busy at weekends of good weather, by no means guaranteed in these parts, as hundreds of Carlisle's citizens enjoyed an escape from their mundane surroundings and arrived by train. A second dock opened in 1885 and the NBR carried useful amounts of freight traffic to and from Carlisle. Silloth was a railway town.

Cleethorpes was a little settlement which had long attracted small numbers of people for a dip in the Humber Estuary but it was 'made' as a seaside resort by the MS&LR which later became the GCR. Cleethorpes gained a place on the railway system in 1863 as an extension from Grimsby. The station was right by the sea. A pier was built in 1872 and, as traffic built up, the station was enlarged to six platforms in 1880. The MS&LR was involved in the building of a promenade, ornamental gardens and various of the other amenities required by an increasingly popular seaside resort, particularly, in this case, one largely given over to trippers. As one historian said: 'At Cleethorpes, the railway company turned showman'. The commitment of the railway company to developing the resort was demonstrated when it bought the pier. Cleethorpes prospered particularly from the 1880s, making little pretence at offering anything more than a cheap and cheerful short escape particularly for folk in industrial parts of the East Midlands and the West Riding of Yorkshire. Cleethorpes was a place made by the railways.

Skegness was also primarily a tripper's destination, in this case mainly for industrial workers and their families from Leicestershire and Nottinghamshire. This previously small and select watering place was joined to the railway system in 1873. Before that, coaches met trains at Firsby or Burgh on the GNR's East Lincolnshire line which opened in 1848. Skegness was at the end of a short branch from Firsby which, although promoted by an independent company, was worked from the start by the GNR. Skegness had a population of only 349 in 1871 but a sizeable station was built in anticipation of large amounts of holiday traffic. It opened in 1873 and trains began to bring encouraging numbers of visitors. The Earl of Scarborough who owned much of the land nearby, through his agent collaborating with the GNR, decided to develop a purpose-built, planned seaside town. This was a bold step involving considerable investment but it proved successful and Skegness came to have the attractions expected of a resort largely patronised by working-class visitors. A pier, fine floral displays and even a narrow-gauge tramway were among the attractions. While the town itself had not become a large one by the First World War, the venture had proved a very successful one because Skegness was attracting around three-quarters of a million visitors annually by the time the war broke out in 1914. Like Cleethorpes, Skegness owed what it came to be, a cheap and cheerful seaside resort, to the railway. Skegness grew but its permanent population remained small. In 1901 2,140 and only 3,775 in 1911.

The GNR made much of the potential of Skegness for excursion traffic. They put on day excursions from King's Cross and employed John Hassall to design posters advertising the town's attractions. Hassall was a prolific and highly skilled artist who did a lot of commercial and other work but he is remembered most of all for his 'Skegness is so bracing' poster. This depicts a cheery looking and rather rotund fisherman, galumphing joyfully along a beach. Like the best commercial art, it was highly effective because it was simple, eye-catching and to the point. He was paid nine guineas for it in 1908 and although it made his name, he rather resented the relative lack of recognition accorded to others of his works that he thought had more merit. He did another well-known railway poster for the London Underground with the tagline 'No need to ask a P'liceman!' This shows a burly police officer directing a lady to a map of the Underground as a more reliable source of information than he could provide.

In 1861, Saltburn found itself as the terminus of an extension of the line of the S&DR from the nearby small seaside resort of Redcar in the North Riding of Yorkshire. Essentially it had been built as a branch from a line to mineral workings further down the coast. The thrusting Pease family's main concern was to exploit iron ore reserves just to the south, but they were perceptive enough to see Saltburn's potential as a seaside resort. The location of the station was on a clifftop amidst spectacular coastal scenery. The Pease family set up a subsidiary company to negotiate with the major local landowner, Lord Zetland, who was happy to sell at an appropriate price. A small town began to develop on top of the cliffs overlooking the previous settlement of fishermen's cottages. A spacious planned town was built focussed on the station, its crowning glory being an enormous and imposing hotel with commanding views over the sea. A unique feature of this hotel, *The Zetland*, was that the railway literally ran right up to the hotel so that the well-to-do guests who it was hoped to attract would simply step off the train under cover and immediately enter the hotel. The railway company built a few homes for its employees and engaged in some speculation by building some tall terraced dwellings. The hotel had its ups and downs and was eventually taken over by the NER, successor to the S&DR. Other seaside attractions followed but Saltburn was never promoted as a 'kiss-me-quick' kind of place, leaving that role to Redcar. Instead, it attracted visitors attracted by its natural delights and affluent residents and retirees. Through trains ran from York and there were connections in many directions available at Darlington and York. Railways played a major part in Saltburn's development.

At Hunstanton, the Le Strange family owned much land on which they decided to develop a select seaside watering place on a site south of the existing village which came to be known as Old Hunstanton. They employed Herbert Butterworth, an architect of national repute, to design many of the buildings. Integral to this plan was the construction of a railway line from King's Lynn which had gained a through route from London in 1847. The line to Hunstanton opened in 1862 and was later absorbed by the Great Eastern Railway. A large hotel was built, and a pier opened in 1870. Hunstanton at that time was the only resort along a long stretch of coast but it was also distant from large centres of population. The same could be said of Skegness, further north, but it benefitted from reasonably direct routes from centres of population in the East Midlands. It took some effort to reach Hunstanton by rail and this meant that its role became that of a successful, quietish middle-class resort which, however, never expanded into a sizeable town nor, perhaps, ever sought to do so. It had excellent sands, unique striated cliffs and was the only one of East Anglia's seaside resorts that faced westwards. Until the start of the age of the privately-owned motor car in the 1950s, most of Hunstanton's visitors arrived courtesy of the GER.

Folkestone before the railway arrived can perhaps best be described as a decayed Kentish fishing village with a profitable side-line in smuggling. Tentative efforts were made to turn the place into a genteel seaside watering place in the early nineteenth century and some accommodation had been built for visitors on the high cliffs just west of the town. This had met with little success and the place continued to stagnate until, in 1843, the SER decided to buy the rundown harbour and establish a packet service across the Channel to Boulogne. This was unexpected but the local response was enthusiastic and hotels and other buildings quickly followed. Between 1841 and 1861 the population doubled, to nearly 10,000.

Two forces were behind the development of Folkestone, the major local landowners and the SER, but they were not pulling in the same direction. The landowners wanted to make the town a seaside resort and desirable place in which to live, the SER's interests were focussed on making a success of the place as a ferry port. Local people resented the presence and intrusive nature of the branch line to the harbour. This was graded in parts as steeply as 1 in 30 and when a steam train climbed up from the harbour, it made a noise that could be heard for miles. Windows rattled all along the route when as many as four small steam locomotives participated in this brutal physical process. Another bone of contention was the inconvenient position of what passed as the town's stations and approaches were constantly being made to the SER to do something about it. The company was unimpressed. The townspeople did not want to push the company too far because the harbour provided jobs and the railway, despite the shortcomings of the stations, brought the visitors that that were helping to make Folkestone an increasingly successful seaside resort of the rather superior sort. From time to time the SER threatened that it might take its packet sailings elsewhere. Over time, differences between the railway company and the townspeople faded away. The company invested heavily in the harbour, ensuring its long-term future as a packet station. The town recognised the contribution that the railway was playing in making the town a success in late Victorian England.

Bognor had long been a small and insignificant seaside hamlet but, towards the end of the eighteenth century, Sir John Hotham, who was what we would now call a 'venture capitalist', bought much cheap land in the vicinity with the idea of developing a seaside resort to rival Brighton and enrich himself as he did so. Work started in 1787 on building a planned, well laid-out and spacious town which he modestly named after himself as 'Hothamton'. He was successful and by the 1800s affluent people were taking up residence attracted by the town's reputation for a healthy climate. In due course, royal and aristocratic patrons were visiting what was becoming a highly fashionable health resort and sea-bathing place. Such visitors tended to be capricious and, to widen the town's appeal, a pier was erected in 1865. It had been felt that further development was being held back by the lack of a direct railway link so, in 1864, the LB&SCR opened a short branch from Barnham Junction on the Brighton to Chichester line. This eased access to Bognor, visitor footfall increased thanks to the railway but Bognor certainly never became a second Brighton.

Littlehampton was a modest port at the mouth of the River Arun. The influence of the railway was rather greater than at Bognor, the developing of a seaside watering-place largely following on the opening in 1863 of a short branch of the LB&SCR from Ford, again on the Brighton to Portsmouth line. Briefly, the LB&SCR operated cross-channel steamers from Littlehampton to St Malo, Honfleur and the Channel Islands. Littlehampton settled gently into the role of a sedate seaside resort lacking the raffish delights that attracted much larger crowds to Brighton.

The railways did allow larger numbers to reach these towns more easily but a daytrip from London which involved using the LB&SCR's line from Three Bridges through Horsham and Pulborough was a slow haul. There were not many other sizeable centres of population close by on which these towns could draw for the trippers' market before the age of private motoring.

The more successful seaside resorts were among the fastest growing towns in Victorian and Edwardian Britain. All the major resorts were rail-served by 1881.

The business at railway resorts fluctuated. Their patrons could be capricious. Although all resorts wanted a share of the market, they did not necessarily want a share of the same market. We have seen how some wanted to keep themselves socially exclusive while others were prepared to go to almost any lengths to widen their appeal for a mass working-class clientele. Either type of resort might, however, find itself apparently drifting out of fashion for no obvious reason and making changes to the character of its provision in order to keep the visitors coming.

Many seaside resorts, like their inland counterparts, were affected by outbreaks of disease. Epidemiology was a nascent science but outbreaks of diseases such as typhoid, scarlet fever and diphtheria were common in this period and the crowds might desert a place badly affected, never to return. In 1893, for example, Worthing was affected by a serious outbreak of typhoid which killed 155 people. By the end of August that year, there was not one holiday visitor in the place and the town took years to recover. It was served by the LB&SCR. The railway company may have lost potential income to the tune of about £15,000 as a result of this unfortunate occurrence, which showed the symbiotic nature of the relationship of the railways and the towns they served. The railways brought the bulk of a resort's visitors. Both railway and town gained income when things worked well. If the town was affected by events like those at Worthing, the railway also lost out.

Large amounts of money could be made in the nineteenth century by speculative builders who developed seaside settlements which went on to become popular resorts. The acquisition of a suitable site and even the building of the kind of amenities expected was, however, no guarantee that the place would 'catch on'. Early in the twentieth century, the Ravenscar Estate Company bought a site between Whitby and Scarborough for a brand-new resort. Just a few buildings were erected close to the railway station before momentum was lost and the developer went bankrupt around 1913. What had seemed like a good idea failed, probably because the site was too exposed to cold winds howling off the North Sea. Evidence of just how strong the winds could be occurred when shelters were built on what was going to be the promenade and they were promptly blown down. The Furness Railway bought land at Seascale on its coastal route from Barrow-in-Furness to Whitehaven with the intention of developing a major seaside resort complete with promenade, floral gardens and other amenities including at least one grand hotel. Seascale never developed beyond being a small seaside settlement still visited today by those who like a quiet stroll along the sands. Fashion has always been capricious but here are two locations which could have developed into resorts that would have largely depended on the railways to bring their visitors, but which totally failed to meet the expectations of their developers.

Relations between railway companies and the business communities of the resorts they served were not always amicable or at least were not necessarily going in the same direction at the same time. The running of large numbers of special holiday trains caused railway companies numerous problems. Among these were the provision of the necessary operating staff and rolling stock, the availability of paths for trains converging on a particular place in close succession and sufficient platform space and storage sidings for the empty rolling stock. Expensive non-revenue-earning train movements might be required to move rolling stock to where it was needed. Bad weather might slash the take-up for day excursions.

In a sense, this was the problem identified by Dr Richard Beeching when making his recommendations for the future of Britain's railways in the 1960s. The nub was the provision of expensive facilities which were only likely to be fully used for a small part of the year. Trains packed to the gunwales with holidaymakers may have generated money, but the fares were often discounted and the trains were costly to run. Sometimes the council of a seaside resort might try to lean on a railway company to lay on more trains or provide more platforms to handle holiday traffic, but such decisions could not be made lightly by railway companies, few of whom made substantial profits in the nineteenth century. Extra platforms, for example, might involve the cost of purchasing expensive new land. Sometimes there were disputes between local authorities and a railway company over excursion traffic. The locals might want more such trains to add to the cumulative spending power of visitors. The railway company might want to cut down on trains that were, at best, only marginally profitable. The NER agreed to meet the extremely worried Town Council at Saltburn in 1873 when there were rumours that excursions were to be discontinued. At Deal, the local businesspeople petitioned the council to approach the SER to change its policy and start running excursions to the town.

Over time, antipathy between local authorities and railway companies tended to lessen and cooperation rather than confrontation came to be seen as mutually beneficial. In 1902-23 the Town Councils at Brighton and Eastbourne, two rival resorts located close to each other joined forces to approach the L&NWR to lay on through services from the north of England. They met a favourable response and such provision lasted for many years. This was a recognition of the mutuality of interest and the dependence of the towns concerned on the railways for bringing them the visitors whose spending was so critical for their economic wherewithal.

*Chapter Fifteen*

# Railways and Smaller Towns

Most of the early long-distance trunk railways were planned to provide communication between major centres of population. These places had the potential to provide worthwhile levels of business from their existing manufacturing and commercial activities and it was hoped that the railways would themselves generate growing levels of such activity. The idea that these railways might generate much passenger traffic was very much a secondary consideration. Railway companies varied in the criteria they applied in choosing the alignments of their planned routes. It came as a considerable surprise to the directors of the L&MR when they found that people wanted to travel their route simply for pleasure.

The possibility of significant amounts of passenger traffic then became one among other factors to consider when deciding on the alignment of new lines. Some companies directed their engineers to find the shortest possible route, irrespective of geographical obstacles. This might mean avoiding major intermediate towns as originally happened, for example, with the North Midland Railway which, on its way from the Midlands to Yorkshire, would normally avoid a town the size of Sheffield. Other companies were prepared to follow more circuitous alignments if that cut the cost of expensive engineering works. Sometimes diversions from the ideal route were forced on railway companies by powerful landowners opposed to a particular railway or railways in general. On occasions in the early days, a company would encounter opposition from the influential burghers of a town who made it clear that they did not want anything to do with a railway.

Thetford was one such place. Usually, early opposition to a railway turned at a later stage to a fervent desire to be on the railway network.

This all made for inconsistency in how intermediate locations on long-distance routes were served. Few companies thought it necessary to attempt to serve every settlement of significance along a proposed route. The choices they made for places to serve sometimes seem very arbitrary. When, by the mid-1840s, there was a general awareness of the economic benefits that could accrue for a place served by a railway, it was understandable that towns might feel affronted if major lines chose to avoid them. Examples of places of some substance that early lines avoided included Tewkesbury, Saffron Walden, Kendal and Stony Stratford. The first three all eventually gained places on the railway but only on secondary or branch lines. It may be significant that none of them developed into large towns. We can only speculate as to how they might have fared had they found themselves served by main line railways. By 1850, towns that did not have railway stations, even on minor lines, began to be concerned that they would be condemned to stagnation or even decay. Sometimes, the people of influence in a town which had been bypassed would approach the company operating the nearest main line and petition them to build a branch to their town. This sometimes worked but if it did not, the townspeople might find the resources to promote their own branch line to a convenient spot on the main line. Aylesbury, spurned by the London & Birmingham, opened a line to a junction with the latter company at Cheddington. To be served by a railway line made a place feel that it was, somehow, 'on the map'.

## Gains from being served by a railway

Windsor was an ancient town dominated by the presence of the royal castle and of Eton College. Slough, three miles away, had a station on the main line of the GWR and the company wanted to build a branch to Windsor but had an uphill struggle against the College which did not want any railway and the Crown which wanted to impose difficult conditions on the route it would use to approach the town. It was 1849 when the GWR eventually reached the town to be followed shortly after by a branch of the L&SWR. The choice of two routes to and from London gave the town a great boost in terms of tourism. Most of the hugely increased numbers of visitors used the trains. The railway made a major and sustained contribution to the economic fortunes of the town. No one, however, would call Windsor a railway town.

Benefits of a very different sort accrued for Rye as a result of it gaining a place on the railway system. It was an ancient place but was sadly faded by the nineteenth century, its port having become insignificant and a major source of income, the smuggling trade, having gone into steep decline. The Town Corporation was badly run and in serious debt. In 1845, plans were proposed for a line from Ashford in Kent to Hastings which would cross flat land just north of the town. The Corporation was able to make money by selling the land needed for the railway and, in doing so, settling its debts while managing to require the railway company to spend money on improving the harbour and the navigability of the River Rother. The town gained from these transactions and a boost in the number of visitors to its picturesque delights. The railway company benefitted by obtaining the land for its station at less than the original asking price. Financially, however, the company, found itself operating a service which never made them much money. Rye was never a railway town but, almost fortuitously, the railway proved to be of lasting benefit to it.

There were, of course, many towns that found themselves conveniently served by stations on the early main lines. Examples could be Berwick-on Tweed, Neath, Lichfield or Belper. Detailed local studies would be necessary to determine in what ways, if indeed at all, these towns gained by having fairly early access to the railway. None of these places had become large towns by 1914. Some other towns which were on the railway scene at an early date became important railway junctions. Tonbridge, Ely and Rugby could be cited as examples. The railway had a much larger presence in Rugby than in the other two, but none of them grew into large towns. Clearly the possession of a busy railway junction was not of itself guarantee that a town would grow significantly in the Victorian period, let alone be described as a railway town.

Boston was a seaport of ancient origins, and it gained an important station on the GNR's roundabout route from Peterborough to Lincoln and points north. This railway opened in 1848. The GNR built a locomotive works but soon began to run this down in favour of a more convenient engineering plant at Doncaster. Fortunately for the town, the GNR built a sleeper depot, importing much of the requisite timber from Scandinavia through the docks in the town. As the GNR expanded, so the sleeper depot grew and by 1912 it had become a major employer in the town with a workforce of 900 in 1912. With substantial sidings and an engine shed as well, the GNR came to be a major player in the life of the town. It remained a town of medium size, but it is interesting, if ultimately pointless, to wonder how much it would have grown and changed had the GNR continued to concentrate its locomotive building and maintenance there.

Luton stood on the MR's main line to London St Pancras from the north. This town was growing lustily before the railway arrived and it became noted as the largest British town in 1851 without a railway. Its dominant industry was the making of straw hats. It gained minor railway connections courtesy of the GNR in 1858 but in 1868 the MR opened a station on its new independent main line approach to London. It sounds like a joke but its situation on a trunk route between London, the East Midlands and the North of England provided a real boost for the hat-making industry. Now it had access to a national market and railways provided an ideal means of transportation for this product that was light, took up space and was not to be squashed. The local business community was canny enough to know that fashion is capricious, and that the town needed to diversify its industrial base. A working party was set up in 1889 to find ways of attracting new industries. They were very successful. In 1905, the Thameside Vauxhall Iron Works in London moved its growing car-making facility to Luton followed in 1909 by Commer, another automotive company, and in 1910 the Skefko Ball

Bearing Company. Significantly, all these plants were rail-connected. The railways therefore contributed greatly to Luton's early start in the embryonic automotive industry. It would be mistaken, however, to describe Luton as a railway town. The railway installations of the town were not particularly extensive.

Other examples could be given of small or medium-sized towns where the existence of the railway had a beneficial economic effect particularly by acting as a fillip to existing industries or being an instrumental factor in the creation of new ones. There were many other places that were materially damaged by the growth of the railways. Among these were the towns that were astride the county's trunk roads and which gained most of their income from the activities associated with coaching. They can be described as 'coaching towns' in the same sense that we talk about railway towns. The coaching industry had reached a high level of comprehensiveness and sophistication by the 1820s. The major coaching towns had several inns aimed at different levels of the market and these required substantial workforces not only to look after the needs of the passengers but to care for the horses and the conveyances themselves. Local businesses built carts, carriages and other horse-drawn conveyances. Farriers and smiths found plenty of work.

Stagecoaches could not compete with railways over long distances. Some places that were dependent on the coaching industry went into steep decline, an example being Ilchester in Somerset. Boroughbridge on the Great North Road in Yorkshire was a thriving example of a coaching town but the opening of the York to Darlington section of what became the East Coast Main Line saw off the last coaches within eight years. Boroughbridge remained a small town but found other business activity. It even gained a branch from the East Coast Main Line in 1847. It should be remembered that the railways generally stimulated business activity. Many stagecoach operators turned to short-haul activity, often to and from a railhead and the operators of wagons found plenty of business carrying consignments to and from railway goods depots. Few places that had previously depended heavily on handling horse-drawn traffic went into serious decline with the coming of the railways. The1840s to the mid-1870s was a period of largely sustained economic growth.

What could happen in a coaching town was that the buzz of activity generated by road traffic in the town centre might fall away and re-emerge where a station was built on the fringe of the town. Although it was already a bigger place than those we have been mentioning, Derby developed a very active quarter around the station. Here several places offering accommodation, pubs and shops appeared and there was a thriving business for cabs and later horse buses conveying people to and from the town centre a mile away. At Grantham, the station was built on what was then the western fringe of the town along with a residential suburb occupied largely by railway workers' families. Similar developments occurred elsewhere.

Two towns, Bakewell and Llangollen, were examples of places where the coaching trade had been very prominent but, after it declined, they found a new niche as centres of tourism, making full use of their picturesque surroundings. The railways brought the visitors, in both cases in the late 1860s. With much to thank the railways for, they would, however, never be described as railway towns.

Launceston was in decline by the early 1850s, desperately wanting a railway to boost its economy but having seen several attempts to bring a line to the town fail to achieve parliamentary sanction. In 1861, a further proposal for a standard gauge line, the Mid-Devon and Cornwall Railway, was defeated in Parliament. Soon afterwards, a proposal was put forward for a Launceston & South Devon Railway which was planned to join up with the broad-gauge South Devon Railway at Tavistock. Several powerful local landowners were opposed to this, as was the War Office which had become hostile to the broad-gauge because it thought that the existence of two gauges on Britain's railways might be a serious disadvantage in the event of an invasion by hostile forces.

The bill for this project passed the House of Commons to the great joy of the citizenry but still had to go before the House of Lords. A mass meeting was called and a handbill issued. It showed how much the railway was wanted but was a masterpiece of hyperbole. It ran: 'Our Railway. Come to the meeting tonight!! Citizens: The enemy is in the field. Arouse ye! Arouse Ye! And do battle to the enemies of your sacred rights ... now in the hour of trial, stand forth as a Samson to crush tyranny and despotism! Now or never!!' Although this outburst inflicted severe injury on the subtleties of the English language, this time the efforts were successful and the bill became law. The line to Plymouth opened in the summer of 1865.

The L&SWR arrived in the town in 1886 with a station on its rather indirect route from Exeter to Padstow. After all this fuss, Launceston was on the railway map which made places feel they were part of the wider world. However, we have to say that the presence of two railways does not seem to have made much difference to its fortunes. Even with two lines, it was a long haul to the regional centres of either Exeter or Plymouth and it is unlikely that local shopkeepers lost much trade. In common with many other places, the railway would have reduced the cost of coal and other necessities. We can only speculate how the fortunes of the town would have gone had it missed out on railways.

## Towns that lost out during the railway era

It should be remembered that many small towns experienced losses of population from the 1850s. Emigration was running at high levels and large-scale migration was occurring as people went in search of better wages in the towns and cities. The railway was an agency of this population movement but hardly a cause of it. Some towns that suffered depopulation were, oddly enough, places which had early found themselves placed on the railway map. Totnes, Warminster and Moreton-in-Marsh were examples. Clearly, a position on the railway system was no guarantee that the town concerned would prosper and grow. Hadleigh in Suffolk gained a railway in 1846 and experienced a boost for its existing economic activities but its population fell by about 12 per cent between 1841 and 1901 as it suffered from the greater 'pull' of nearby Ipswich and from being the terminus of an obscure branch line.

Every place had its unique features. Devizes in Wiltshire was an ancient market town with a castle and two fine churches. It was a major centre for the manufacture of snuff and for brewing. It was a coaching town and was served by Kennet & Avon Canal. It shared with Salisbury the role of the county town. With a population of around 6,000 in the 1830s it wanted a railway and was big and important enough to expect to get one. Various schemes were mooted but it had to wait until 1857 and 1862 when it gained lines approaching from opposite directions. By this time the place was in the economic doldrums, having lost its coaching trade and witnessing the decline of business on the canal. Perhaps curiously, its population grew between 1850 and 1870 but it received a blow when, in 1899, the decision was taken to make Trowbridge the county town. This town was located on a line from which many connections could easily be made. Devizes, by contrast, was located on a relative backwater, a secondary cross-country route off the main Berks & Hants line of the GWR. The railway played a major part in shaping the future of the two towns although Trowbridge did not grow into a large town as a result of its elevation to county town status. Devizes too remained a small town.

Marlborough, also in Wiltshire, was an old town with an important market function and, situated on the London to Bath road, it had become a coaching centre of importance. It lost the coaching trade almost entirely in 1841 after the opening of the GWR's London to Bath and Bristol route. It agitated for a railway but had to wait until 1864 when a short branch line was opened from Savernake on the GWR's main line from London to Taunton and the West Country. Marlborough had its railway, but Savernake was only a wayside station and the GWR did not choose to provide many stopping trains for people wanting to get to and from Marlborough. The branch might have been a somewhat tenuous link to the wider world, but it did seem to assist the growth of Marlborough College by increasing its accessibility.

This was established in 1843 and grew into a prestigious public school. The town gained another railway in 1881 with the grandiose-sounding Midland and South Western Junction Railway. This line wended its wearisome way from Andover in the south via Marlborough, Swindon and Cirencester, and eventually expired on reaching Cheltenham. It enjoyed useful connections at both ends and even had at its own station at Savernake, but it passed through sparsely populated country with little originating traffic. Trains were few and speeds slothful. Strangely, although Swindon's population growth as a result of the railway works meant that it largely took over its role as a market town and, for a while its population fell, Marlborough somehow hung on and experienced a revival with the dawn of the motor age before the First World War. Its relationship with railways was therefore a rather odd one. It may have helped it to consolidate its position as an educational centre while at least partly depriving of its market function.

An entire book could be devoted to a study of the relationships that existed between the influential people of certain towns and the railway companies that served them especially if, in the view of the townsfolk, they did so very badly. There were towns where a powerful landowner used influence to keep the railway at a distance or would only sell land for railway use at a location inconvenient to the townspeople. At Stamford in Lincolnshire, for example, the Marquess of Exeter sold land to the Midland Counties Railway that lay north of the River Welland in an inconvenient spot for a station. He was playing complicated political games, being concerned to maintain the hold over the electorate which his family had held for a century or more. He wanted to keep Stamford as a 'pocket borough' but this was in the 1830s and 1840s at a time of turbulent economic and social change when the electorate was growing and becoming much less predictable in its behaviour.

A chapter could deal with the often-fraught relationship between a railway company and the burghers of a town which wanted a railway desperately which the company was not keen on providing. In the case of Marlborough, mentioned above, this led to the formation of a local company to build a line to the nearest railhead at Savernake. This suited the GWR well. It had been less than enthusiastic about such a line but, having in effect created the determination of the locals to pay for the building of the line, they then operated it, for a financial consideration of course! Other examples of such arrangements could be given.

There were towns which almost went down on bended knee in beseeching railway companies to connect them to the system. Such entreaties might fall on deaf ears. Caistor in Lincolnshire, a bustling small market town, was eager to be served by a railway but even though Lord Yarborough, chairman of the Great Grimsby & Sheffield Junction and a very prominent local landowner promised them one, the company did not get round to building it. Caistor never got its hoped-for railway. On some long-distance trunk routes, a railway company might make a gesture to a settlement that it avoided by cynically building a station some distance from the town. For example, the MR, when building the Settle & Carlisle line, opened stations called Dent and Kirkby Stephen which were, respectively, four and over two miles from those places, admittedly not very large ones. The GWR was the maestro at this sleight of hand by studiously avoiding towns it had no desire to serve directly for whatever reason by opening a station only vaguely in their vicinity which they would then call something 'Road'.

Mansfield, another old but considerably larger town, exemplified the mutual inability of some urban communities and railway companies to work in harmony. This town had a station on the line of the MR from Nottingham, opened in 1849. This line was extended northwards to Worksop in 1875. Another MR line ran eastwards towards Southwell and Newark. The major issue was the slowness of the passenger service to Nottingham, the natural focus of the district and the gateway to many other places. The locals felt that the growth and prosperity of their town was being retarded by being a railway backwater. Certainly, Mansfield was off any main line of the MR, but that company valued the business potential of the Mansfield district with its quarries, ironworks, textile industries and, increasingly, its coal resources. Such was the industrial development of the town that its population grew from about 8,000 in 1861 to 39,000 in 1911. Despite this substantial growth, the town still felt that it was off the beaten track and was neglected. Many approaches were made to the MR to improve the passenger service it offered the town, but these were quietly rejected to the intense frustration of the townspeople. The fact was that much more money was to be made from the goods and mineral traffic generated in the district and the company was content to leave the Nottingham service as it was. In 1895, there were just over a dozen trains to and from Nottingham which was 17 miles away. They mostly took nearly an hour for the journey. Later, the GCR built a line through the town but the main emphasis of that was also goods and minerals. While Mansfield may have resented the secondary nature of the passenger trains serving the town, it experienced strong economic growth despite having such a poor passenger service to the county town.

Oxford was not a large town in the nineteenth century, but it had a prominence in the life of the nation that had little to do with the size of its population. It was big enough, however, even without the presence of the University, to be a place likely to interest a railway company. The GWR arrived in 1844. About twenty years later, the GWR was looking to concentrate its carriage building and repairing activity on one site rather than in the existing three dispersed sites. It approached the Corporation of Oxford who indicated that it was willing to lease an unused site close to the railway on the town's western fringe and at an advantageous rent. Oxford was conveniently located on the GWR's growing system. The possibilities offered by this development were welcomed in certain local circles. Oxford's prosperous coaching trade had collapsed with the coming of the railways and even traffic on the Thames and the Oxford Canal was in decline. The proposed works held out the prospect of 1,500 jobs and the increased spending power would benefit the city.

It is not surprising that this perspective was not shared by the University. This establishment greatly treasured its air of cloistered seclusion and exclusion and had a lofty disdain for the 'satanic mills'. It exercised a major influence in the city and argued that any economic gain that might accrue from bringing the GWR's facility to Oxford would be negated by the irreparable harm it would be likely to do to the city's character. The issue attracted national interest and a host of academics and others sounded off in the media of the time about the malign influence that this works would have on the city's (meaning the University's) unique character. The University had already succeeded in ensuring that the station was located well away from its various colleges, one of the reasons given was that smoke from the locomotives would damage their stonework.

Oxford did not get a railway works because the GWR took the decision to centralise its locomotive and rolling stock building and maintenance at Swindon. The University by its show of opposition perhaps won a pyrrhic victory but the 'town' as opposed to the 'gown' viewed the situation with gloom. Other places were bounding forwards embracing industry and Oxford, without a sound manufacturing base, looked to be condemned to an ivory-towered existence dominated by the ancient university which paid notoriously poor wages to most of its non-academic staff. It was well into the twentieth century before Oxford gained for itself a significant industrial base around motor manufacturing and, even then, the huge works that developed at Cowley was tucked away out of sight of the University and the tourists.

It is impossible to say whether, or to what extent, Oxford missed out by not gaining the works. Any judgement is bound to be subjective. It is curious, though, that while Oxford became a busy railway centre served by trains to a wide variety of places, its station became notorious for the inadequate and poor services it offered for passengers at such an important location. Even the GWR engine shed was tiny, timber-built and totally inadequate as a base for its sizeable allocation of locomotives. A reader could be forgiven for thinking that the GWR resented the local response to its proposal for the works and wanted to offer minimal facilities to get its own back.

The case of Lincoln is interesting in any consideration of what constitutes a railway town. This is an ancient city, the seat of a bishopric and by the Middle Ages one of England's most important towns. It was an administrative centre, the focus of a large and very prosperous agricultural area and a manufacturer of cloth – the famous Lincoln Green. It was an inland port of some importance located with an outlet to the Trent not too distant and to the North Sea at Boston via the River Witham. It was the meeting point of many major roads, not least the Fosse Way.

There were several agriculture-related businesses located by the Witham and they needed cheaper supplies of coal for fuel. By the late 1830s, the benefits of railways for conveying coal cheaply had become obvious and the city became keenly interested in gaining a place on the growing railway map. It was only to be expected that Lincoln's importance would make it one of the places most likely to be an intermediate point on any main line from London travelling up the eastern side of England to York, Newcastle and perhaps Scotland. It was not to be. The first railway arrived in 1846, this being the MR from Nottingham. Soon Lincoln found itself being served by railways converging from eight directions. This made Lincoln an extremely busy railway centre but all the lines except one were of a secondary nature. Even the one which could be described as a main line was an oddity. This was the Great Northern & Great Eastern Joint Line from St Ives and March to Doncaster. It was an artery for the movement of huge amounts of coal, particularly from South Yorkshire, to meet the massive demand for fuel by London's homes and factories. On an everyday basis, few long-distance passenger trains traversed the Joint Line and those that did hardly qualified as expresses. Despite all these railways, it would not be completely unfair to describe Lincoln as something of a railway backwater. The main line to the North was routed from Peterborough through Grantham, Newark, Doncaster and Selby on its way to York. A decent service offering travel to and from London without changing is something that Lincoln had to wait for until the twenty-first century.

The arrival of the railways in the city generated economic development particularly in the manufacture of agricultural machinery and even steam locomotives. The city took on a predominantly industrial character despite the stunning presence of the cathedral on the hill overlooking what became a grimy working town. The railways brought in its raw materials and fuel and took away the artefacts it made. Lincoln became known for the manufacture of agricultural implements which provided useful experience for the building of railway locomotives. The local firm of Ruston, Proctor and Company built small tank engines mostly for industrial work and were prepared to adapt to meet the needs of customers using unusual gauges. Clayton & Shuttleworth also built some small shunting locomotives.

It is perhaps pertinent in any consideration of the concept of railway towns to question whether Lincoln could be considered under that category. It had two railway stations, many goods depots, impressive warehouses and three engine sheds. All these provided considerable employment. What was perhaps unique to Lincoln was the way in which the railway stamped its presence on its industrial and commercial life. In skirting the bottom of the hill on which the cathedral was situated, the railways had an extraordinary influence on everyday life in the town. They were the source of constant aggravation with their level crossings, there being two, for example, at either end of the larger of the passenger stations, that belonging to the GNR. With infuriating frequency, road traffic was brought to a halt as trains made what seemed like painfully slow progress over these level crossings, a problem that has not even been completely solved in the present century. To add to the intrusive nature of the railway, an avoiding line was built around the south side of the city. Much of the mineral and goods traffic on the Joint Line went this way. Most of this avoiding line was elevated on bridges, viaducts and embankments which were not only highly visible but created divisions in the districts through which it passed. Was Lincoln a railway town?

## Towns that never had railways

The expansion of the railway system was petering out by the 1900s. Reductions in services began to make themselves felt in the second decade of the twentieth century, especially during the First World War. Robust competition was being felt, particularly in cities and large towns, from electric tramways. It has often been argued that Britain was over-provided with railways, an arguably mistaken result of long-term official policy which said that government intervention in the country's business activity should be kept to a minimum and competition encouraged.

By 1914, most towns were served by railways. Three small towns were among the last to gain railway connections. These were Aberayron (1911), Holywell (1912) and Thaxted (1913). There remained a small number of other small, rather disgruntled, towns in England that were not placed on a railway if we define that as being three miles or more from the nearest station. The largest of these in 1911 were Painswick, Kingsclere and Ambleside. All had populations over 2,000.

Painswick was an old centre of Cotswold cloth manufacturing which was much in decline by the mid-nineteenth century. By that time, the town was taking on a different character as a desirable place of residence for what were then called 'gentlefolk'. Despite many of these being retirees who would not necessarily make much use of railways, there were several initiatives to put Painswick on the railway map. They failed. It may be to this that Painswick perhaps owes what is described as its delightful old-fashioned appearance. The GWR put on a motor bus from Stroud in 1905.

Kingsclere in Hampshire was actually not disgruntled. It was a remarkably self-contained place with a busy market and several racing stables and appears never to have felt the need to be put on the railway map. It was a different matter at Ambleside. This was an obscure village tucked away near Windermere in what was then the county of Westmoreland until the Lake District was discovered as a tourist destination. By the middle of the nineteenth century it was well supplied with the hotels and other amenities demanded by quite well-to-do visitors. After a railway was opened in 1847 to Windermere from Oxenholme on the main line between Lancaster and Carlisle, it was hoped that it would be extended to Ambleside in what would have seemed a natural development that would benefit the economic interests of the town. However, there influential landowners in the area who did not want their neighbourhood besmirched by the presence of masses of urbanites, probably of working-class origin, arriving by train. The railway never arrived in Ambleside although connecting buses were laid on from Windermere. We will never know to what extent, if at all, that the town's growth and prosperity was harmed by not having its own railway station.

The case of Beaumaris is particularly interesting. It had a population of about 2,000 but the place was more important than that figure suggests. It was the county town of Anglesey and the location of the island's assizes and quarter sessions. It was a small but active trading port and watering place. Repeated initiatives were made locally to persuade the L&NWR to build a branch from the North Wales main line to Holyhead. The railway loftily dismissed these approaches and in the absence of any serious offers to finance such a branch, Beaumaris remained without a railway. It was therefore condemned to the dubious distinction of being the only county town in England and Wales without a place on the railway system. It could, of course, be argued that although Beaumaris wanted to be on a railway, it does not seem to have wanted it enough to raise the capital to make it a reality. The town did not have champions of sufficient gravity or persuasiveness for the L&NWR to take the case of Beaumaris seriously. Having said that, there were places that offered, at best, marginal financial possibilities, but that managed to find powerful advocates who pulled strings and secured a place on a branch line built by a major company. St Ives and Malmesbury were examples. A large and powerful railway company like the L&NWR was motivated by the pursuit of profit. It considered a branch to Beaumaris and rejected it as unlikely to be financially viable.

Other existing places of sufficient size to be considered as towns in the nineteenth century but which never gained railways include Modbury in Devon, Shaftesbury in Dorset, Burford in Oxfordshire and Abbots Bromley in Staffordshire. They remained small. So too did Brewood in South Staffordshire which had a population of 3,799 in 1831. This place must be unique as it featured six times in plans for proposed railways, none of which were built. It was the ancient market centre for a rich agricultural area but did not attract any industrial development in the nineteenth century and then, along with many other places dependent on agriculture, suffered in the generally depressed conditions of the last quarter of the century. It was between 2 and 3 miles from the Wolverhampton to Stafford line of the L&NWR. It lost population in the nineteenth century and the obvious question is to what extent, if any, was its decline due to the lack of railway facilities?

The great pioneer of the academic study of local history, W.G. Hoskins, in 1948 made an unusual point about the impact of the railways on some small towns. He sounded rather jaundiced when he wrote, 'In the main the coming of the railways to these little places ruined them by breaking their isolation and now too many of them are picturesque but hollow shells'. He was referring, among others, to Kimbolton, Olney, to Godmanchester and St Ives in Huntingdonshire, to Oundle in Northamptonshire and to Uppingham in Rutland. He was unhappy about the loss of character and individuality which saw the demise of locally owned, old-fashioned businesses and the breaking of the intimate linkages between these little towns and the surrounding countryside of which they were the natural centres. He was, of course, correct in identifying this impact made by the railways but was writing at a time when he could not have foreseen the far greater impact that the spread of private car ownership was to have on the form and function of these places. Interestingly, none of the towns he mentioned has grown beyond the category of 'small town'.

### The strange case of Trent

Lewis Carroll's *Alice's Adventures in Wonderland* has the heroine having an encounter with a very large Cheshire Cat sitting in a tree. Fortunately, it is amiable, but it has a rather disconcerting habit of abruptly disappearing and then suddenly reappearing. Alice mentions this to the cat who tells her that he's perfectly happy to disappear slowly which he then proceeds to do, leaving just his grin in the tree. Alice ponders on having seen plenty of cats without a grin but never a grin without a cat.

Trent was a station, a busy and commodious one, without a town, village or even a hamlet nearby. This did not, however, prevent it from becoming a major hub of the MR. It stood in almost total isolation, about 7 miles south-east of Derby and about the same distance from Nottingham. The first line through the future site of the station was that of the Midland Counties Railway linking Derby and Nottingham. This opened in 1839. A station had to wait until 1862 when the MR was in the process of building a complicated web of lines meeting at this point. Eventually, Trent was served by lines to Leicester and the south, to Derby via Chellaston and alternatively via Borrowash; to Burton-on-Trent via Repton and Willington; up the Erewash Valley towards Chesterfield and to Nottingham via Beeston. The choice of destinations available from Trent was wide-ranging. They included London, Leicester, Nottingham, Derby, Sheffield, Leeds, Manchester, Birmingham, Lincoln and eventually Carlisle, Glasgow and Edinburgh.

Trent became the exchange station par excellence with almost no originating traffic but heavy usage by passengers changing trains. The only pedestrian access was along ill-lit and ill-frequented country footpaths to and from nowhere in particular. Almost the only dwellings visible were the station master's house and ten cottages for railway employees. The station consisted of one long island platform with full facilities including a refreshment room and bookstall. Unknowing passengers could be seriously confused when trains to some destinations left from opposite sides of the island platform and proceeded in opposite directions.

Something of the essence of the place was captured by a nineteenth century observer who wrote:

> You arrive at Trent, but where that is I cannot tell. I suppose it is somewhere near the River Trent, but then the Trent is a very long river. You get out of your train to obtain refreshments and having taken them you endeavour to find your train and your carriage. But whether it is on this side or that, or whether it is going north or south, this way or that, you cannot tell.

Despite the number of trains calling and the variety of destinations on offer, including London and even Scotland, Trent did not attract anything significant in terms of housing development during the period under review. It was, however, an early railway spotter's paradise because on weekdays scarcely more than a few minutes went by without the approach of yet another train being indicated by a multitude of MR lower quadrant semaphore signals. Perhaps Trent was a railway nowhere.

*Chapter Sixteen*

# Navvy Settlements

The extraordinary burst of railway building which so altered the face of Britain particularly in the period from 1830 to 1900, could not have taken place without the employment of vast numbers of men, largely using muscle power, to build bridges, viaducts, embankments, cuttings, culverts and tunnels, some of which were structures of a monumental scale. Not even the building of the Edwardian castles in Wales in the late thirteenth century or the great cathedrals and monasteries of the Middle Ages, prodigious projects though they were, could stand any comparison with the almost frenzied level of railway construction activity that the country witnessed for much of this time.

The physical work was undertaken by men often but rather misleadingly labelled as 'navvies'. In fact, the navvies were the aristocrats of the constructional labour force, and they did those parts of the projects that required the greatest skills, and which were frequently also the most dangerous tasks. Where mere brawn was required, unskilled labourers were engaged. There was a marked hierarchy in these labour forces of which the navvies were unquestionably the aristocrats. However, for the purposes of simplicity, we will refer to all these men as 'navvies'.

Many parts of Britain are hilly and difficult terrain for railway construction given the need wherever possible to keep gradients to a minimum. Large amounts of labour were often needed sometimes in remote places far distant from towns and villages. This meant that the contractors engaged in the works often had to build what sometimes were very large encampments of temporary buildings to provide sleeping and living accommodations for their workers and families. Even in sites much closer to established communities, such encampments might be needed if there simply was insufficient accommodation nearby. The arrival, in a small rural community, of many hundreds of men and their dependants was always likely to create a temporary housing crisis which sometimes could only be tackled by either the contractor making some provision or the navvies themselves exercising self-help and digging themselves in. After all, they had the skills to do that. At their worst, navvies might be housed in hovels scooped out by themselves with earth floors and built with any materials that came to hand. They would be cold and damp, and sometimes in winter might be decorated with icicles. One sod cabin measuring 27 feet by 12 occupied during the buildings of the Edinburgh to Hawick line in 1846, housed twenty people. Conditions could be dire.

Contractors were often understandably unwilling to provide anything other than the most basic for what, even if it was prolonged, was still a temporary situation. When work was being done on Bramhope Tunnel in Yorkshire, for example, the contractor provided sixty huts made from turf and several others consisting of brick and stone. In a few cases, railway companies built cottages for their navvies which were intended to become permanent dwellings for railway employees when the construction work was completed. This rebounded on the North Midland Railway at Clay Cross in Derbyshire because by the time the navvies had moved on, they had trashed the cottages which were ruinous.

The best accommodation, if it can be called that, might be provided by contractors on major projects where the work would perhaps take years. Examples were sites located by the Forth Bridge and at Sudbrook for the building of the Severn Tunnel. At the latter, the contractor put up well-built dwellings of stone and brick and even a coffee house, a school and a hospital. Visitors, either voyeurs or sometimes others genuinely concerned about the physical and spiritual welfare of the navvies, sometimes commented on how well kept the navvy dwellings might be. Missionary societies might build chapels and reading rooms in their attempts to lure the navvies away from the 'demon drink'.

The navvy settlements did not just contain navvies and labourers but all manner of camp followers. There were always women, sometimes actual wives but others who were little better than prostitutes and occasionally women, usually elderly, taken on to cook and clean, for example. Near Ais Gill on the Settle and Carlisle line we know that there were enough navvies to attract people described as shopkeepers, bakers, grocers, dressmakers and a shoemaker. Large sites usually attracted sellers of beer and spirits.

A feature of the navvy settlements was disease, often the result of overcrowding and poor sanitation which meant that typhus and cholera might be rampant. Smallpox was another frequent visitor. To put this in context, it needs to be said that environmental conditions in the encampments were not necessarily a great deal worse than in many industrial towns. Given the intrinsic danger of working on the construction sites, it is hardly surprising that undertakers frequently had rich pickings as they rather ghoulishly followed the construction work as it moved on from one place to the next. Sexually transmitted diseases were perhaps only to be expected among workforces largely consisting of fancy-free youngish men.

Many stories exist about racially motivated battles between, for example, English and Irish navvies, and about navvies drinking pubs dry and, when no more drink was available, wrecking the alehouse. Some navvies, it has been alleged, worked in a permanent state of intoxication and, for bravado, took appalling risks with what was already extremely hazardous work. Undoubtedly there were incidents of this sort but, taken as a whole, the work done by the navvies was on a heroic scale. At least in the early days working with little or nothing in the way of mechanical aids, they used their brawn to shift unrecorded vast amounts of soil, rock and other materials. Many of the tunnels, cuttings, viaducts and other works they created can still be seen. The temporary camps which accommodated them have disappeared except in precious photographic records. They deserve a brief mention in any work on railway towns and settlements.

# Select Bibliography

Andrews, Michael, *Barrow-in-Furness and its Railway*, Barrai Books, 2020.
Bagwell, Philip S., *Doncaster 1853-1990, Town of Train Makers*, Doncaster Books, 1991.
Biddle, G., *Railways in the Landscape*, Pen & Sword Transport, 2016.
Billson, Peter., *Derby and the Midland Railway*, Breedon Books, 1996.
Brooke, David, *The Railway Navvy. 'That Despicable Race of Men'*, David & Charles, 1983.
Challoner, W.H., *The Social and Economic Development of Crewe 1780-1923*, Manchester University Press, 1950.
Chambers, Susan, *Crewe, A History*, Philimore Press, 2007.
Christiansen, R., *Rail Centres: Crewe*, Ian Allan, 1993.
Coleman, Terry, *The Railway Navvies*, Hutchinson, 1965.
Dixon, John & Pickard, Geoff, *Railways around Saltney*, Privately published, 2006.
Drummond, Diane, *Crewe: Railway Town, Company and People*, Routledge, 1995.
Evans, A.K.B. & Gough, J.V. (eds.), *The Impact of the Railway on Society in Britain*, Routledge, 2003.
Girouard, Mark, *The English Town*, Yale University Press, 1990.
Gosling, David, *Gorton Tank. A Pictorial Review of the Gorton Locomotive Works Manchester*, Lightmoor Press, 2020.
Grosse, Philip, *The Railways of Carnforth*, 2nd edition, Barrai Books, 2017.
Hoskins, W.G., *Midland England*, Batsford, 1948.
Hoskins, W.G., *The Making of the English Landscape*, revised edition, Hodder and Stoughton, 1988.
Irons, R. & Jenkins, S.C., *Woodford Halse: A Railway Community*, Oakwood Press, 2009.
Jackson, Alan A., *Semi-Detached London*, George Allan and Unwin, 1973.

Lloyd, David W., *The Making of English Towns*. W&N, 1984.
Marshall, Peter, *Burntisland. Fife's Railway Port*, Oakwood Press, 2001.
Parker, Richard, *Neyland. A Great Western Outpost*, Kestrel, 2002.
Reed, Hayden J., *The Back Line. A History of the Eastern reaches of the Great Northern Railway's Derbyshire Extension*. Book Law Publications, 2019.
Rolt, L.T.C., *A Hunslet Hundred*, David & Charles, 1964.
Saint, Andrew (ed.), *London Suburbs*, Merrell Publications, 1999.
Smith, Sidney, *Rides on Railways*, Published 1851, Philimore (Reprint), 1973.
Simmons, Jack, *The Express Train and other Railway Studies*, Atlantic Transport, 2004.
Simmons, Jack, *The Railway in Town and Country 1830-1914*, David & Charles, 1986.
Smith, D.N., *The Railway and its Passengers, A Social History*, David & Charles, 1988.
Thomas, J., *The Springburn Story*, David & Charles, 1964.
Thomas, David St. J., *How Railways changed Britain, A New Social and Economic History*, Railway and Canal Historical Society, 2015.
Thompson, F.M.L. (ed.), *The Rise of Suburbia*, Leicester University Press, 1982.

## Sample websites

https://vaguelyinteresting.co.uk
https://familypedia.fandom.com
https://www.wikiwand
https://www.locomotion.org.uk
https://m.famousfix.com
https://www.jstor.org

# Index

Aberdeen 177
Aberystwyth 32, 215-6
Acton 12
Agricultural Change in Nineteenth
    Century 24
Alderley Edge 12, 154
Altrincham 12
Ashby-de-la-Zouch 188
Ashford (Kent) 82-3
Aylesbury 230

Barrow-in-Furness 15, 141-3
Barry Docks 13, 170
Barry Island 171
Bath 14-5, 18, 180-2
Battersea 11, 50
Bearsden & Milngavie 12, 116
Bermondsey 131, 136
Berwick-upon-Tweed 231
Beyer Peacock & Co 109
Birmingham 30, 161
Birmingham & Derby Junction
    Railway 71-4, 143
Birmingham & Gloucester
    Railway 19
Birmingham to Stratford Line 155
Blackheath 119
Blackpool 14, 32, 193-8

Bognor 224-5
Bo'ness 174
Boston 78, 232
Bournemouth 32, 200-3
Bow Works of North London
    Railway 134
Bradford 32, 146-7
Braithwaite & Ericcson, loco
    builders 135
Brentford 138-9
Bricklayers Arms 11, 135, 136
Brighton 14, 32, 205-7
Bristol 161, 171-2
Builth Road 64
Burntisland 177-8
Burton-upon-Trent 15, 143-5

Caledonian Railway 12, 105
   at Grangemouth 174
   at Shields Road 113
   at Springburn 105
Cambrian Coast Resorts 216
Cambrian Railways 64, 80-2, 216
Cambridge 18, 72
Canal System 21-2, 25
Cardiff, coal exports 169-70
Carlisle 10, 104-6, 218
Carlyle, Thomas 7

Carnforth 90-1, 142
Carstairs 65
Census Returns, National 16, 20-1
Central Wales Line 63-4, 188
Cheltenham 19, 182-5
Cheshire Lines Committee 153, 199-200
Chester 106-7
  and Great Western Railway 106-7
  and L&NWR 106-7
Chester & Crewe Railway 39
Chester & Holyhead Railway 159-60, 214
Churchbury Loop 127-8
Cleethorpes 14, 220-1
Coaching Industry 21, 233
Coal industry and railways 27
Colwick 156-60
Commuting 118-9, 120-1, 128-9, 130
Consett 15, 149-50
Corkerhill (Glasgow) 84
Coventry 145-6
Craven Arms 63-4
Crewe 9, 17, 39-45
Cromer 217-8
Croydon 117, 123-4

Darlington 76-7
Derby 71-6
  Great Northern Railway at Friargate 76
Dickens, Charles 133
Didcot 59

Didcot, Newbury & Southampton Railway 59, 165
Doncaster 21, 77-80
Dover 13

Ealing 12, 124-5
Earlestown 91-2
Eastbourne 207-8
Eastern Counties Railway 99
Eastleigh 50-1
East London Railway 136
Edale Valley Line 156
Edge Hill (Liverpool) 160
Edinburgh 12-13
Electric trams 120, 130
Ellesmere Port 22
Ely 9-10, 231
Enfield 126
Eton & Windsor 231
Exeter 31, 72

Faringdon 18
Fleetwood 13, 165-7, 177
Folkestone 13, 223-4
Frome 18
Furness & Midland Junction Railway 90-1, 113
Furness Railway 90, 141-3, 226

Gateshead 161
Glasgow 11, 31, 110-3
Glasgow & South Western Railway 84, 105, 113
Gloucester 22
Gooch, Daniel 43

Goole 167-8
Gorton and Openshaw, Manchester 11, 108
  and Beyer-Peacock 109
  and Great Central Railway 109
  and Manchester, Sheffield & Lincolnshire Railway 108
Grand Junction Railway 39, 41, 86
Grangemouth 172-3
Grantham 92-3, 234
Great Central Railway 53, 88, 97
Great Eastern Railway 83, 117, 125, 175-6
  and commuter traffic 120-1, 126-30
  at Cromer 218
  at Hunstanton 223
  Stratford Works 134
Great Northern Railway 51-2, 143
  at Bradford 147
  at Colwick 156-9
  at Doncaster 77-80
  at Grantham 93
  at Peterborough 100-3
  at Skegness 221-2
  and North London suburbs 125
Great Northern & Great Eastern Joint Railway 83, 241
Great Northern & London & North Western Joint Railway 158
Great North of Scotland Railway 65-6
Great Western Railway 12, 18, 19, 44, 120, 160, 170, 172-3, 216
  at Bath 180
  at Newton Abbot 88-90
  at Shrewsbury 94-5
  at Swindon 7-8, 33-8
  at Torquay 204
  Birmingham to Stratford Line 155
  Brentford Branch 138-9
Grimsby 13, 176-7

Harrogate 186-7
Harwich 13, 175-6
Hatcham Ironworks, loco builders 135
Heaton Park & Prestwich 12, 153-4
Helensburgh 116
Hellifield 9, 56-7
Highbridge 69
Highland Railway 188-9
Horncastle 17
Hornsea 32, 152
Horse trams 119
Horwich 9, 49-50
Hounslow 21
Hull 13, 148-9, 152
Hull & Barnsley Railway 148-9
Hunslet (Leeds) 113-4
  locomotive builders at 114
Hurlford 84
Hunstanton 32, 223

Ilfracombe 216
Immingham 13, 168-9
Industrial Revolution 28-30
Isle of Wight 217
Inverurie 65, 69

*John Bull,* Magazine 7-8

Kendal 18, 230
Kilmarnock 84
Kingston-upon-Thames 122-3

Labour Party 68-9
Lancashire, Derbyshire & East
  Coast Railway 52, 62
Lancashire & Yorkshire Railway 12,
  49-50, 61, 154
  at Blackpool 194-7
  at Bradford 147
  at Horwich 49-50
  at Preston 97-8
  at Southport 199
  at Wigan 97-8
  in the Fylde Peninsula 166
Lancaster & Carlisle Railway 18, 63,
  90, 105
Landowners and Railways 24-5
Langwith Junction 62
Launceston 234-5
Leamington Spa 116
Leeds 30, 113-4
Lewisham 119
Lincoln 17, 241-2
Littlehampton 225
Liverpool 13, 30, 160
Liverpool & Manchester Railway
  23-26, 229
Llandrindod Wells 187-8
Llandudno Junction 63
London 31
  Industrial Activity in 134
  North-east Suburbs 120-2

Physical Impact of Railways 131
Population in 1801, 30
Railway District around Euston &
  St Pancras 131-2
London & Birmingham Railway 86,
  99, 145
London & Brighton Railway 72, 136,
  206
London, Brighton & South Coast
  Railway 117, 136, 137-8, 206-7,
  225
London, Chatham & Dover
  Railway 82-3, 134
London & Greenwich Railway 117,
  119, 131, 136-7
London & North Western Railway
  41, 56-7, 63-4, 90, 125, 143,
  160, 188
  and North Wales resorts 214-5
  at Blackpool 194-7
  at Carlisle 105
  at Colwick 160
  at Crewe 8-9, 39-45
  at Earlestown 91-2
  at Morecombe 212
  at Peterborough 100-3
  at Preston 97-8
  at Rugby 86-8
  at Shrewsbury 94-5
  at Wigan 95-6
  in the Fylde Peninsular 166
London & South Western Railway
  47-8, 122, 131-2, 134, 164-5,
  216, 217
  at Eastleigh 50-1
  at Bournemouth 202-3

Longhedge Works (LC&DER) 83, 134
Lowestoft 13
Luton 232
Lytham-St Anne's 194, 198

McCorquodale, Printers & LNWR 42, 92
Manchester & Birmingham Railway 39, 154
Manchester & Leeds Railway 61
Manchester Northern Suburbs 12, 153, 154
Manchester, Lincolnshire & Sheffield Railway 108, 176, 220
Manchester Southern Suburbs 12, 116, 152, 154
Mansfield 238
March 83-4
Margate 14
Marlborough 236
Maryport & Carlisle Railway 105
Melton Constable 9, 69, 92
'Metroland' 117
Metropolitan Railway 117
Middlesborough 20, 140-1
Midland Counties Railway 71, 86, 237
Midland & Great Northern Joint Railway 92, 218
Midland Railway 19, 56-7, 59, 61, 91, 125
  at Bradford 146-7
  at Burton-upon-Trent 143
  at Derby 72-6
  at Morecombe 210-12
  at Peterborough 100-3
  at Trent 247
  at Wellingborough 84-5
  Edale Valley Line 156
Midland & South Western Junction Railway 164-5, 185, 237
Miles Platting 49
Milford Haven 177
Morecombe 210-12
Morris, William 66

Nantwich 39
New Brighton 116
Newcastle-upon-Tyne 151
New Cross 11, 135-6
Newhaven 13
Newton Abbot 89-90
Newton-le-Willows 91-2
Newquay 32
Neyland 172-3, 177
Nine Elms 50, 122, 134
Norfolk & Suffolk Joint Railway 218
Normanton 60-2
North British Locomotive Company 111
North British Railway 12, 54-5
  at Carlisle 105
  at Grangemouth 173
  at Silloth 219-20
  at Springburn 111
North Eastern Railway 46, 61, 63, 151-2
  at Carlisle 105
  at Darlington 76-7
  at Harrogate 186
  at Hull 148-9

at Middlesborough 141
at Saltburn 222
at York 104
North Kent Line 119
North Kent resorts 211
North London Railway 120, 134
North Midland Railway 61, 71, 76
North Staffordshire Railway 44, 143, 214-5
North Wales resorts 214
North Western Railway 56
Norwich 31
Nottingham Suburban Railway 154-5

Old Oak Common 135
Oswestry 80-2
Oxford 239-40

Paignton 204
Parkeston Quay 175-6
Peterborough 10, 20, 66-7, 99-103
Peterhead 177
Pontypool Road 64-5
Preston 9, 97-8
Preston & Wyre Railway 165, 193

Railways, Growth of Leisure Travel 26
  as Housing Landlords 22
  Revolutionary Impact of 32
  In the Industrial Revolution 25-30
Railway Hotels 73
Railway Towns, Nature of 66-70

Railway Servants, Amalgamated Society of 44
Rainhill Trials 29, 30
'Rational Recreation' 69
Ravenscar 226
Reform Acts 1832 27-8
Riccarton Junction 54-5
Richmond-on-Thames and Twickenham 117
Robert Stephenson & Co 77
Rowsley 58-9
Rugby 86-8, 231
Rye 231

Saffron Walden 230
Sale 12
Salisbury 95
Saltburn 222
Saltley District, Birmingham 11, 161
Saltney 35, 159-60
Saxby & Farmer, makers of signalling equipment, 135
Scarborough 14, 32, 208-10
Sea-bathing 190
Seaside Resorts 190-2
Seascale 226
Selhurst & Norwood Junction 11
Shardlow 22
Sheffield 30
Shields Road (Glasgow) 11, 112-3
Shildon 9, 45-6
Shrewsbury 94-5
Shrewsbury to Chester Railway 159
Silloth 218-20

Simmons, Prof Jack 8, 33
Skegness 14, 221-2
Smith, Sydney 40-1, 47-8, 66
Solihull 116
Somers Town 132
Somerset & Dorset Joint Railway 182, 202
South Devon Railway 90, 204
South Durham & Lancashire Union Railway 63
South Eastern Railway 82, 117, 136-8, 224
South Eastern & Chatham 82-3
Southampton 13, 164-5
Southend-on-Sea 14, 32
Southport 116, 151-2, 198-200
South Wales Railway 172-3
Southwark 131
Spa Towns 179-80
Springburn (Glasgow) 11, 110-2
Stamford 21, 237-8
Steel Making 26-7
Stockton & Darlington Railway 46, 76-7, 140-1, 222
Stony Stratford 21, 230
Stourport-on-Severn 22
Stratford Works 134
Stratford-on-Avon & Midland Junction Railway 53
Strathpeffer 188-9
Streatham 117
Styal Line 155
Surbiton 12, 122-3
Swindon 8-9, 17, 33-38

Tebay 62-3
Tewkesbury 19, 230
Thames Tunnel 136
Thomas, Jimmy 69
Torquay 204-5
Totnes 235
Towns, Growth of in Nineteenth Century 30-1
Towns without Railways 243-5
Trade Unionism in Early Railway Days 68
Trent 246-7
Trent & Mersey Canal 143
Tuxford 51
Tynemouth 151

Urbanisation in Nineteenth Century 30-2

Walthamstow 126
Webb, Francis William 42-3
Wellingborough 84-5
Wellington, Duke of 24
Westbury 60
Westerham 18
Westinghouse Brake Co, King's Cross 135
West Kirby 116
West Lancashire Railway 195
Weston-super-Mare 203
Wigan 9, 95-6
Willesden Junction 135
Wilmslow 12, 153-4
Wimbledon 117

Windsor 231
Withernsea 152
Wolverhampton 161
Wolverton 9, 46-9
Woodford Halse 9, 53-4
Woodhead 16

Woolwich 119
Workington 20

York 10, 103-4
York & North Midland Railway 61, 104, 209